Enhanced Indexing Strategies

Enhanced Indexing Strategies

Utilizing Futures and Options to Achieve Higher Performance

TRISTAN YATES

WILEY

John Wiley & Sons, Inc.

Published by John Wiley & Sons, Inc., Hoboken, New Jersey.
Published simultaneously in Canada.

For general information on our other products and services or for technical support, please contact our Customer Care Department within the United States at (800) 762-2974, outside the United States at (317) 572-3993 or fax (317) 572-4002.

Wiley also publishes its books in a variety of electronic formats. Some content that appears in print may not be available in electronic books. For more information about Wiley products, visit our web site at www.wiley.com.

Library of Congress Cataloging-in-Publication Data:

Yates, Tristan.
    Enhanced indexing strategies : utilizing futures and options to achieve higher performance / Tristan Yates.
        p. cm. – (Wiley trading series)
    Includes index.
    ISBN 978-0-470-25925-2 (cloth)
    1. Index mutual funds.   2. Stock price indexes.   3. Investments.   4. Portfolio management.   I. Title.
    HG4530.Y365 2009
    332.64′5–dc22

                                                            2008019098

Printed in the United States of America.

10 9 8 7 6 5 4 3 2 1

Contents

Preface

What if we could borrow money at 5 percent and reinvest it at 10 percent annually for years or even decades? This simple idea proved to be the seed for an ambitious project, a book created to show investors how to use futures and options on index-linked securities to earn very high portfolio returns. After more than a year of writing and research, here is that book.

To achieve our goal, we start with the highest performing and most reliable investment available in the marketplace, the index fund. In the past several years, literally hundreds of index-related products have been introduced in the marketplace, most designed to capture a narrow slice of returns in the broad markets and provide investors with the capability to mix and match different funds in order to build custom portfolios.

Ironically, this wide variety of investment products creates a security selection problem that is very similar to the one that indexing was created to avoid. In this book, we show exactly why some indexes perform better than others and how to successfully combine products into portfolios that deliver better risk-adjusted returns than Standard & Poor's 500 Index (S&P 500). These index portfolios are the basis of our leveraged portfolios.

The next step is to apply leverage, and the most cost-effective way to do this is by using derivatives such as futures and options. With these instruments, it is possible to not only borrow money to invest at a low rate of return, but also, when using options, to implement hedging strategies that help reduce the risk of catastrophic losses.

A key difference between this book and others on option trading is that here options positions are used to capture long-term pricing trends rather than short-term market movements. On average, the index rises 10 percent a year, but some years it gains 25 percent and in others it loses 25 percent, and the aim is to develop and present a variety of option strategies that can capture appreciation in volatile conditions across many years. Six chapters are devoted to implementing specific long-term strategies.

As a result, this book discusses some options strategies in depth but omits others that would be inappropriate to those goals. The focus is primarily on long calls and call spreads, LEAPS options, and hedging strategies. Previous exposure to options strategies is definitely helpful, but not required, but a solid understanding of investing and index funds is obligatory, and a facility with Excel is assumed.

CHAPTER BY CHAPTER

The first and introductory chapter in any book on indexing is usually quite tedious, as it presents material that we've already encountered in a dozen other similar books, forcing us to skip ahead to the point where we can find something new. Thankfully, for both the reader and the author, this book does not have a chapter like this.

Instead we start Chapter 1, "Owning the Index," with the story of an ambitious project by the University of Chicago that could be considered the genesis of modern index investing. It goes on to discuss how both active and index investing can work in a semi-efficient market; whether there is momentum or mean reversion in the markets; how to interpret market cycles; why some indexes are designed for low volatility and others for high performance; how, exactly, the small-cap and value premiums deliver results; and what the potential factors could be for a four- or five-factor model. Every effort was made to ensure that the reader—including the reader who has studied the index for decades—will be treated to new material and different ways of looking at the index.

The second chapter, "Applying Leverage," covers the use of leverage in investment portfolios. To many people, *leverage* is a dirty word, associated with excessive greed and devastating financial losses. But realistically, without leverage to provide purchasing power, the price of every asset in the marketplace would be lower. We begin the chapter with a defense of the practice, or at least an explanation, provided during one of the stock market's most difficult periods by none other than Merton Miller, the Nobel Prize–winning economist.

The first concept covered in Chapter 2 is the leverage ratio, and portfolios are shown that both gain and lose value over time as a result of leverage. Special attention is given to underwater investments, which are investments in which the level of debt is greater than the value of the assets due to falling prices. Sources of portfolio leverage that can be applied to index investments are also introduced, including margin loans, futures contracts, and options. Because the most difficult but most important part of managing a leveraged portfolio is reinvesting and compounding gains, the chapter also examines three different types of reinvestment strategies, and also reviews rebalancing and dollar-cost-averaging techniques that incorporate leverage.

Chapter 3, "Indexing with Synthetics and Futures," is the first strategy chapter of the book, and shows how to build a leveraged diversified index-based portfolio with synthetics, which are options positions that replicate a leveraged stock or index position. By holding options on four different indexes, an investor can earn annual returns of 15 percent with decreasing leverage, but with some initial risk of margin calls. Next, we show how to substitute futures to reduce the margin risk and ramp up the leverage to get higher returns.

Chapter 4, "Capturing Index Appreciation with Calls," begins with an intuitive approach to options pricing that can help investors understand exactly why an option is priced at a certain level, and how to pair the right option with a specific strategy. Next, the Black-Scholes model is introduced and applied to a number of index call options in an effort to determine which ones are best at capturing appreciation and what returns can be expected.

A useful piece of analysis is found at the end of the chapter: a historical comparison is made between the closing level of the VIX and the volatility experienced during the next week, and during the next thirteen weeks. We show that the VIX is not a useful predictor of return, but is an important predictor of future volatility, with some caveats.

Chapter 5, another strategy chapter, builds a leveraged covered call portfolio using short options and long futures. Covered calls have a fascinating risk-reward relationship and can often provide risk-adjusted returns significantly higher than those of long-only portfolios, which makes them an excellent candidate for leverage.

At maximum leverage, the covered call portfolio is capable of losing more than its total investment, and the chapter focuses not only on leverage ratios and asset allocation, but also introduces a possible adjustment using the VIX and the research discussed above that can act as a market timing mechanism and reduce potential losses from the strategy.

Chapters 6 and 7 are related to a specific strategy, Rolling LEAPS Call Options. Chapter 6 shows how to use LEAPS call options to create a leveraged long-term position on the index by rolling the option over again and again for many years. During that time, the underlying asset appreciates and the roll forward costs decline, building large amounts of equity and multiyear annual returns in the 15 to 20 percent range.

Rolling LEAPS call options is one of the most predictable leveraged strategies, in that all of the cash outflows can be calculated to a relatively high degree of precision. This makes budgeting very easy and reduces much of the risk associated with reinvestment.

In Chapter 7, we model the Rolling LEAPS Call Option strategy during one of the market's worst periods and see the results. Then, we use various rebalancing and reinvestment strategies in order to raise the level of return.

Chapter 8, "Long and Short Profits with Call Spreads," explains how to combine long and short options to create profitable positions. We begin the discussion with one of the most popular spread positions, the bull call spread, and explain why it is profitable in theory but not in practice, because of the volatility skew, the effect of the bid-ask spread, and the difficulty of early exit.

Two other spread positions are introduced that have much more profit potential: the diagonal call spread and the calendar call spread. Each of these positions limits the risk, but can provide profits many times larger than the original cost of the position.

The chapter also introduces a new asset allocation concept in which funds are rapidly and repeatedly cycled through short-term investments, and suggests how to calculate the ideal asset allocation using the Kelly criterion, a gambling technique. This method has the potential to create extremely high payoffs over time, but would also experience large drawdowns at certain points.

In Chapter 9, "Cycling Earnings Using Spread Positions," we apply the cycling technique to a diagonal call spread strategy using one-year call options, and then extend the strategy to a biweekly variation using front-month calls. These are extremely profitable strategies, but have a very wide distribution, in which some portfolios have doubled or tripled, but others have lost value. A relatively simple method is also presented to simulate weekly volatility in order to effectively model the short-term strategy.

Chapter 10, "Practical Hedging with Put Spreads," and its strategy counterpart Chapter 11, "LEAPS Puts and Three Ways to Profit," are two of the most important chapters in the book, as together they demonstrate how to prevent catastrophic portfolio losses. We show why simply buying put options is not cost-effective, and then introduce put spread strategies such as the collar and the speed bump that will provide similar portfolio protection at a much lower price.

Portfolio protection allows more aggressive investment, which can create higher returns, and Chapter 11 validates this concept using a highly leveraged index fund with a hedge in place that allows it to avoid catastrophic losses while paying a relatively small price in terms of performance. We show that over a ten-year period this portfolio is expected to grow to five times its initial value.

Chapters 10 and 11 also cover other profitable index-related strategies using put options, including holding calendar put spreads and using LEAPS as security for a put-writing strategy. Each of these strategies generates high returns, but also presents some challenges when it comes to reinvestment.

Chapter 12, "Managing the Leveraged Multistrategy Portfolio," is the capstone chapter that explains how to combine the above concepts and strategies into a single investment portfolio. It begins by addressing the question of whether to index commodities in addition to equities, and then explains why one of the most well-known and widely used leveraged index funds in the marketplace, the ProShares Ultra S&P 500, has underperformed its underlying index, and what we can learn from this situation.

Finally, we emphasize that managing a leveraged investing portfolio is similar to managing any type of project or process, and requires setting objectives, carrying out associated tasks, and monitoring and measuring results. In the context of portfolio management, this requires selecting indexes and strategies and determining the level of exposure, calculating the expected returns and the possible range of returns, and then monitoring the portfolio to ensure that it is performing in accordance to projections.

And then, we encourage you to get started. Many investors, when presented with a variety of choices, suffer from "analysis paralysis" and end up deferring their investment indefinitely. These are often the kind of people who won't buy when the index is up because they feel they have missed the gains, and then won't buy when it's down because they are concerned about more losses. But the data present a crystal-clear message: Every day that you are not invested in the index is a missed opportunity for profit.

PERSONAL ENRICHMENT

I would also like to offer one more lesson from my experience, which is that the study and practice of index investing is a path to enrichment. But I don't mean only financial rewards, although of course those are substantial over time. The benefits go far beyond that.

Students of indexing have access to a wealth of information on the subject, ranging from introductory articles to papers by Nobel Prize–winning economists. They also have the benefit of pricing data sets that go back for decades and inexpensive computing resources that make examination of this data possible, assuming that one has the proper mathematical and statistical foundations.

The challenge is to put all of this together into practical and useful techniques and recommendations for investors. It is a never-ending task because every day new products are announced, new research is published, and the existing indexes add more data points to their history. The ongoing effort is a mental marathon that develops both intellectual curiosity and strong analytical capabilities in those who choose to pursue it.

What I have found is that as the study of indexing enriches the mind, the egalitarian nature of the discipline enriches the soul. Not only are the authorities in the field always willing to share valuable knowledge and data, but they also seem to share the same conviction, which is that everyone, everywhere, deserves the benefits of index investing, regardless of their starting level of wealth or financial knowledge.

The accumulated expertise that is being created in this field is leading to the creation of hundreds of billions, perhaps trillions, of dollars, and all of that wealth will have a profound effect on the lives of millions of individuals across all levels of society. I find it difficult to think of anything more exciting or uplifting, and am proud to be a part of this collective effort. I have no doubt that you will also find the study and practice extremely rewarding.

I should also mention that this book, and very likely my financial writing career, would not have been possible without the help of three editors who gave me early opportunities and exposure, and I would like to express my appreciation. Those editors are David Jackson at Seeking Alpha, Chad Langager at Investopedia, and David Bukey at Futures & Options Trader.

And lastly, I would like to thank the team at John Wiley & Sons. Wiley was the only publisher that I ever considered for this book, a decision that has been validated throughout this process again and again, and I thank them immensely for this opportunity and their efforts.

CHAPTER 1

Owning the Index

I s indexing a strategy or a philosophy? In this chapter we make the case that it's a little of each, and tell the story of how fifty years ago a combination of advances in computing technology and research in risk management set the groundwork for a revolution in both the science of and attitudes toward investing.

While the financial industry was initially slow to embrace the practice of indexing, the brightest minds in financial academia have been researching the subject for decades, and here we present a collection of some of the most interesting and practical findings, including the results of one groundbreaking paper published by Eugene Fama and Kenneth French in 1964, and another by the same team in 2007.

One of the most researched topics in the long-term behavior of indexes is whether there are patterns or trends in the pricing of indexes that can be identified and possibly exploited. Many investors have beliefs and assumptions that are based upon little hard evidence, and in this chapter we present the most up-to-date research in this area.

THE STORY OF INDEXING

The Standard & Poor's 500 Index (S&P 500) was created in 1957, but the first index fund didn't appear until 1973, and index funds didn't become mainstream until the mid-1980s. Why the delay?

We might not yet have index funds today if not for advances in computer technology. Robert Noyce, of Fairchild Semiconductor, invented the first practical integrated circuit in 1959, making possible computers that didn't require roomfuls of transistors and that cost tens of thousands of dollars, rather than millions. Data processing became widely available to organizations.

This new computing power was applied to historical stock data. In 1960, the University of Chicago Graduate School of Business realized that there was an opportunity to create a database of common stock prices and calculate the expected return on equities. With the help of a $300,000 grant from Merrill Lynch, the university formed the CRSP, or Center for Research of Securities Prices.

The CRSP completed this project in 1964, and the project was able to include market data from 1926 onward, a thirty-eight-year data sample with between two and three million pieces of information. The expected return on New York Stock Exchange (NYSE) stocks was found to be 9 percent, and the results were published on the front page of the *Wall Street Journal.*

The CRSP's data set still plays a dominant role in finance, and the vast majority of academic research studies use its data as a source due to its completeness and accuracy. We'll revisit its contributions later, when we look at the research on different types of stocks and indexes.

With this data, researchers began to study the performance of individual investors and mutual funds, and they found a surprising result. The S&P 500 was beating all of them. Not every day, not every year, but over long periods of time the index delivered higher results than most market participants were getting either individually or from their investment funds.

And when the results were adjusted for risk, the gap was astonishing. Individual investors and mutual funds had lots of up and down years in which they would gain or lose large sums. In contrast, the S&P 500 had extremely low volatility and could deliver much more consistent returns, without the white-knuckle roller-coaster ride often associated with focused stock portfolios. Less risk allows investors to invest more of their money with the confidence that it will still be available next week or next year.

Even so, this research was largely confined to the academic community, and there was little demand for an S&P index fund. Even if Wall Street money managers understood the issue, they had little incentive to change, and individual retail investors didn't even know what they were missing.

John Bogle started the first index fund for retail investors on December 31, 1975, and he had little competition. Evangelizing new ideas can be a lonely business, and his fund was initially ignored and then laughed at. His timing wasn't ideal either, as the market performed poorly for the next five years. Eventually, the fund's performance statistics overcame the skeptics. The Vanguard S&P 500 Fund beat 84 percent of his competition over the twenty-year period from 1980 to 2000, and by the 1990s, indexing was established in the marketplace.

With success came competition. New indexes were created to capture returns from other asset classes, such as bonds or small-cap stocks, and new funds were created around those indexes. Today, new indexes and associated funds are launched every day to capture smaller and smaller subsets of the market. Ironically, that presents investors with the challenges in security selection that indexing was originally designed to avoid.

Another factor currently driving new index construction is a feedback loop between the financial media and investors. Narrow-sector or country indexes are very useful to reporters and sell-side analysts who are covering a specific segment of the market, as they provide definitive statistics that can be compared to other investments. For example, an analyst might compare ten commodity ETFs and publish the results, which in turn helps to market those investments.

But additional choices are always good for educated and informed investors. The S&P 500 can be viewed as an accidental success, and many of these new indexes offer better risk and reward. We'll cover higher performance indexes in much more detail later in this chapter.

As the universe of investment choices grows, so does the availability of options and futures, both of which can be used to gain additional leverage and capital efficiency on the original index. We're at a unique point in history in which indexing and derivatives are mainstream financial products, and are now cheap and widely available to both institutional and retail investors, and at the same time a large body of academic research has emerged to support both indexing and specific investment styles.

INDEXING: STRATEGY OR PHILOSOPHY?

Active investors and index investors both have the same goal—to profit from their invested capital—yet they have very different philosophies and approaches, and seem to view the financial markets through opposite ends of the spyglass. Is one view right and one wrong? Or is there a way to reconcile the two perspectives?

Active Investment Selection

Active investing begins with the assumption that at certain points a stock price is trading above or below fair value, and that an investor can identify and profit from that differential. The process is research intensive, and ultimately decisions are subjective, combining fundamental financial and technical analysis with qualitative factors such as predicted future trends or investor psychology.

Most active investors have an area of expertise, perhaps a country or industry or perhaps a style, such as small growth companies. Specialization allows them to identify consistent patterns in the market and provides an edge over other investors.

After the capital is committed, stock prices can move for a variety of reasons that have nothing to do with the initial analysis. A price increase could be due to the company's improved prospects, industry trends, macroeconomic factors, a bull market, market demand for a specific type of stock, a favorable geopolitical outlook, or perhaps simply because of luck.

The decision to sell is the most complex and important of all financial decisions. An active investor usually has more investment opportunities than available capital, and is constantly faced with the choice between closing a position and taking a certain profit or loss and moving the capital to another opportunity, or holding the existing position and hoping it improves.

Successful active investing means having some ability to anticipate the behavior of other active investors. Even deep-value investors have to trust that other active investors will eventually agree with their fundamental evaluations and insights, or they could be stuck holding a position for years, waiting for the valuation to improve.

In television commercials, active investing is often presented as a pursuit for a retiree or small-business owner. In actuality, most of the capital assets in the market are managed by multibillion-dollar funds with experienced management and enormous research capabilities. These funds are generally risk-averse, partly by mandate and partly because it's so easy for an investor to move their money elsewhere.

Index Investing and the Efficient Markets

Index investors don't conduct any research, at least not on individual securities. Their goal is not to profit from pricing anomalies, but to capture the average return of an asset class while reducing risk to the lowest level possible through very broad diversification. Their assumption is that the buying and selling activity of all of the active investors in the market has already pushed prices close to their fair value. This doesn't mean that markets are completely efficient, but only that they are efficient enough for indexing to work over long periods of time.

For example, consider a market with 100 stocks, with every stock trading at either 10 percent above or 10 percent below its fair value at random. Every stock in this market is mispriced, but on average, the market is exactly fairly priced.

Or consider a market in which all stocks are overpriced in some years and underpriced in others. An index investor that bought when stocks were overpriced would suffer short-term losses as the market oscillates to underpricing, but would then earn huge gains as the market shifts back to a higher pricing level.

Index investors have only a single market view: that over long periods of time, the index will provide a reasonable rate of return. Their view is not affected by the actions of individual stocks or industries, and even major geopolitical events may only slightly change the level of their near-term projections, but not affect their long-term expectations.

Because index investors are not trying to time moves in and out of individual stocks, their holding period is essentially infinite and their transaction costs are very low. They do not have to watch the market every day or research dozens of stocks. Indexing is very time efficient, but nevertheless requires knowledge of the various securities available and expertise in portfolio management.

As only the largest investors can afford to construct indexes cost-effectively, an index investor's efforts are focused on building a broad portfolio of fund investments that captures and combines the returns of various asset classes, such as U.S. equities, bonds, or foreign stocks. This requires a detailed understanding of the discipline of portfolio management and of the different products available in the marketplace.

Reconciling Indexing and Active Investing

Many index investors look down on active investors and view their attempts to forecast the market as little more than educated guesses and wishful thinking. However, index investors and value investors, a subset of active investors, actually have many characteristics in common. They both have long horizons and believe that markets are efficient in the long run; after all, an efficient market is the only mechanism aside from chance that could reward a value investor.

Index investors hold many more positions than active investors. This diversification reduces investment focus, but also reduces risk. It would be extremely unlikely that an active investor could construct a portfolio with lower volatility than the S&P 500 unless he or she purchased more than one hundred large stocks, which would in turn make in-depth analysis impossible.

In the past five years, the S&P 500 index fund has delivered better performance than 61 percent of actively managed mutual funds, which means that the average mutual fund has less return and more risk. But this still implies that there are actively managed funds that have higher returns, and perhaps also higher risk-adjusted returns. PIMCO Director Bill Gross was able to beat the S&P 500 for 15 years in a row with a value investing style.

The success of active investing, value investing, and index investing seems to suggest that the market is at least somewhat efficient in the long term, but inefficient enough in the short term for some active investors to make profits in excess of the average. Index investing depends upon both active and value investors to set prices in the marketplace, and the profits from indexing come from the continual appreciation of the average price level over time.

In exchange, index investors provide liquidity. At any price, and in any market, they are willing buyers for a security. Although their purchases are individually infrequent, collectively they can provide a steady stream of buy and sell orders at current price levels. This liquidity helps the capital markets function efficiently.

This philosophy of how markets reward investors is flexible enough to recognize that many different styles of investing will work in many different types of markets. In this book, we will not call active investors fools or gamblers, as many books and articles on indexing do. We as indexers should appreciate their efforts to set prices, and in turn we hope that they will appreciate our market participation and additional liquidity.

Our only advice to active investors is that, especially for large-cap stocks, the discipline of investing should be approached professionally. Billion-dollar mutual funds and hedge funds have a number of advantages over the typical trader, including former industry CEOs on the board, access to proprietary data sources, and low trading costs. These funds are eager to take investors' savings, and it's all too common to see amateurs who experience losses respond by taking on additional risk and ultimately turn a modest failure into a major disaster.

INDEX RISK AND REWARD

Individually, equities are very risky, but when combined into broad, diversified portfolios, the risk plummets. This wasn't clearly understood until Harry M. Markowitz and William F. Sharpe studied risk management in the 1960s.

Prior to that point, investors were encouraged to hold only a few high-performing stocks in order to get the highest returns. Sharpe's focus on risk-adjusted returns reframed the problem and changed the debate into how to get the highest return for the lowest risk. Two investments could be compared by assuming an identical risk tolerance and then calculating the expected return, given that constraint.

Meanwhile, Markowitz showed that every additional investment an investor could hold in their portfolio had the potential to reduce risk. The logical conclusion, given an efficient market with every asset priced at or near fair value and taking into account a market's volatility, is that an investor should own every investment available in proportion to the market. This portfolio strategy is called a market-cap weighted index.

Of course, this is an academic perspective, and, as we will show in this chapter and the next, there are many assets that add additional volatility but do not appear to provide additional return, and market-cap weighting may not be optimal. But currently, the market-cap weighted total stock market index is the most analyzed index in both academia and the financial industry, and the S&P 500 is an excellent proxy, so that's where we will begin the analysis.

Drift and Noise

Stock price returns have been studied for at least one hundred years in order to detect technical patterns, with very little success. Instead, index returns have been found to be a random walk with an upward drift.

On a daily basis or even weekly basis, the upward drift, or index drift as it's also called, is imperceptible. The mean weekly return of $100 invested in the S&P 500 index is 21 cents. It's a fraction of a percent of return combined with typically zero to three points of noise that results in additional upward or downward movement. It took researchers many years of studying market returns to determine that index drift even existed.

Mathematically, the index is considered a submartingale. A martingale is a random series in which each number is equal to the previous number plus a random factor. For a martingale, the most accurate prediction for the next number is the previous number, because the random factor is unpredictable and is only a source of error. A submartingale is a class of martingale in which the base number is steadily increasing over time, but still has a random component.

The up and down weeks of the index tend to cancel each other out, leaving a small drift. For every year since 1950, we analyzed the number of up weeks and down weeks and their respective contributions. The result is that the index moves upward about 43 points a year, and then downward about 34 points a year. The difference, 9 points, is the average appreciation.

The data is similar if we look at the index on a daily, weekly, monthly, quarterly, or annual basis. Most of the moves of the index are small and have very little effect, often being canceled out by another small move. Then there are a few large moves that are canceled out by other large moves. But the result is that there are a few more positive moves than negative moves, and that's where the appreciation comes from.

Years that are classified as "up years" or "down years" are simply years in which there were more positive returns than negative. The effect of random noise in short-term returns, such as 3 months or 6 months, is vast. It doesn't start to subside until we get to longer periods such as multiple years.

Over long periods, index drift overwhelms the noise (see Table 1.1). Here we show the average return, the average standard deviation, and a standard deviation range for different holding periods. On average, holding an index for four years was worth about forty points of return with a forty-point standard deviation.

The combination of noise and index drift helps explain why both buy-and-hold and trading strategies work on the index. Buy-and-hold focuses on the drift, and trading profits from the noise. There is some reliability associated with each effect, and an investor who purchases the index at a random point and waits for it to rise will likely not wait long on average—both the drift and the noise have the potential to push the price upward.

As a test, we took the closing dividend-adjusted monthly prices for the S&P 500 from 1950 to 2006, and then calculated how many days it took to generate a 1 percent increase, using daily closing prices. Based upon average appreciation, we would expect the results to be about five weeks. But sometimes it takes only one day, and sometimes it takes many years.

Given the random and independent nature of the noise, it is simply not safe to make directional bets on the index as part of an indexing strategy. All of the statistics show that, on average, the longer an investor is invested in the index, and the more money they invest, the more they will make. Short positions depart from this principle and will tend to lose money over time.

Every investment starts with a view, and the view of an indexer should be that in the short term, the index is unpredictable, but in the long term it will move upward. That's the view that we will build our investment strategies around. That doesn't mean that we can't create short-term strategies, only that they will tend to have more value and certainty when repeated over periods of months or years as a part of a long-term strategy.

Momentum, Mean Reversion, and Market Cycles

Can we do better than to merely treat the index as a martingale? There are two other predictive models that are widely assumed to exist and are commonly applied to the index: mean reversion and momentum.

Mean reversion is the tendency for a price or factor or economic indicator to revert to a mean value over time. For example, U.S. gross domestic products (GDP) growth rates tend to be mean reverting over a period of a few years. The average annual rate for the United States over the past twenty-eight years is 3 percent, and after years in which it is lower, it tends to rise, and vice versa (see Table 1.2).

The correlation between one year's GDP growth and the average growth for the next two years is –0.33, and based upon that statistical relationship, the best guess possible for next year's growth would be 3.0 percent, plus or minus a small adjustment based on the current value.

TABLE 1.1 S&P 500 Index Returns, Average by Holding Period (January 1950 to September 2007, rolling sets)

Weeks	1	2	4	8	13	26	52	104	208	364
Avg. Return	0.17%	0.34%	0.68%	1.36%	2.22%	4.47%	9.10%	18.56%	39.79%	77.65%
Avg. Stdev	1.95%	2.74%	3.93%	5.56%	7.08%	10.43%	15.56%	23.28%	38.38%	61.53%
10% Best	2.33%	3.38%	5.07%	7.52%	10.44%	17.84%	29.06%	50.39%	90.61%	159.65%
10% Worst	−2.10%	−3.02%	−4.11%	−5.23%	−6.21%	−8.84%	−12.33%	−9.25%	−7.16%	1.22%

Source: Yahoo! Finance (source for all market statistics).

TABLE 1.2 U.S. GDP Growth Data Series: 1979 to 2006

Year	GDP Growth Rate (%)
1979	3.16
1980	−0.23
1981	2.52
1982	−1.94
1983	4.52
1984	7.19
1985	4.13
1986	3.47
1987	3.38
1988	4.13
1989	3.54
1990	1.88
1991	−0.17
1992	3.32
1993	2.67
1994	4.02
1995	2.50
1996	3.70
1997	4.50
1998	4.17
1999	4.45
2000	3.66
2001	0.75
2002	1.60
2003	2.51
2004	3.91
2005	3.22
2006	3.32
Average	3.00
Standard Deviation	1.78

Source: U.S. Department of Commerce.

Note that this does not imply that current GDP growth rates can be used to predict future growth with any reasonable accuracy. There is still a vast amount of noise in the series, and growth is often above or below the average for three years out of four. Like index returns, GDP growth is a noisy variable with a large random component.

Momentum is the opposite of mean reversion, and is the tendency for a variable to keep moving in the same direction. At some level, GDP growth also has momentum, as a very low value is very unlikely to be followed by a very high value. Momentum and mean reversion are not mutually exclusive, so long as they exist in different time frames.

Market commentators and analysts use terms such as mean reversion and momentum to describe stock prices, but there are specific mathematical definitions that can be applied to the 80-plus years of available stock market data. At this point, neither mean reversion nor momentum has been conclusively found in the broad stock market index by any leading academic researcher.

This doesn't necessarily suggest that the effect doesn't exist. Mean reversion could certainly be active across multiple sectors, and perhaps there are target P/E ratios for each industry and for the overall market that help push stock prices down after a rise, and momentum effects that tend to keep them higher in the same conditions. But when all of the effects are added together, they are undetectable, or at least have been up to this point.

> *As Ronald Balvers, Yangru Wu, and Erik Gilliland commented in their 2000 study of mean reversion in stock index prices in 18 countries, a serious obstacle in detecting mean reversion is the absence of reliable long-term series, especially because mean reversion, if it exists, is thought to be slow and can only be picked up over long horizons.*

The result is that there is no way to tie either mean reversion, momentum, or even valuation to a long-term timing model regarding the stock market that tells an investor to get in and out at certain points. Analysts or commentators that suggest that we should avoid investing in the market because it has either risen sharply recently, or fallen sharply recently, are likely making emotional decisions based upon recent volatility, because academically there's very little basis for any conclusion of that sort.

People often see patterns in data that simply aren't there. When stock prices rise, they see momentum, and when prices fall, they see mean reversion. The assumption seems to be that, based upon prior behavior, conclusions can be drawn regarding the future direction of prices. However, that line of thought has been discredited for more than one hundred years.

Clearly, there are stretches where the market goes up or down for a long period of time, and we'll take a closer look at one shortly. The question is whether these cycles are predictable and/or persistent. Identifying a market as a bull or bear is of little value if we don't know how long the present conditions will last.

Still, we should mention that the index does have a few patterns that have been identified. These patterns aren't enough to change our long-term view, but may suggest altering an investment strategy slightly at certain points.

The first is that the S&P 500 does have a tendency to rebound after a large decline. According to a study by M. Bremer and R. Sweeny, after a daily decline of more than 10 percent, the index will recover 1.78 percent in the first market day, and 2.64 percent over the three-day period. This is simply an average, however, and may be skewed by the 1987 crash and large rebound.

There is also a seasonal affect to stock market returns. Henk A. Marquering studied U.S. stock market returns from 1973 to 2002, and found that monthly returns in the winter months (defined as December to May) are about three times higher than returns in the summer months. This effect was also found in other European markets. It could be considered a superset of the January effect, in which stock market returns are consistently higher in that month.

And, stock market returns are significantly lower on Mondays. Why? Nobody knows, but the effect has been documented in academic studies going back to 1973, including one by Ken French in 1980.

Cycles and Regime Change

Think the markets are unpredictable now? Take a look at this classic quote from *Business Week*:

> *The masses long ago switched from stocks to investments having higher yields and more protection from inflation. Now the pension funds—the market's last hope—have won permission to quit stocks and bonds for real estate, futures, gold, and even diamonds. The death of equities looks like an almost permanent condition—reversible someday, but not soon.*
>
> *At least 7 million shareholders have defected from the stock market since 1970, leaving equities more than ever the province of giant institutional investors. And now the institutions have been given the go-ahead to shift more of their money from stocks—and bonds—into other investments. If the institutions, who control the bulk of the nation's wealth, now withdraw billions from both the stock and bond markets, the implications for the U.S. economy could not be worse.*
>
> *Before inflation took hold in the late 1960s, the total return on stocks had averaged 9% a year for more than 40 years, while AAA bonds—infinitely safer—rarely paid more than 4%. Today the situation has reversed, with bonds yielding up to 11% and stocks averaging a return of less than 3% throughout the decade.*

(From "The Death of Equities," *Business Week*, August 13, 1979)

As this issue of *Business Week* went to publication, the Dow Jones Industrial Average was trading at 887 and had been in decline for three years, and pension funds, cited as the only hope left for the market, had just been given approval to diversify into alternative investments. Inflation, energy, and commodity prices were at all-time highs. Never before and never again would the publication be so pessimistic.

As predicted, things did get worse. By October the Dow Jones Industrial Average (DJIA) was trading at 815, and by March 1980, it was 785. Then the market improved, and finally got above 1,000 again in March 1981 before enjoying an incredible bull market in the mid-1980s.

But was the market clearly in a down cycle? The arithmetic average monthly return from January 1975 to December 1979 is 0.38 percent with a 4.23 percent standard deviation. There are nine months with a greater than 5 percent return, including a 14.4 percent return in January 1976, and a 10.6 percent return in April 1978. In some months the index was trading in the 900s, and in other months the Dow was back down below 750 (see Table 1.3).

By assigning a singular direction to the Dow and by labeling that period, or any period, as simply a bear market, we risk overlooking important details, such as the positive average monthly return and the occasional high

TABLE 1.3 Monthly DJIA Returns during the 1976 to 1979 Bear Market

	1976	1977	1978	1979
Jan.	14.4%	−5.0%	−7.4%	4.2%
Feb.	−0.3%	−1.9%	−3.6%	−3.6%
Mar.	2.8%	−1.8%	2.1%	6.6%
Apr.	−0.3%	0.8%	10.6%	−0.8%
May	−2.2%	−3.0%	0.4%	−3.8%
June	2.8%	2.0%	−2.6%	2.4%
July	−1.8%	−2.9%	5.3%	0.5%
Aug.	−1.1%	−3.2%	1.7%	4.9%
Sep.	1.7%	−1.7%	−1.3%	−1.0%
Oct.	−2.6%	−3.4%	−8.5%	−7.2%
Nov.	−1.8%	1.4%	0.8%	0.8%
Dec.	6.1%	0.2%	0.7%	2.0%
Monthly Avg.	1.48%	−1.55%	−0.14%	0.42%
Range	850 to 1,000	800 to 1,000	740 to 875	800 to 890

All Four Years

Monthly Average	0.05%
Monthly Standard Deviation	4.21%

returns. These two details, when combined with the appropriate strategy, are enough to generate profits, as we'll show in one of our early strategy chapters.

The best, or at least most cited, evidence for market cycles comes from the recent NASDAQ boom and bust in the late 1990s and early 2000s. However, by that point the NASDAQ had become largely a tech sector index, and its huge market cap had distorted even the larger S&P 500, sharply reducing the industry diversification benefits of index investing.

For example, near the NASDAQ peak, in a column written by Jeremy Siegel for the *Wall Street Journal*, called "Big Stocks Are a Sucker Bet," he explained that of the 33 largest U.S. stocks by market capitalization, 18 were technology stocks, and that their market-weighted PE was 125.9. Half of the assets in S&P 500 index funds were invested in "story stocks" with no earnings.

During the last half of the 1990s, as the composition of the S&P 500 changed, so did the volatility. The S&P 500 had traditionally been a very low-risk index, but the VIX jumped from an average of 12 to 15 to the mid-20s and sometimes even the low 30s. (The VIX and volatility is covered in more detail in the next section.)

The lesson is that traditional bull and bear market classifications are not nearly enough to base investment decisions on. Trying to jump into and out of different markets virtually guarantees buying before corrections and selling well before a bull market ends.

Still, indexes do change fundamentally at times, and it's important to recognize what that shift is and when it occurs, particularly with regard to the expected return distributions. Academics often refer to these types of shifts as a "regime change" in order to avoid other market labels with different connotations.

Volatility-related regime changes are, according to studies, somewhat related to changes in macroeconomic variables, financial leverage, and trading volume. At the extremes, such as the period after the 1929 depression when stock prices were moving 10 percent a month, increased volatility may be due to legitimate uncertainty about whether the economic system will survive.

Understanding Volatility

Volatility is a measure of the downside risk of a security. As a rule, volatile securities are expensive to own because they are expensive to hedge. As risk increases and prices become more unstable, option prices climb, and more capital is required to hold a position.

Typically, volatility is quoted as an average based upon annualized historical thirty-day volatility, which is actually the standard deviation of twenty-two days of market returns. We can divide by 3.4 to convert the annualized number to a monthly figure, or 7.2 to find the weekly result.

For example, if the annualized volatility of the S&P 500 was 12 percent, which is a typical value, that means that prices moved by an average of 3.5 percent a month, or 1.7 percent a week. Sixty-six percent of daily, weekly, and monthly returns are expected to be within one standard deviation, and 95 percent within two standard deviations.

As time gets shorter, the expected range of returns decreases, but only at the square root. The square root of 12 is 3.4, the number of months in a year, and 7.2 is the square root of 52 weeks, the number of weeks in a year. This nonlinear relationship between time and the expected movement of a security is critical for understanding options strategies, forecasting expected returns, and managing risk, and will be covered in more detail later.

We've shown the annualized volatility for selected indexes, calculated using weekly returns. Volatility for an index of 10 or less is considered very low, 15 to 20 is about average, and in the 30s or 40s is considered very high. Consider that a security with a volatility of 40 has a 33 percent chance of gaining or losing more than 40 percent in a year and would also be expected to gain or lose about 10 percent in the coming month (see Table 1.4).

Low or high volatility does not change the average return for the index. Academic theories such as the Capital Asset Pricing Model (CAPM) say that investors avoid assets with high volatility and expect a premium for them, but experience with any hot asset class shows that volatility on the upside can often attract investors rather than dissuade them.

Table 1.5 shows the relationship between annualized volatility, also known as IV, and monthly price change expectations. When the IV for an investment hits 35 or 40, 10 percent monthly movements become commonplace.

Implied volatility, also known as IV, is the option market's future estimates of volatility, as opposed to historic volatility, or HV, which are calculations from actual daily returns. IV affects option prices, and can be backed out of the price of an option if interest rates and dividends are known.

There are several interesting characteristics related to implied volatility that have been widely studied, but are still not well explained. For example, IV for puts is often higher than IV for calls on the same security, IV for in-the-money options is higher than IV for out-of-the-money options, and IV for longer-term options is higher than IV for shorter-term options. Intuitively, IV should be identical for all of the options on a single security, but this is clearly not the case.

IV is also higher than historic volatility in most cases for most time periods. The reasons for this gap are not well understood, and may be related to downside volatility crash protection. We'll later show a volatility arbitrage

TABLE 1.4 Selected Index Returns and Volatility

Index	Oct 1987 to Sep 2007				Jan 2002 to Dec 2006			
	Monthly Return		Annualized		Monthly Return		Annualized	
	Avg. Return	Avg. Volatility	Avg. Return	Avg. Volatility	Avg. Return	Avg. Volatility	Avg. Return	Avg. Volatility
Dow Jones Industrial Average	0.90%	4.02%	11.31%	13.93%	0.55%	3.54%	6.80%	12.26%
S&P 100	0.82%	4.13%	10.30%	14.31%	0.44%	3.58%	5.41%	12.40%
S&P 500	0.84%	3.95%	10.56%	13.68%	0.57%	3.46%	7.06%	11.99%
Russell 2000	0.94%	5.08%	11.88%	17.60%	0.97%	4.77%	12.28%	16.52%
NASDAQ 100	1.40%	7.65%	18.16%	26.50%	0.86%	5.77%	10.82%	19.99%

TABLE 1.5 Converting Actual or Implied Volatility (IV) to Monthly Change

Volatility	% Change 1 STD (66%)	% Change 2 STD (95%)
10	2.9%	5.8%
15	4.3%	8.7%
20	5.8%	11.5%
25	7.2%	14.4%
30	8.7%	17.3%
35	10.1%	20.2%
40	11.5%	23.1%

(often referred to as "vol arb") strategy that exploits this difference, but it is not risk-free, as volatility can rise sharply and unexpectedly.

In academic theory, implied volatility is the market's best guess of future volatility, and should utilize all available information and be at least somewhat predictive. In reality, it is both predictive and reactive and is heavily correlated to recent negative returns. High volatility can emerge and dissipate quickly, often spiking and then fading after a few weeks.

At the same time, there is a background level of volatility for every index that is related to long-term trends. An argument can likely be made that this is the "true" volatility, or expected return distribution at a weekly or monthly level, and the short-term spike represents only the expected volatility at a daily level. Still, a temporary market drop will often affect IVs on options months or years into the future.

In order to help measure volatility, the CBOE calculates and distributes the VIX, a volatility index derived from a weighted average of a range of options on the S&P 500 index, with the goal of measuring the implied volatility of a 30-day at-the-money option on that index. Other similar indexes are being created for the NASDAQ and the Russell 2000.

Using the VIX and the above divisors for monthly return distributions, we can estimate the market's expected downside risk for the current period. For example, if the VIX is 18, then we can assume that the market believes that the one standard deviation gain or loss for the S&P 500 over the next 30 days is 5.3 percent, or 18 percent divided by 3.6.

Also, by using historical VIX quotes, it is often possible to estimate previous option prices for the S&P 500 or highly correlated indexes. This can be useful for backtesting various options strategies.

Note that the VIX can move very quickly in a matter of days or hours, whereas 30-day historic volatility is a moving average and thus has some inherent smoothing and takes a little longer to rise and fall. Ideally, we would like to know the "instant" volatility, in other words what the return distribution is at that exact moment, but unfortunately that's impossible and can only be estimated later from the future analysis of returns.

HIGH PERFORMANCE INDEXES

Different indexes have very different performance characteristics. For example, the OEX and the S&P 500 have extremely low volatility, and the Russell 2000 has higher volatility but higher performance. This diversity is a direct result of how the index is constructed and the types of stocks it contains.

The S&P 500 has made a tremendous contribution to index investing and to the wider economy—it is even one of the leading economic indicators. Still, it would be fair to say that its construction is more of a product of the 1950s than the twenty-first century. At this point, we know much more about individual stock returns and volatility and portfolio management than we did sixty-five years ago.

The S&P 500 was and still is designed with stability in mind. Companies are selected primarily for size, but also on the basis of financial strength, and the overall composition of the index is carefully managed to provide broad industry representation. Once a company is included in the index, it rarely gets removed except under the worst of circumstances. This creates an extremely stable portfolio with low turnover and low volatility. Note that it is not necessarily the portfolio with the lowest possible volatility—it is very likely that there are still stocks in the S&P 500 that have too much volatility and don't provide enough return in compensation.

The CAPM states that every investment has a beta, or correlation, to the broad market, and the higher this beta, the more return investors should demand from the investment. However, CAPM is much more a theory than an actual observation. In the marketplace there are many highly volatile stocks that have provided low historic returns and that still have high betas, and thus low risk-adjusted returns. The S&P makes no effort to remove these stocks.

Two other "old-school" indexes also seem antiquated given today's knowledge. The Dow Jones Industrial Average consists of only thirty U.S. stocks, selected by hand and price-weighted, and thus is neither a broad measure of the economy nor an academically defensible weighting. The NASDAQ-100, also known as the NDX or QQQQ, is a list of the top 100 companies that happen to be listed on that exchange rather than the NYSE and meet other minimal requirements. It is neither diversified by sector nor broadly representative.

A better approach for index construction would be to mine the CSRP data and find out which types of stocks performed better than others, and build a high-performance portfolio around just those stocks. This was done more than forty years ago, almost immediately after the data set mentioned at the beginning of this chapter was first created.

Small Cap and Value Premium

In 1964, Eugene Fama and Kenneth French studied thirty-eight years of market returns, trying to determine if certain stocks performed better than others. They were originally looking for evidence of CAPM, the model that assumes that beta and volatility drive stock price performance. Instead, they found that the influence of beta on stock returns was very weak.

However, they found that two other factors, size and book-to-market, explained more than 90 percent of stock market returns. Since that time, additional factors have been shown to have additional explanatory value; we'll discuss those shortly.

Book-to-Market is a valuation metric that is closely correlated to other similar metrics such as Price-to-Earnings or Price-to-Cash-Flow. It's a way of measuring whether a company is cheap or expensive relative to its peers. Size is simply smaller market capitalization versus large market capitalization. Small stocks and value stocks have significantly better returns.

Size and Value have been defined in the model as SMB (Small minus Big) and HML (High Book-to-Market minus Low Book-to-Market). These values are the premium that a small-cap or value portfolio delivers over its polar opposite. These values have been tracked for more than forty years and updates are posted monthly on Ken French's web page (see Table 1.6).

For example, in one study, Fama and French created 25 stock portfolios based on five divisions of size and five divisions of Book-to-Market. The small-cap value portfolio has a nine point advantage over Large Growth, and isn't significantly more volatile (see Table 1.7).

The three-factor model has been well examined, and the paper in which it was introduced is the most widely cited in financial academia. The results have been duplicated repeatedly across many different data sets, including later market returns, financial companies (originally excluded from the sample), and international stocks.

Of course this research has profound implications for the broader traditional indexes such as the S&P 500, the NASDAQ-100, and the Dow Jones Industrial Average. All of these indexes are heavily biased toward large-cap and growth stocks. That has led to suggestions that the indexing industry should move away from market-cap weighting to either equal-weight or weights based on some fundamental factor, such as revenue or dividends and the creation of products such as the WisdomTree Index ETFs.

HML and SMB can be viewed as additional investments that are included with the purchase of a value and/or a small-cap stock. Both HML and SMB have positive expected returns for every period, but also wide standard deviations. As is true with the index return, defined in the study as Rm-Rf (Market return minus Risk-free return, such as the rate on a U.S.

TABLE 1.6 Fama & French Factors

Factor	Jan 1950 to Dec 2006					Jan 2002 to Dec 2006				
	Avg. Monthly Return	Volatility	Annualized Return	Volatility	Rm-Rf Correlation	Avg. Monthly Return	Volatility	Annualized Return	Volatility	Rm-Rf Correlation
Rm-Rf	0.64%	4.19%	7.94%	14.53%		0.46%	3.62%	5.69%	12.55%	
SMB	0.19%	2.81%	2.26%	9.72%	0.27	0.54%	2.60%	6.63%	8.99%	0.33
HML	0.36%	2.92%	4.46%	10.10%	−0.26	0.70%	2.18%	8.78%	7.55%	0.38

Source: Kenneth R. French Data Library.

TABLE 1.7 25 5×5 Size and Book-to-Market Portfolios

Annualized Return
Book-to-Market

Size	Low		Mid		High
Small	9.2%	16.0%	16.5%	19.4%	21.2%
	11.2%	15.1%	17.6%	18.2%	20.0%
Medium	12.3%	15.6%	15.8%	17.5%	19.1%
	13.1%	13.5%	16.6%	17.0%	17.8%
Large	12.0%	12.8%	14.1%	14.2%	15.0%

Annualized Volatility
Book-to-Market

Size	Low		Mid		High
Small	26.8%	22.6%	19.3%	18.1%	19.3%
	23.5%	19.3%	17.2%	16.9%	18.9%
Medium	21.5%	17.4%	15.9%	15.8%	18.0%
	19.2%	16.4%	15.7%	15.6%	17.9%
Large	15.7%	14.7%	14.1%	14.5%	16.6%

Source: Kenneth R. French Data Library.

government bond), the longer the horizon, the more the return matters and the less effect the noise has.

This suggests that over long periods of time, that is, five or more years, a small-cap and/or value portfolio is virtually guaranteed to beat a large-cap or growth portfolio, even with its additional risk (see Table 1.8). And this also means that on a daily basis, the statistics favor the outperformance of these securities, if only by a slight amount.

In the following, we've compared the returns from the S&P 500, the Russell 2000, and the Russell 1000 value for various periods. As shown previously in Table 1.6, SMB is positively correlated with the Rm-Rf, which means that in bull markets, SMB will generate higher returns, but in weaker markets, it will punish a portfolio. This is why many investors avoid small stocks regardless of the premium, although the additional return appears to more than compensate for the risk over long periods of time.

On the other hand, HML, the value premium, is negatively correlated with Rm-Rf, which means that these stocks can provide a cushion in a down market, but will lag in up markets. Still, it should be noted that both of these correlations are relatively weak and may not hold for shorter periods of time.

Holding both premiums, the small-cap and the value, combines the relative outperformance, but allows the correlations to cancel each other out, becoming roughly zero. That creates an asset with a beta of 1, but with almost double the equity premium.

However, it should be mentioned that there is a momentum effect to small cap and value returns, and there will always be periods where small

TABLE 1.8 $1 from 1950 Invested in...

	Large Caps			Small Caps		
	Growth	**Neutral**	**Value**	**Growth**	**Neutral**	**Value**
1955	2.53	2.77	3.63	2.39	2.70	2.90
1960	4.61	5.24	7.02	4.83	5.45	6.05
1965	8.00	10.35	14.10	6.01	8.92	11.82
1970	9.95	10.53	19.50	12.81	18.70	25.85
1975	9.44	12.04	27.43	6.21	14.90	26.67
1980	15.90	28.62	70.65	24.92	57.72	116.82
1985	28.93	57.44	172.42	44.35	167.70	380.74
1990	60.88	120.64	384.73	54.92	303.80	699.01
1995	106.95	198.10	674.10	80.59	586.36	1,418.64
2000	388.61	502.66	1,488.86	183.20	1,392.03	3,418.68
2005	311.42	752.28	2,110.27	158.72	3,007.44	9,036.47

Source: Kenneth R. French Data Library.

cap and value underperform the broader market. The outperformance is only a tendency over longer periods of time.

Stock Migration

The size and value premiums are well known, but not widely exploited. The overwhelming majority of assets, and especially indexed assets, are in large-cap portfolios that are tilted toward growth. The issue preventing more widespread adoption may be that both factors take time to deliver returns in excess of their volatility and may be incompatible with a mutual fund industry that's focused on next quarter's performance.

There is also one other key difference between index portfolios constructed around small-cap and/or value stocks and the more traditional index portfolios such as the S&P 500. The portfolios are much more dynamic.

Fama and French revisited their research in 2007 and started tracking the movements of stocks in and out of the size and value portfolios. They divided the stock universe into three value categories and two size categories, and assigned each stock to a portfolio in June of every year, based on its book-to-market ratio and market capitalization.

What they found is that stocks moved in and out of the value category very frequently. Almost thirty percent of value stocks moved to core, the center category, and almost thirty percent of the stocks in core moved to value. As these stocks migrated from value to growth and back, they were bought and sold by the virtual portfolio, generating returns in the process (see Table 1.9).

Value stocks also had a better chance of being acquired, and when they were, the premiums were higher. This positive migration (from value to core) and the opportunity to benefit from an acquisition is the explanation

TABLE 1.9 Migrations between Growth, Neutral, and Value Portfolios (by percentage of stocks, annual average)

From	To	Percent
Big Neutral (BN)	Big Growth (BG)	12.5%
	Big Value (BV)	9.2%
Big Growth (BG)	Big Neutral or Value (BN/BV)	13.3%
Big Value (BV)	Big Neutral or Growth (BN/BG)	20.3%
Small Neutral (BN)	Small Growth (SG)	10.9%
	Small Value (SV)	20.1%
Small Growth (SG)	Small Neutral or Value (SN/SV)	27.0%
Small Value (SV)	Small Neutral or Growth (SN/SG)	16.5%

Source: Fama & French, "Migration" (CRSP Working Paper No. 614, 2007).

for the value premium. Small-cap stocks also migrate—a few grow and become large stocks, creating huge premiums in the process. An individual small-cap stock is a lottery ticket with an expected payoff higher than its cost, but with an extremely high volatility. Individually, small-cap stocks and value stocks are more risky than large-cap and growth stocks, in that they have a higher chance of failure. In the study, each year on average, 2.5 percent of small-cap value stocks were removed from the portfolio due to failure, compared to 2.2 percent for small-growth and 0.2 percent for large stocks. In absolute terms the percentages are still very low and don't affect the premium significantly.

The phenomenon of migration makes us question what it really means to be an index. The Dow Jones Industrial Average and S&P 500 are relatively stable collections of companies. Of course, mergers and acquisitions take place, and new firms are added to the list, but the average turnover is relatively low, about 5 percent for the S&P 500.

But the Fama and French value portfolio changes every year. It could change every month or every day. It buys stocks when they are relative values and then sells them when prices rise. Similarly, the small-cap Fama and French portfolio buys small stocks and sells them when they get big. And when these two strategies are combined, the portfolio outperforms the market by eight points a year, on average. Did Fama and French develop a factor model, or did they in fact create two rule-based trading systems that have delivered higher returns than the broad market for more than eighty years?

The pair is modest when discussing their achievements. Their explanation is that markets are efficient, and that there is no market outperformance without additional risk, which means that small-cap and value stocks have to carry more risk. That may be true of the small-cap index, due to the positive correlation between Rm-Rf and SMB, but value stocks have the opposite effect—they deliver higher returns but reduce some of the risk associated with equities. Many others believe that behavioral factors are involved.

There have been many studies that show that investors chase outperformance. Most are naturally attracted to securities that have risen lately and mentally screen out those that have performed poorly from their investment choices. Behavioral finance could certainly account for the effect.

Another explanation may simply be that small-cap and value stocks are more risky individually, but this risk is reduced dramatically when hundreds of stocks are held in a portfolio. The pricing then is rational at the individual level, because it takes into account the risk of total loss, but not at the aggregate index level when diversification is applied.

Additional Factors

Another argument for the behavioral explanation comes from the momentum factor. There are two studies that are the cornerstone of momentum theory. The first, by Narasimhan Jegadeesh and Sheridan Titman (1993), shows that stocks that have done well over the past six months outperform "losers" by 1 percent a month on average for the next six to twelve months. This is sometimes known as the "smart money" effect, as it's assumed that the dumb money follows the smart money and contributes to their total return. However, Werner F. M. DeBondt and Richard Thaler (1985) show that loser stocks in the past three to five years outperform winners by 25 percent over the next three years. This implies long-term reversals are an important phenomenon in the market, and that many investments left for dead can come roaring back to life—for example, telecom or energy in recent years. Models that use momentum as a fourth factor (see Table 1.10) in explaining stocks returns refer to it as UMD, or Up minus Down, or alternately, WML (Winner minus Loser), or MOM (Momentum); however, not all use the same time or portfolio definition.

Ken French calculates the factor using 2 to 12 month returns, and averaging the difference between the momentum effect on a large-cap and small-cap portfolio. The results from 1950 through 2006 are 0.84 percent a month with a 3.65 percent standard deviation, making it definitely a significant, if somewhat unpredictable, factor. MOM is not correlated with the broader market, which is somewhat unexpected.

While no indexes have been constructed around the momentum factor, there is some industry discussion that mutual funds often use stock momentum in their selection process. It follows that it could also be used to select broad portfolios full of stocks with high momentum factors, such as countries, industries, or even styles.

While momentum is commonly accepted as a fourth factor, even by Fama and French, there is no real agreement on a fifth factor. One approach that has been used is to identify a new market beta and use this variable as both a systematic risk indicator and a factor explaining individual stock market returns.

For example, Lubos Pastor of the University of Chicago found that returns were greater for less liquid stocks. Ten portfolios were created based upon liquidity, and the top decile, that is, the least liquid stocks, had 9 percent higher returns than the lowest liquidity, even after controlling for size, value, and momentum.

In another study, researchers created a volatility beta for the total stock market that measured an individual stock's sensitivity to market volatility, that is, the VIX. Stocks that had more sensitivity delivered better returns.

TABLE 1.10 Momentum Factors

Factor	Jan 1950 to Dec 2006				Jan 2002 to Dec 2006			
	Avg. Monthly Return	Volatility	Annualized Return	Volatility	Rm-Rf Correlation	Average Monthly Return	Volatility	Annualized Return	Volatility	Rm-Rf Correlation
Mom	0.84%	3.66%	10.54%	12.67%	−0.06	0.31%	4.34%	3.74%	15.02%	−0.58

Source: Kenneth R. French Data Library.

Regardless, given that at this point there is no momentum-based index fund or other investable asset in the marketplace, even if a fifth factor were conclusively found, it could be a long time before index funds were constructed around it.

FORECASTING INDEX RETURNS

Modeling stock returns has always been difficult for academics and researchers, primarily for three reasons:

1. Volatility varies across at least two dimensions. There is a long-term volatility that changes slowly, and shorter-term volatility that spikes upward when the market declines.
2. Prices jump between trading periods. An index may close at 1,550 and then open at 1,540 the next day because of negative news or events before the open.
3. Return distributions are not normal distributions. It is not exactly clear what they are, but usually they are modeled as log normal. Log normal variables are the multiplicative product of many small independent factors, such as the daily rates of return on a stock.

The models in use in academia and on Wall Street are random walks with generalized autoregressive conditional heteroskedasticity, or GARCH, which are then modified for discontinuities (that is, jumps), fatter tails, and other variable distributions such as a student-T. For example, one model, EGARCH, is an exponential model that provides for both positive and negative shocks.

Thankfully, in this book we can use much simpler models because the objective is to calculate a reasonable set of monthly or annual price changes, rather than the continuous stream of price ticks that traders use. Still, as we progress, we will apply some of the techniques listed above to generate prices with higher frequencies or more complex volatilities.

SUMMARY

The practice of indexing owes its existence to several key events, including research into portfolio diversification, a data analysis project for the University of Chicago, and the Vanguard fund, the first index fund for retail investors. Today, indexing is firmly established in the investing marketplace, and new products are being introduced constantly.

Indexing strategies work because the market is at least somewhat efficient, meaning that in the aggregate and over long periods of time, the market price of a set of securities should trade in line with its fair value. However, the success of indexing does not preclude active investing strategies from working, and, in fact, indexers need active investors to continuously adjust the market prices of securities through their trading activity.

While many investors believe the pricing trends of the indexes are influenced by previous prices and thus exhibit either momentum or mean reversion, and market analysts often cite these two reasons for either market rallies or declines, the research in this area has found no significant relationship between past pricing trends and future prices. The index can best be described as a small amount of upward drift with a large amount of random noise.

As a short-term investment, the index is wildly unpredictable, as the high level of noise makes the price changes over periods of weeks or months essentially random. But over longer periods of time the index delivers. For holding periods of four years, gains average 40 percent or more and losses are scarce. This creates an opportunity for long-term leveraged investments to benefit through the investment and compounding of additional capital.

The S&P 500 has long been used as a proxy for the market-cap weighted U.S. stock market index, because from its inception it has contained a cross-section of the largest listed firms. But analysis from Fama and French in the 1960s revealed that shares of larger firms tend to underperform smaller firms, and that shares of firms with a higher book-to-market ratio underperform those of other firms. The publication of the three-factor model has led to both the creation of new high-performance indexes, and an ongoing search for additional factors.

CHAPTER 2

Applying Leverage

I n the last chapter, we introduced indexed investments and demonstrated how their built-in diversification can provide the ability to efficiently capture long-term returns but with lower volatility than individual securities. In this chapter, we will apply financial engineering and portfolio management techniques to create related investments, but with new risk and return profiles that allow us to achieve higher returns with less capital.

We begin with an in-depth explanation of the leverage ratio and its effects on risk and returns, and in the process show how even investments with negative equity still have value, and provide some guidelines for investors that can help them understand how much leverage is too much. Then, we introduce and compare several leveraged investment tools available to index investors, including margin, futures, and options.

The last portion of the chapter is devoted to leveraged portfolio management and reinvestment. Expertise in these areas can mean the difference between low volatility and high returns, or sky-high volatility and a fund collapse, and we encourage readers to study that portion carefully.

LEVERAGED INVESTMENTS: CONSERVATION OF RISK

The year is 1990, and Merton Miller has just won the Nobel Prize in Economics. At the awards ceremony, he gives a speech on corporate leverage.

At this time, "corporate leverage" is the dirtiest pair of words in finance. In the 1980s, financiers begin issuing junk bonds and taking over large, well-known corporations through leveraged buyouts. After the purchase, valuable assets would be liquidated and jobs cut, and the remaining firm would be burdened with debt or sold to the highest bidder.

For the investors and upper management, the outcome was sky-high profits, but for the lower-level managers and workers, it was chaos. It's no coincidence that Oliver Stone's film *Wall Street* was released in 1987 and featured an ethically challenged corporate raider, Gordon Gekko (Michael Douglas), as the villain who gets his comeuppance.

Thirty-five years prior to the Nobel awards ceremony, Miller and Franco Modigliani, another Nobel laureate, had discovered that, in the absence of external factors, a firm's capital structure or dividend policy had no impact on the firm's value. This research argues against leveraged buyouts (LBOs) because theoretically a pure financing transaction should have no effect on the ultimate value of a company and could never *create* value.

But there were two environmental factors that changed this analysis. The first is the corporate deductibility of paid interest, sometimes known as a tax shield. This effect reduces the after-tax cost of debt financing and creates situations where profitable companies can be made more valuable by replacing large amounts of equity with debt.

The second is the control premium—gaining control of a company provides the new owner with the ability to change management and obtain the financial benefits of restructuring. This potential payoff creates an incentive to acquire the company, and issuing debt is a relatively fast way to raise large amounts of capital, and it enables the new acquirer to reap the rewards.

Both of these effects contributed to the profitability of these transactions, and issuances of high-yield corporate debt soared in the latter part of the decade. LBO transactions became both more common and more ambitious, their targets growing larger and larger.

But by 1989, the party had ended. The U.S. economy entered a recession, and the junk bond market collapsed, as companies were no longer able to pay the high yields. In 1990, there was more than $20 billion in junk bond defaults.

Even worse, many of these bonds were owned by savings and loan institutions, resulting in a credit crunch and the potential for the collapse of an important part of the banking system. Increased government regulation and high profile criminal indictments for racketeering and securities fraud also served to reduce demand, and consequently market liquidity, for high-yield corporate debt.

Junk bonds and corporate excess were to blame, said the financial press and mainstream media. But was this really true? According to Miller in his speech, not at all. The ownership structure of a corporation or any investment has nothing to do with its inherent risk. He referred to this principle as the conservation of risk, and as an essential corollary of their research in the 1950s on the affect, or lack thereof, of financing on a firm's value.

His analysis was that as the impending recession impacted the projected profitability and reduced the value of U.S. corporations, any owner also would have been affected, whether they were a stockholder or a bondholder. Rising and falling asset prices will always affect owners, no matter what their ownership structure is, and owning a corporation through the purchase of high-yield bonds was just another way of financing an investment.

The fears that were attributed to junk bonds and leverage should have been directed at the economic outlook. When certainty returned to the financial markets, U.S. corporations and all investments based on their ownership, including stocks and both investment-grade and junk bonds, would also recover.

Unless, of course, the government heeded the calls to heavily regulate junk bonds and thus retarded both their development and the overall recovery. When financial and economic problems occur, people look for someone to blame, and leverage was, and still often is, the obvious scapegoat.

When asset prices rise, every investment based upon ownership of that asset gains value, including traditional and junk bonds, stocks, futures, and options. And when the underlying asset falls, all of those investments lose value. Investing using leverage starts with the understanding and appreciation that leverage is another form of ownership, and that owning any asset provides both rewards and risks, depending upon its future performance.

Leverage could have been regulated out of existence in 1990, following the junk-bond market collapse and the stock market crash of 1987, in which derivatives played a part. Instead it survived and then thrived. High-yield debt is now commonplace in the bond markets, and highly leveraged equity products such as futures and options are widely available to retail investors.

There's no question that excessive leverage is dangerous to the firms that employ it, as the portion of the asset they own is highly volatile. Yet, without leverage, the modern financial system would not exist, and many investments would have to be made at a higher cost, or might not even take place. In these next sections, we show both the enormous benefits and the considerable dangers inherent in the practice of using borrowed money to invest.

USING THE LEVERAGE RATIO

To understand the impact of leverage on an investment, we first have to quantify it. While there are many different ways to write a debt-to-equity ratio, in this book, a leverage ratio is used that is equal to total assets divided by total equity. We like the leverage ratio because it can easily be applied to both expected return and volatility as a multiplier.

An unleveraged portfolio has a leverage ratio of 1, while a portfolio that has twice as many assets as equity would have a leverage ratio of 2. Leverage ratios below 1 are possible by holding a portion of assets in risk-free securities (that is, U.S. treasury bonds).

The formula for the expected return on the leveraged investment, given the expected return on the unleveraged investment, the cost of debt, and the leverage ratio is:

$$rE = (L \times rA) - ((L - 1) \times rD)$$

where rE = % rate of return on equity
      rD = % interest on debt
      rA = % rate of return on underlying assets
      L = leverage ratio

For example, if an investor can borrow money at 5 percent and invest it at 10 percent, and can borrow twice the amount of their initial investment, creating a leverage ratio of three, their expected annual return is 30 percent − 10 percent = 20 percent.

When discussing rates of return of 20 percent, its important to remind our readers just how much of a difference a few percentage points can make over time. As Table 2.1 shows, just increasing the rate of return from 10 percent to 12 percent will give an investor a 43 percent higher return over 20 years.

If multiple sources of capital are used with varying capital costs, the cost of capital in the formula can be a weighted average, or the formula can just be extended. Second sources of capital, even at high interest rates, can often be used to generate extremely high returns.

Suppose that a portfolio manager can borrow at 5 percent interest for up to 50 percent of the equity of an investment, and then borrow at 10 percent interest for another 25 percent of the equity, for a total leverage ratio of 4. Assuming a 10 percent rate of return on the underlying assets, the expected rate of return is:

$$4 \times 10\% - (2 \times 5\%) - (1 \times 10\%) = 40\% - 20\% = 20\%$$

TABLE 2.1 Growth of $10,000 (over various periods of time at various rates)

	5 Years	10 Years	15 Years	20 Years
10%	16,105	25,937	41,772	67,275
12%	17,623	31,058	54,736	96,463
15%	20,114	40,456	81,371	163,665
18%	22,878	52,338	119,737	273,930
20%	24,883	61,917	154,070	383,376
22%	27,027	73,046	197,423	533,576
25%	30,518	93,132	284,217	867,362

This specific example is also illustrative because the rate of return on the investment is the same as the interest rate on the more expensive loan. Is it still worth it to borrow in this case? Yes, because each $1 borrowed at the higher rate can be combined with $2 borrowed at the lower rate.

We could look at the problem another way, through loan profitability. Each $1 that is borrowed at the lower rate of 5 percent will earn 5 cents a year, after the cost of capital. Each $1 we borrow at the higher rate, 10 percent, will earn 10 cents a year, because it allows the investor to borrow an additional $2 at 5 percent. Every line of credit has an expected value tied to the investor's ability to reinvest the proceeds at a higher rate.

Leverage magnifies the gains and losses and thus increases the risk. The leverage ratio can be multiplied by the volatility of the unleveraged investment in order to find the volatility of the investor's equity at any time.

Table 2.2 shows the results of an index fund that is leveraged several times. The model assumes an average annual return of 10 percent and a volatility of 15 percent and a 5 percent cost of capital. Note that a one standard deviation range encompasses 66 percent of the expected returns for a security. One-third of returns will still be outside this range, and the investor should be prepared for this level of volatility.

TABLE 2.2 Expected Return and Volatility of a Leveraged Index Fund

Leverage Ratio	Expected Return	Expected Volatility	Range, 1 Std	
			Low	High
1.00	10%	15%	−5%	25%
1.50	12.5%	22.5%	−10%	35%
2.00	15%	30%	−15%	45%
2.50	17.5%	37.5%	−20%	55%
3.00	20%	45%	−25%	65%

This helps show that a leveraged asset's volatility very much depends upon the volatility of the underlying asset and the amount of leverage applied. Because the index itself has low volatility, even at 2× leverage the investment is still less volatile than many investments, such as gold or emerging market indexes, based upon current market conditions.

In Table 2.3, we've presented an example of a highly leveraged investment held for ten years. As the value of the assets increase and the investment builds equity, the leverage ratio falls, which also reduces the volatility associated with the investment. This effect can make leveraged investments less risky over time.

If held indefinitely and appreciation continues, the leverage ratio would fall to almost 1, as the debt would become infinitely small compared to the equity. The volatility would also decrease, making the portfolio less risky as it accumulates equity.

UNDERWATER INVESTMENTS

The gains in leverage primarily come from compounding. When assets are able to compound at a higher rate than debt, huge profits can be created. The problem is that risky assets also have the potential to compound negatively in any period, wiping out investors equity. And as the amount of equity decreases, the asset becomes even more leveraged and more volatile.

In Table 2.4, the value of the assets in a highly leveraged portfolio falls five percent in each of the first three years as a result of an extended market downturn.

TABLE 2.3 Growth of 5× Leveraged Investment during Ten Years

Year	Assets	Debt	Equity	Leverage	Cap Gains	% RoE
0	50,000	40,000	10,000	5.0		
1	55,000	42,000	13,000	4.2	3,000	30.0%
2	60,500	44,100	16,400	3.7	3,400	26.2%
3	66,550	46,305	20,245	3.3	3,845	23.4%
4	73,205	48,620	24,585	3.0	4,340	21.4%
5	80,526	51,051	29,474	2.7	4,889	19.9%
6	88,578	53,604	34,974	2.5	5,500	18.7%
7	97,436	56,284	41,152	2.4	6,178	17.7%
ROI	22.4%					

Assumptions: Assets increase at 10% a year and Debt increases at 5%.

TABLE 2.4 Leveraged Investment in a Downturn, Years 0 to 3

Year	Assets	Debt	Equity	Leverage	Cap Gains	% RoE
0	50,000	40,000	10,000	5.0		
1	47,500	42,000	5,500	8.6	−4,500	−45.0%
2	45,125	44,100	1,025	44.0	−4,475	−81.4%
3	42,869	46,305	−3,436	NA	−4,461	−435.2%

As the equity declines, note the changes that take place. While the value of the assets is falling, the debt continues to compound, wiping out the equity. As a result, the leverage ratio increases sharply, and in the third year cannot be calculated, as there is no equity remaining in the investment.

Will this investment recover? Statistically, in any period the assets are expected to compound at a faster rate than the debt, and this would help the portfolio increase in value and eventually build equity. In Table 2.5, we estimate the expected recovery time by compounding both assets and debt at a regular rate.

If the portfolio performs as expected, during the next seven years it would build some equity, but the 10-year ROI is only 6.3 percent. Of course, this is just an estimate, and one or two more years of poor returns could push the expected recovery time out to years or even decades.

Leveraged investments are a race between debt and equity, and the random nature of equity returns means that it can pull ahead or fall behind at any point. Still, the odds will always favor the investment recovering at some point in the future.

Underwater investments are very common, especially in real estate. In 2003 and 2004, there was speculation that large parts of Equity Office Properties, the large public commercial office real estate investment trust

TABLE 2.5 Estimated Recovery of the Leveraged Investment, Years 4 to 10

Year	Assets	Debt	Equity	Leverage	Cap Gains	% RoE
4	47,156	48,620	−1,465	NA	1,972	NA
5	51,871	51,051	820	63.3	2,285	NA
6	57,058	53,604	3,454	16.5	2,635	321.3%
7	62,764	56,284	6,480	9.7	3,026	87.6%
8	69,041	59,098	9,942	6.9	3,462	53.4%
9	75,945	62,053	13,891	5.5	3,949	39.7%
10	83,539	65,156	18,383	4.5	4,492	32.3%
ROI	6.3%					

(REIT) owned by Sam Zell, were underwater. But in 2007, he was able to sell the company for $39 billion to Blackstone in the largest leveraged buyout in history. Leverage and rising real estate prices changed his fortunes quickly.

Donald Trump wasn't as fortunate with the Trump Taj Mahal in Atlantic City. This investment was financed with high-yield debt, and went through bankruptcy twice, diluting his ownership. The underlying asset was and still is extremely profitable, but has never been able to increase in value faster than the interest on the debt, due in part to the 1990 recession, the high level of competition, and the initial high yields.

Out-of-the-money long-term call options and equity futures can also be viewed as underwater investments, as the asset price has to appreciate before the security develops any intrinsic value.

If an underwater leveraged investment can be seen as the result of a portfolio meltdown, melt*ups* are not only possible, but also more probable.

Examine the portfolio in Table 2.6, which in the first three years grows at 20 percent, significantly above expectations. Over the next four years, the assets return the market average, 10 percent.

During the first three years, the RoE (Return on Equity) surges but then falls. As the portfolio builds equity, the leverage ratio falls, and this makes the portfolio less risky. However, as a consequence the RoE also has to decline as there is less borrowed money to invest per dollar of equity.

At this point, the investor could choose to either pay down their debt to further reduce risk and leverage and help lock in gains, could choose to increase debt in order to increase the leverage ratio and get higher expected returns, or could just leave the portfolio as is and be content with the reduced expected RoE and volatility.

TABLE 2.6 Effect of Early Gains on Leveraged Investment Growth

Year	Assets	Debt	Equity	Leverage	Cap Gains	% RoE
0	50,000	40,000	10,000	5.0		
1	60,000	42,000	18,000	3.3	8,000	80.0%
2	72,000	44,100	27,900	2.6	9,900	55.0%
3	86,400	46,305	40,095	2.2	12,195	43.7%
4	95,040	48,620	46,420	2.0	6,325	15.8%
5	104,544	51,051	53,493	2.0	7,073	15.2%
6	114,998	53,604	61,395	1.9	7,902	14.8%
7	126,498	56,284	70,214	1.8	8,820	14.4%
ROI	32.1%					

How does the random nature of market returns affect this analysis? To help answer this question, one hundred leveraged portfolios with seven years of random returns were generated. Each portfolio has $10,000 of equity initially leveraged 3×, and the underlying security has indexlike returns and volatility of 10 percent and 15 percent, respectively. The cost of debt is 5 percent.

Excel is well suited to the task of creating random portfolio simulations like this and it's an excellent exercise for helping to model potential market conditions. In order to value the portfolio assets, $30,000 is grown at a variable rate for seven years, using the following calculation to obtain a random rate given the previously defined parameters for a normal distribution of index returns:

$$= \text{NORMINV(RAND(), .10, .15)}$$

At the same time, the $20,000 debt increases at a constant rate of 5 percent a year, compounding to $28,142. The average equity at the end of seven years is $28,424, a 16.1 percent return on the original investment of $10,000. The portfolios are ranked in Table 2.7.

At the end of seven years, only two of the one hundred portfolios were underwater, that is, had debt higher than equity. Eleven other portfolios

TABLE 2.7 Percentile Rankings of Leveraged Portfolio Scenarios

	Assets	Debt	Equity	Return
Worst	19,450	28,142	−8,692	−198.0%
5%	34,195	28,142	6,053	−6.9%
10%	36,421	28,142	8,279	−2.7%
20%	41,444	28,142	13,302	4.2%
30%	43,966	28,142	15,824	6.8%
40%	47,679	28,142	19,537	10.0%
50%	55,523	28,142	27,381	15.5%
60%	59,042	28,142	30,900	17.5%
70%	63,741	28,142	35,599	19.9%
80%	72,101	28,142	43,959	23.6%
90%	82,111	28,142	53,969	27.2%
95%	90,828	28,142	62,686	30.0%
Best	100,206	28,142	72,064	32.6%
Avg.	56,566	28,142	28,424	
Stdev	17,535	NA	17,535	

Results of 100 3× leveraged index portfolios.
Seven-year timeframe, compounding debt.

still had equity but had taken losses. Thus 87 out of the one hundred port-folios broke even or better.

At the other end of the extreme, more than twenty-five portfolios had generated more than $40,000 in equity, a 22 percent return, and seven had generated equity of more than $60,000, a sixfold return in seven years.

The average return of this leveraged investment is impressive, but it is the outliers that are truly astonishing. Many leveraged investments have a "lottery ticket" effect in which rapidly compounding gains can create very large amounts of equity very quickly, and a single investment more than makes up for other losses in a portfolio.

DEBT AND INTEREST EFFECTS

In the previous examples, we've compounded our interest into our original investment. In practice, this is not always possible, and interest has to be paid when it is incurred or sometimes even prepaid, as we'll see with long-term call options.

Interest payments are usually made out of investor cash flow or accu-mulated assets, but can also come from the investment itself in the form of dividends. Large-value stocks in particular are known for paying high dividends, and this can help offset the carrying costs of these investments when leveraged. At the time of this writing, the Wilshire Value ETF (ELV) pays a 2.44 percent dividend, which could offset a significant fraction of the cost of debt required to hold the security.

If an investment pays no dividends but only has capital gains, then the investor could regularly sell shares to meet interest payments. When the market is down, this results in selling at a loss, and the investor needs to ensure that the leverage and volatility are not so high that a few inter-est payments at the wrong time could wipe out a significant fraction of portfolio.

Regularly paying the interest can be positive, as it prevents the debt balance from accumulating and compounding. During the investment, the assets will continue to grow and compound, building additional eq-uity. Over long periods of time, asset compounding drives extremely high returns.

If we calculate the return on investment (ROI) for two leveraged invest-ments, one that allows debt and interest compounding and accumulation and one that requires immediate payments, the first investment will come out far ahead, because the ROI of an interest payment is only the inter-est rate itself. In practice, of course, an investor could periodically borrow against equity to offset the loss of cash flow.

Ideally, if the leveraged asset appreciates quickly, additional capital can be borrowed and returned to the investor, and the investment position can still be maintained and then sold later for a profit. This can result in a very high ROI and is the basis for many successful real estate investments.

Debt often has tax benefits, as accumulated interest can be applied against income or capital gains, lowering the effective interest rate. Using accumulated debt, it is theoretically possible to defer capital gains taxes indefinitely while taking deductions for interest.

Three Commandments of Leveraged Investing

1. Money can be borrowed at a low rate of interest and invested at a higher rate. (For multiple sources, use weighting.)
2. Cash or cash flow is available to meet interest payments
3. Loan terms will not require a forced sale if the level of equity declines significantly

SOURCES OF LEVERAGE

Analysis of return on investment, interest rates, and tax deductions can obscure much more important issues regarding debt. Of course the interest rate has to be competitive, but generally, the key issues are how much can be borrowed and when does it need to be paid back. This is known as debt availability.

In this section, we'll review common sources of investment leverage, both for cost-effectiveness and for debt availability.

Margin Loans

When most retail investors think of leverage, they immediately think of buying stocks on margin. Margin is available to virtually any investor with a brokerage account. Conventional brokerage accounts require 50 percent initial margin, which means that for every $1 of equity, $1 of additional debt can be taken on, creating a maximum leverage ratio of 2.

Interest rates on margin can be somewhat competitive, or very uncompetitive, depending upon the broker. Some brokers who specialize in low margin provide interest rates of 5.5 percent on high margin balances, while others are close to 10 percent for retail investors, which would make borrowing to invest obviously prohibitive. Interest is charged periodically but compounded.

The biggest problem with broker margin is that the loan can be called if the equity position deteriorates. If a 30 percent maintenance margin is required, and then if the assets underperform the debt and the amount of equity falls below 30 percent of the value of the assets, then the position will be liquidated, resulting in a forced sale at a loss.

Thus the problem with margin loans is that we have very poor availability of debt. The low initial leverage provided, combined with the possibility of suddenly losing access to our line of credit due to a margin call, generally discourages investors from utilizing the full potential of margin.

A simulation was created in which an investor has $10,000 to invest, and can borrow with margin at 6.5 percent and invest in an index fund that pays 10 percent a year, on average, but with a 15 percent standard deviation. The investment is held for five years, or until the investor receives a margin call based upon a 30 percent requirement. The results are summarized in Table 2.8.

As expected, higher levels of initial margin led to higher profitability, but increased the odds of a margin call significantly. When the leverage ratio was over 1.8, there was a 10 percent chance of receiving a margin call during the five-year period. At 2.0× leverage, the likelihood of a margin call is significant enough that the average ending equity starts to decline, as compared to previous levels of margin.

From this data, we could infer that a leverage ratio of 1.6× offers a good risk/reward tradeoff, as profits are about 8 percent higher over the five years and the probability of a margin call is only about 3 percent. However, if the volatility of the index comes in higher than expected, then even that level of equity may be insufficient.

TABLE 2.8 5-Year Margin Call Probabilities at Selected Leverage Ratios

Leverage Ratio	Equity ($)	Margin Call	Benefit (over no leverage)
1.00	15,952	0.00%	
1.10	16,179	0.00%	+1.4%
1.20	16,432	0.00%	+3.0%
1.30	16,634	0.03%	+4.3%
1.40	16,880	0.30%	+5.8%
1.50	17,112	1.18%	+7.3%
1.60	17,299	3.14%	+8.4%
1.70	17,431	6.31%	+9.3%
1.80	17,575	10.63%	+10.2%
1.90	17,684	15.59%	+10.9%
2.00	17,604	21.51%	+10.4%

Futures

A common misconception about futures contracts is that they can be used to predict the market's opinion of the future value of a security. This is because S&P futures are often used to predict whether the stock market will open higher or lower every day, and fed funds futures can be used to detect a market bias toward a future interest rate cut. The commodity futures market also provides signals about price expectations.

But for equities, there are no future expectations built into pricing. Instead, the market price is merely a simple cost of capital calculation. If a stock is priced at $100 today, the futures price will be higher because capital is required for the seller to hold the position. The cost of capital is equal to the broker interest rate, minus expected dividends.

Although every futures contract has a settlement date, gains and losses in a futures contract are immediate, due to the margin required to hold the position. Every contract has a specific margin requirement, but typically broad indexes require 5 percent margin to hold the position, while a stock future requires 20 percent. This margin is used as security for the broker to ensure that the investor will be able to meet their obligations.

These low-margin requirements mean that investors can create very large investment positions with very little capital. At 5 percent margin, an index futures contract is a 20:1 leveraged position, and thus on an immediate basis the investment has 20× the return and 20× the volatility.

Futures could be considered the "purest" form of leveraged investment. If the security appreciates at a higher rate than the embedded cost of capital, a long position will be profitable. Futures contracts also have a high degree of standardization, and this results in lower transaction costs and high liquidity.

Futures contracts as a source of capital rate extremely well on both cost of capital and the amount of leverage available, but have availability issues, because even though leverage is high, any downturn in the security requires additional margin and could lead to a forced liquidation. Thus the 20× leverage limit is theoretical, not practical.

For example, an investor with $50,000 could potentially control $1m of the index, but would be foolish to do so because they would have no extra cash to meet obligations if the index declines. If prices fell at all, the broker would immediately liquidate their position. Futures contracts are best used in conjunction with either a large cash reserve, or with options to hedge against market declines.

Options

Options were originally asset-price hedging instruments, but their utility has grown well beyond that, due to the realization that they can be used as a low-cost substitute for the underlying investment. This is because as the underlying stock or index increases, the value of the hedge will change accordingly.

For example, if an investor writes a put option on the S&P 500 and creates a potential liability if prices fall, a leveraged position is now created on the index that will gain or lose value depending upon the movement of the underlying. The short put option is now a potential substitute for the security itself.

Fischer Black, Myron Scholes, and Robert C. Merton, two of whom won the Nobel Prize in economics in 1997, are credited with the discovery in the 1960s that any option can be modeled as a portfolio of shares of stock and risk-free bonds, the proportions of which constantly change as the price and volatility of the underlying stock increases or decreases (the Black-Scholes option pricing model).

The risk-free debt built into options is the same debt as that used to calculate the pricing of futures contracts, and the associated cost of the capital is also known as the broker rate. The use of equity and debt makes any option a leveraged position that could theoretically be replaced by futures. Of course keeping the right proportions of futures contracts would be a full-time job.

Because each option is unique in its underlying security, strike price, and expiration date, each underlying security may have a hundred options trading on it. For many, perhaps most or all of these options for some securities, liquidity may be poor and bid/ask spreads relatively high.

The primary advantage of options over futures is that hedged, leveraged positions can be constructed that capture investment profits efficiently but limit liability. Constructing and managing these positions is a complex effort, and the majority of this book is devoted to that task.

Example: Synthetics

A synthetic is an options position that is specifically designed to replicate the performance of an underlying security. While often referred to as a "synthetic stock," here we use the term synthetic as it can be applied to many different types of investments, including indexes.

A synthetic is created by buying a call option and selling a put option on the same security at the same strike and expiration date. This creates a dollar for dollar movement in the value of the security and the options position, but with much less capital.

Here's an example of a synthetic created with SPY, the S&P 500 ETF:

SPY is trading at @153.99 on 10/16/2007
Buy call @ 150 exp 3/22/2008 for 11.65
Sell put @ 150 exp 3/22/2008 for 5.55

Each option position by itself is a bullish position and hedging instrument, but when combined, the pair has the same payoff as SPY when held to expiry. The break-even point for the synthetic listed above is 156.10, and this is directly reflective of the cost of capital, which is the broker rate modified for the dividend yield of the underlying.

Capital is required to enter and hold the position, and incorporates both the initial cost of the long call, and the margin required to hold the short put option. Because this option has unlimited liability, the broker will require cash or equity to be held in the account to offset this liability, and this requirement will be adjusted constantly depending upon the price movement of the underlying. Each broker will have different margin requirements, and minimums will be set by the exchange.

Replacing 100 shares of SPY with one long call and one short put contract would free up cash that could be either deposited in risk-free bonds, or used for other investments. Some cash would have to be maintained for hedging costs, both as initially calculated, and then based upon potential decreases in the price of the SPY.

A synthetic stock position can be maintained indefinitely. Options can be "rolled forward" to future expiration date by simply replacing the two options with the same options but with a later expiration date. In the next chapter, we'll use this technique to create a long-term leveraged position on the index.

Other Debt Sources

Many investors or institutions have the ability to borrow against their assets or future cash flow. For example, a real estate investor could borrow against their holdings and invest in index funds or ETFs in order to diversify and earn additional capital gains. From one point of view, this would be a leveraged investment.

Lines of credit tied to assets are generally low cost, and the debt is available as long as the asset is owned. In effect, these loans are borrowing against net worth. Credit based on future cash flow tends to be related to credit scoring, and usually is of a higher interest rate.

The benefit in using external, nonmarket sources of credit is that cost and availability are not tied to the equity in the investment itself. This means that even if the investment loses value in the short term, the loan can still be maintained as long as payments continue to be made.

For example, suppose an investor opens a $100,000 line of credit based on their home equity, and then uses the first $10,000 as margin for $200,000 worth of index futures contracts. If the broker rate built into the futures contracts is 5 percent, but the index is assumed to appreciate at 10 percent, then the investor is expected to make $10,000 a year, not including interest on the line of credit.

On the other hand, if the value of the futures contracts declines in the short term, they can use their additional home equity to meet margin requirements. Because the debt is not tied to the value of the securities, the investor is in a position where they can avoid mark-to-market losses and margin calls.

MANAGING A LEVERAGED PORTFOLIO

The goal in portfolio management is to reduce risk while maintaining or increasing potential return. The challenge in managing leveraged portfolios is that the stakes are higher. Debt is unforgiving and borrowed capital is expensive, and if mistakes are made in portfolio management, the underlying debt still has to be paid back.

High volatility investments not only increase the risk of total loss, but also can make investors very nervous about continuing with an investment strategy. There are psychological affects associated with volatility that can change behavior, making nervous investors eschew risk and seek safety, leading investors to sell assets and abandon strategies at the worst time.

Lower volatility also decreases hedging costs and makes higher degrees of leverage possible, which indirectly increases returns. In this section, we'll investigate portfolio management techniques that can reduce volatility and increase returns at the same time.

Portfolio Sizing

The most common and most dangerous mistake that most leveraged investors make has little to do with the cost of capital, rates of return, diversification, or any other leveraged investing or portfolio management concept. It is simply attempting to hold too large a position in a risky investment.

The dilemma that investors face is that markets do reward investors for risk, and the greater the risk taken on, the higher the profits, in general. This creates a temptation to take on larger and larger risks to get a higher level of returns, and sets up a situation where an investor can be rewarded several times for their mistakes, and then severely punished, wiping out all of their previous gains.

Consider a middle-class investor who uses $25,000 to purchase $500,000 worth of S&P futures contracts. If historical S&P 500 annual volatility is approximately 12.5 percent, we can calculate that the underlying portfolio can easily gain or lose 3.6 percent a month. (3.6 percent = 12.5 percent divided by sqrt(12)). This represents a potential $18,000 gain or loss before index drift and interest costs every month.

If the position is held for three months, and we include 5 percent annual interest costs, then the average gain is approximately 0.3 percent a month, or $4,500 total. Meanwhile, our one standard deviation gain or loss has grown over that period to $31,250, or $500,000 × 12.5 percent/sqrt(4). The investor is equally likely to end these three months up $36,000 or down $27,000. If the former, then there will likely be a strong temptation to reinvest the gains and increase the position and thereby take on more risk. If, instead, the investment loses the money, the investor could be wiped out by a margin call and decide to never invest in anything aside from treasury bonds again. Leveraged investing would be blamed for the loss, when in fact it was just too large a position with too much risk.

Portfolio sizing can be viewed as an optimization problem between expected future return and short-term liquidity requirements. The objective is to calculate the ideal portfolio size so that there is both the greatest chance of meeting short-term cash obligations and the opportunity to obtain the largest portfolio at a future date.

Institutions also face portfolio-sizing problems and sometimes make deadly mistakes. It is very common to see hedge funds or even financial institutions take on outsize risks in the hopes of large returns, and end up in serious trouble. Nick Leeson, Orange County, Long-Term Capital Management, and Amaranth Advisors are all well-known examples.

One approach is to estimate the largest possible loss of a portfolio in a given period. This is very similar to what large financial institutions do with their Value-at-Risk (VaR) metric, and to what we've done above. By calculating the likelihood of investment losses exceeding a specific amount by a specific date, risk can be measured and monitored.

Still, Value at Risk is driven by key assumptions regarding the volatility of an investment, and these volatilities can change suddenly, making a portfolio that seems secure suddenly extremely volatile. But at least VaR is an attempt to answer the question, given the available data.

Depending upon the structure of the investment, the investor may not be concerned about short-term losses, but rather with the ability to hold the position to profitability. In this case, focusing on the required cash flows to hold the position—that is, interest payments—is the best approach, and is often the limiting factor in portfolio size.

If the above investor had been able to put a hedge in place and maintain it, for example by rolling put options forward, the portfolio could be sized by combining both the required interest and the expected cost of maintaining the hedge. The objective then is to ensure that there is enough cash or expected cash flow on hand to maintain the investment for four or five years, by which time the probabilities strongly favor profitability.

Thus we have four components to sizing a portfolio:

1. Affording the initial equity
2. Affording the interest payments
3. Managing potential short-term losses
4. Maintaining a hedge or margin (if required)

This book has an entire chapter, Chapter 10, devoted to hedging, but it's worth mentioning here that smart hedging allows investors to take on more risk than they otherwise would and receive higher returns in the process. It is an important tool for aggressive investors seeking the highest return, and not only for the overly cautious.

Portfolio Allocations

Portfolio management theory is based upon the concept that holding multiple risky assets is generally less risky than holding any one asset individually. The laws of statistics and of large numbers help to cancel out the individual price movements, but still leave some risk, often labeled as systematic, that can't be diversified away.

By selecting assets with high returns as compared to their impact on systematic risk and total portfolio risk, an investment can be created with very high capital efficiency and risk adjusted returns. A portfolio like this is ideal to apply leverage to because its overall volatility is low and returns are predictable.

Of course, it is impossible to predict with any certainty what a specific asset's returns and volatility will be in the near future. Generally, portfolio managers use historical averages, but the current values can change quickly. For example, large bank stocks can be very stable and boring, except when there's some sort of credit crunch or financial crisis, and then they get very volatile very quickly.

By only using recent returns and volatility, it is possible to fall into a trap where assets are selected for the portfolio when conditions look favorable, and then sold when problems emerge, in effect buying high and selling low. A better approach is to use estimates based upon very long-term averages, and to understand that any investment is capable of diverging from either historical or recent trends.

It is theoretically possible to have an asset that has high volatility, but a low correlation to the overall portfolio, so that adding this asset to a portfolio actually reduces risk. In practice, these are difficult to find. Most risky assets will make a portfolio more volatile.

As an exercise, let's compare the dividend-adjusted performance of the S&P 500 to an equal-weight portfolio of nine sector funds, named Blend. Each sector ETF contains a subset of the stocks in the S&P 500.

XLB	Materials
XLE	Energy
XLF	Financials
XLI	Industrials
XLP	Consumer Staples
XLU	Utilities
XLK	Technology
XLY	Consumer Discretionary
XLV	Health Care

Table 2.9 shows that during the period examined, January 1999 to December 2006, the S&P gained on average 3.9 percent per year with 14.1 percent volatility. The S&P 500 has lower volatility than most, but not all, of the individual sectors. Consumer staples and health care sectors have lower volatilities. The numbers presented are annualized numbers based on monthly averages.

The result is that Blend, the equal weight portfolio, has both a higher return and lower volatility than the S&P 500. Have we built a better index? Very likely.

By keeping the proportion of each sector constant, the portfolio allocates its resources to higher performing sectors, on average, and avoids some of the volatility at the same time. The Diff column shows the performance advantage of Blend vs the S&P 500. The Blend portfolio has higher performance and/or lower volatility in most, but not all years.

Blending sectors is not an optimal portfolio, simply a starting point. We could reduce our exposure to exceptionally volatile sectors, like technology. Of course we know how technology fared in our historical data, but even without this knowledge, we could still see that in 2000, volatility was 15 points higher than any other sector and contributed significantly to our overall portfolio volatility.

A second portfolio, LoCorr, was created that is an average of only four sectors: Consumer Products, Utilities, Energy, and Financials. These were chosen for their low volatility, and, except in the case of Financials, a low

TABLE 2.9 Sector ETF Portfolio Compared to the S&P 500 ETF

Annualized Returns

	SPY	XLB	XLE	XLF	XLI	XLP	XLU	XLK	XLY	XLV	Blend	LoCorr	Diff
1999	11.5%	17.2%	29.1%	−0.1%	15.5%	−11.5%	−2.9%	37.3%	1.7%	12.1%	10.0%	3.7%	−1.4%
2000	0.5%	−6.2%	22.4%	33.0%	18.4%	17.3%	19.9%	−18.9%	8.2%	−1.3%	9.3%	23.2%	8.8%
2001	−15.2%	9.3%	−17.2%	−9.7%	−13.5%	−3.3%	−11.3%	−30.1%	7.1%	−6.0%	−9.0%	−10.4%	6.2%
2002	−21.3%	−9.3%	−12.1%	−13.2%	−22.6%	−21.5%	−26.1%	−33.2%	−22.4%	0.7%	−18.3%	−18.2%	3.0%
2003	34.6%	40.2%	33.8%	37.8%	41.7%	15.4%	34.0%	49.0%	42.6%	19.0%	34.5%	30.2%	−0.2%
2004	6.4%	16.1%	36.4%	5.4%	13.9%	9.3%	24.0%	−3.1%	9.2%	−4.0%	11.3%	18.8%	4.9%
2005	10.1%	13.9%	59.9%	9.8%	6.5%	2.0%	17.3%	10.0%	0.1%	11.5%	13.6%	22.3%	3.5%
2006	14.3%	17.0%	2.9%	18.3%	15.1%	16.1%	17.0%	10.8%	19.8%	8.9%	13.9%	13.6%	−0.5%
1999 to 2006	3.9%	11.4%	17.0%	8.9%	7.8%	2.1%	7.3%	−0.8%	7.0%	4.8%	7.2%	8.8%	3.3%

Annualized Volatility

	SPY	XLB	XLE	XLF	XLI	XLP	XLU	XLK	XLY	XLV	Blend	LoCorr	Diff
1999	14.2%	33.6%	21.1%	22.9%	21.3%	16.3%	14.8%	24.6%	23.0%	14.1%	14.5%	10.4%	0.3%
2000	17.0%	26.1%	25.3%	27.2%	19.6%	20.8%	24.2%	44.4%	23.2%	18.1%	15.9%	18.3%	−1.2%
2001	19.4%	23.1%	20.1%	14.9%	27.4%	10.9%	10.7%	43.6%	24.9%	23.2%	18.1%	10.7%	−1.3%
2002	20.2%	25.6%	20.3%	20.6%	18.3%	14.2%	22.0%	44.6%	20.0%	15.2%	19.4%	17.2%	−0.8%
2003	10.3%	18.2%	17.7%	15.0%	12.7%	7.7%	17.5%	12.4%	15.4%	9.9%	10.2%	11.6%	−0.1%
2004	7.9%	13.6%	13.2%	9.1%	10.4%	9.6%	8.2%	14.8%	10.3%	11.0%	7.5%	5.8%	−0.4%
2005	8.1%	16.5%	25.8%	7.9%	9.8%	5.4%	10.5%	13.1%	13.0%	6.9%	8.2%	11.2%	0.0%
2006	5.5%	11.9%	17.9%	7.6%	9.7%	4.2%	9.4%	12.4%	9.8%	8.2%	5.3%	7.1%	−0.2%
1999 to 2006	14.1%	21.6%	20.7%	17.1%	17.4%	12.5%	16.1%	29.9%	18.3%	13.9%	13.5%	12.7%	−0.7%

SPY Correlation

SPY	XLB	XLE	XLF	XLI	XLP	XLU	XLK	XLY	XLV	Blend	LoCorr
1999	0.66	0.39	0.67	0.62	0.27	0.19	0.77	0.93	0.86	0.91	0.50
2000	0.43	0.47	0.58	0.75	-0.18	0.03	0.80	0.51	0.88	0.80	0.16
2001	0.79	0.52	0.88	0.88	0.43	0.22	0.95	0.87	0.85	0.96	0.54
2002	0.85	0.74	0.95	0.92	0.70	0.68	0.93	0.92	0.87	0.98	0.77
2003	0.77	0.34	0.90	0.91	0.82	0.55	0.89	0.88	0.36	0.97	0.63
2004	0.84	0.14	0.80	0.85	0.51	0.48	0.85	0.88	0.60	0.98	0.62
2005	0.75	0.56	0.54	0.85	0.72	0.20	0.92	0.84	0.38	0.97	0.61
2006	0.73	0.23	0.69	0.57	0.17	-0.03	0.89	0.73	0.25	0.93	0.22
1999 to 2006	0.68	0.48	0.74	0.81	0.35	0.37	0.87	0.80	0.76	0.93	0.54

correlation to the S&P 500 index. The LoCorr portfolio has a higher average return and lower volatility than either the SPY or the Blend portfolios.

Creating index portfolios using historical data is always educational and can produce results that are better than any single index during that time; however, we can see from the sector funds how much return, volatility, and correlation can change from year to year, making predictions difficult. For example, Health Care sector correlations changed significantly and apparently irreversibly in 2003.

Focusing on only the correlations—as some portfolio managers do—ignores the big picture, which is that holding more high-quality assets provides higher average returns and lower volatility. In our last chapter, we sought to find the best index from all of the options in the marketplace. But the results show that it's better to build than to buy, and we'll use that approach in the next strategy chapter to develop investments that are comparable, if not superior, to any broad index.

Rebalancing with Leverage

In the above example, holding multiple sectors in equal proportions would only be possible if the portfolio was rebalanced regularly by selling shares of winning funds and transferring the assets to the relative losers.

Rebalancing can be done on any frequency. According to reports, David Swensen, who manages the Yale endowment, rebalances the billion-dollar fund daily. Simulating rebalancing in a model is simple, as the average return of the portfolio simply becomes the weighted average return for all of the assets in that period.

In some cases, rebalancing can improve performance, for example, if assets are shifted from lower performing to higher performing investments. In theory, shifting assets from an appreciated investment that has a higher valuation to one with a lower valuation should create higher returns. In practice, assets simply aren't this predictable unless hundreds of investments are held, such as in a value portfolio.

The primary benefit of rebalancing is the reduction of volatility through the preservation of asset allocation. Lower volatility in an unleveraged portfolio makes higher degrees of leverage possible. Unfortunately, quantifying the exact benefit is only possible ex post facto.

To rebalance a leveraged portfolio, rebalance the assets and ignore the debt and equity, as they cannot be changed except through reinvestment, which is covered in the next section.

Sometimes investors are psychologically resistant to rebalancing because they don't want to sell assets that look as though they will continue appreciating and put the proceeds into something else perceived as "dead money." This is a mental bias based upon the perceived ability of past performance to predict future results, and is inconsistent with historical investment returns.

However, rebalancing does incur transaction costs and trigger taxable events, so it's not necessary to do it constantly. Asset allocation is unlikely to diverge significantly in a one-month or three-month period unless the underlying assets are highly volatile.

Dollar Cost Averaging and Liquidity Preference

One of the fears of investors is that they will make a large investment in the market, and that prices will immediately fall, wiping out a significant portion of their investment. Because of this, investors with lump sums to invest are generally recommended to dollar cost average their way into the market, that is, invest a fixed amount every period over time.

The reasoning behind dollar cost averaging is that risk is reduced because instead of having a single entry point into the market, an investor's entry point is a weighted average of the market prices on several dates, and this makes profitability more likely. However, this reasoning is flawed.

If the underlying trend of the index is higher, but with random drift, then every day that assets are held out of the market is an opportunity cost. Investing a lump sum over a period of several months will result in higher average costs, not lower. This means that fewer shares are purchased, and the investment has less time for the assets to compound, resulting in reduced gains.

Also, by keeping assets in cash over the dollar cost averaging period, the investor is in effect selecting a lower leverage ratio. For example, an investor with $100,000 who invests $5,000 a month for ten months will have a leverage ratio of 0.05 for the first month, 0.10 for the second month, and so on, until they are fully invested.

What of the original concern—that an immediate crash could wipe out the portfolio? The response then has to be, what if a crash comes in twenty months when the lump sum is fully invested? A crash is no more likely to occur today than in twenty or forty or sixty months when the investor is fully invested, and the portfolio will have missed out on the appreciation in the meantime.

For every price trend that we can think of that would benefit from dollar cost averaging, we can think of another that would result in lower earnings or even losses. For example, the market could rise sharply during the dollar cost averaging period and then collapse thereafter, resulting in both higher average prices and a huge decline.

The probabilities say that the more money an investor has invested for the longest period of time, the more money they will make. The logical conclusion of this is not to dollar cost average, but to size the investment portfolio correctly to achieve the long-term results required, and then to immediately make the investment.

Dollar cost averaging is psychology, not finance or portfolio management. If an investor is not comfortable having a certain sum of money at risk, then giving that investor a false sense of security by rationalizing that only a little bit of money will be invested at a time doesn't actually solve the problem; it simply defers it.

Note that dollar cost averaging is the preferred way to invest cash flow, as that's how the cash comes in, and it plays a role in reinvestment, as we'll see below. But it is not recommended for investing lump sums, except perhaps over very short periods where the expected loss is extremely minimal.

Reinvesting Leveraged Gains

A leveraged investor has the option to increase their investment at any time by issuing new debt, or decrease their investment by selling assets and paying down debt. This changes the portfolio's asset and debt amounts and leverage ratio, but keeps the level of equity the same, aside from any transaction costs.

Investing more assets increases expected gains, but also puts more capital at risk. Failing to invest is a missed opportunity, but taking a too large investment position with a leveraged portfolio can create catastrophic and unrecoverable problems if prices fall.

Futures contracts, securities bought on broker margin, and unhedged options all have the ability to trigger a margin call and potentially a forced liquidation of the portfolio, wiping out the entire investment. Preventing situations where this occurs is critical.

The primary way to accomplish this is to keep the level of leverage low. For example, as previously discussed, a futures contract has a 5 percent margin requirement, which can theoretically provide 20:1 leverage. But how risky would a portfolio be with just 2:1 leverage?

Clearly a 50 percent decline in the underlying security would wipe out the portfolio, but a very long flat market could potentially wipe out the investor also. Futures contracts have a cost of capital built-in, and a long string of 1 percent annual returns would eventually erode an investor's equity. Still, either occurrence has a very low probability.

High volatility leveraged portfolios that are unhedged, marked to market, and require margin are the most dangerous portfolios, as all of these factors can combine to create a situation where a few months of bad returns can wipe out most of the equity in an account. Their only protection is diversification, but, in downturns, a wide variety of assets are often affected simultaneously.

Reinvesting leveraged gains or adjusting the portfolio after losses is a risk management exercise in which we balance expected gains against possible losses. In the rest of this chapter, we will present one reinvestment strategy that is commonly used but has significant dangers, and two others that can both reduce volatility and increase returns.

Also, the risk/reward equation can be changed significantly by hedging with options, which we discuss more extensively in the next few chapters, or by finding other solutions such as external debt that avoid margin calls and mark-to-market losses.

Constant Leverage Trap   One solution that is often considered in leveraged portfolio management is to select a specific target leverage ratio and maintain that ratio over time. This is typically the result of a risk assessment in which the investor calculates that they are comfortable with a certain amount of volatility, but no more. For example, if the S&P 500 has an average volatility of 15 percent, and the investor is comfortable with 22.5 percent volatility, then a 1.5× leverage ratio could be maintained over time.

This technique has some academic support, in that the emphasis of portfolio management is on trying to secure the greatest return given an acceptable level of risk. This suggests that by leveraging the most efficient investment—the total stock market, to a target level—an optimum investment strategy could be maintained.

But this doesn't work well in practice. The problem is that, in the short term, the only way to adjust leverage is by buying or selling portfolio assets. This means that any portfolio that tries to maintain a constant leverage ratio over time is going to be selling whenever the market goes down and buying when it goes up.

The effect of this poor market timing is to accumulate large amounts of assets during market rallies and peaks and sell them during corrections. Not only does this increase volatility significantly, it also retards performance.

Table 2.10 shows the effect on a portfolio that attempts to maintain a target leverage ratio of 2 by readjusting every week. During this example period, the market had a brief rally, and then a dip, and then recovered, ending flat for the ten weeks. Yet, the portfolio has lost value, even though this example assumes no cost of capital.

How did this happen? The evidence is in the fund returns as compared to the index returns. All of the fund returns are double the amount of the index return, as would be expected by leverage and a zero cost of capital for borrowed funds. The initial 2 percent return is doubled to 4 percent, and the next 1.96 percent return is doubled to a 3.92 percent return.

By the end of the ten weeks, however, there is a shortfall. It's not a math or a rounding error. It is a mathematical effect that occurs when both

TABLE 2.10   Constant Leverage Trap

Week	Index Price	Index Return	Fund Return	NAV
0	100			100.00
1	102	2.00%	4.00%	104.00
2	104	1.96%	3.92%	108.08
3	106	1.92%	3.85%	112.24
4	102	−3.77%	−7.55%	103.76
5	100	−1.96%	−3.92%	99.70
6	98	−2.00%	−4.00%	95.71
7	96	−2.04%	−4.08%	91.80
8	95	−1.04%	−2.08%	89.89
9	98	3.16%	6.32%	95.57
10	100	2.04%	4.08%	99.47
Volatility		2.43%	4.85%	

negative and positive investment returns are doubled and those returns are compounded. The doubled negative returns have a larger affect on the portfolio than the doubled positive returns.

Compare:

$$+5\% \times -5\% = 1.05 \times 0.95 = 0.9975 = -.0025\%$$
$$+10\% \times -10\% = 1.1 \times 0.9 = 0.99 = -1\%$$

The portfolio loss of −0.53 percent may look small, but this shortfall is over only ten weeks. Over time, this slippage accumulates, and in the real world, higher transaction and ongoing interest costs also play a factor. The result is that a constant leverage portfolio can underperform not only other leveraged portfolios, but even the underlying itself, as we'll see in the last chapter of this book.

Maintaining constant leverage over time through buying and selling assets is also a form of a dynamic or delta hedging strategy. These strategies are often modeled in academic papers; for example, the Black-Scholes model has, at its core, a delta hedged options portfolio.

In the real world, these strategies not only don't work, but it is theorized that they have the power to destroy the financial system. This is according to none other than Warren Buffett, who referred to derivatives as financial weapons of mass destruction in his 2003 shareholder letter.

One of the contributors to the stock market crash of October 1987 was the widespread use of portfolio insurance, a dynamic hedging technique that buys and sells S&P 500 futures to offset portfolio gains and losses.

When market prices fell, liquidity collapsed, and those transactions were no longer possible.

Investors need to be extremely wary of derivative portfolio management strategies that require trading whenever the market makes a move, especially if the transaction "follows the trend"—that is, is in the same direction as the overall market. These strategies tend to perform well in rising markets, but have significant volatility and can collapse spectacularly if a correction occurs and market liquidity evaporates.

Constant Asset or Debt Reinvestment   Instead of keeping the leverage ratio constant over time, a better approach is to keep either the debt or assets constant in the short term, and increasing slowly in the long term. Both of these reinvestment strategies minimize transactions, reduce volatility, and can improve long-term performance.

A constant debt reinvestment strategy is similar to having no reinvestment strategy at all. The portfolio manager sets an initial level of debt, and then pays the interest monthly or quarterly over time using asset sales or dividends. This is an excellent strategy for investing future cash flow or for utilizing external debt that's not linked to asset prices.

For example, a portfolio manager could combine $100,000 of debt with $50,000 of equity, and then pay the interest every month through stock sales. The initial leverage ratio would start out at $3\times$, but then would decrease over time as the underlying assets appreciate.

Paying the interest prevents the debt from compounding, but allows the assets to continue to grow, eventually dwarfing the debt and reducing both the leverage ratio and the portfolio volatility.

Or, the debt could be slowly increased over time to implement a gradual reinvestment strategy. For example, the investor could borrow an additional 10 percent a year, say, $10,000 the first year, $11,000 the second year, and so on, and use the proceeds to make new investments. Directing the cash to investments that have underperformed in the past year could also help to rebalance the portfolio.

It is also possible to keep the level of invested assets constant despite market fluctuations by increasing or reducing the level of debt. This is exactly the opposite of the constant leverage strategy, and is best illustrated by the following example.

A portfolio manager combines $100,000 of debt with $50,000 of equity and invests it in a portfolio of index funds. If the portfolio increases in value, to $160,000 for example, the investor will sell $10,000 worth of assets and pay down the debt.

If instead, the portfolio falls in value by $10,000, the manager responds by borrowing additional funds and reinvesting the proceeds. The leverage ratio climbs higher, as does the expected return and volatility of the portfolio. When the market recovers, the portfolio benefits from the leverage and then pays down the debt.

This adjustment could be done monthly or quarterly, and keeps exactly $150,000 of assets invested in the market after the transaction. Over time, as investment gains accumulate, the debt would be reduced, which also reduces the leverage and the interest costs. At some point, the portfolio would be debt free.

Then, the level of assets could be increased every year to create a larger exposure to the market over time. Otherwise, eventually all of the debt would be paid off, and the surplus would accumulate in risk-free bonds, and the leverage ratio would fall below one.

The primary benefit of a constant assets strategy is reduced volatility. If the amount invested in the market is exactly the same every month or every year, then that helps to reduce the volatility of the overall portfolio. Then as gains come in, the leverage ratio is reduced, further reducing risk. It can also be a very profitable strategy in volatile or cyclical markets.

Of course, the danger is that prices may fall so far that the portfolio cannot sustain the level of debt required by the model. However, the portfolio manager could also simply cap the level of debt at some safe, reasonable level, thereby creating parameters for both the portfolio asset and debt levels.

SUMMARY

This chapter analyzes the effects of using financial leverage in portfolios. When assets can be invested at a higher rate of return than the associated debt, leveraged investments can be extremely profitable. Over periods of years, an investment can have a rate of return that is several points higher than the underlying, especially if investment gains are allowed to continue compounding.

The leverage ratio, as calculated by assets divided by equity, is the simplest way to measure leverage as it can be used as a multiplier for both the expected return and expected volatility. An index–based portfolio with a leverage ratio of 2 will have returns that are twice as high as the index, not including the cost of capital. However, the volatility will also be twice as high.

As the portfolio builds equity, the leverage ratio falls. This reduces the potential volatility of the portfolio, but also the expected return. In order to maintain the same level of leverage, an investor would have to borrow and invest more; otherwise, over time, the portfolio would be equivalent to an unleveraged fund.

When the underlying assets are volatile, as is the case with an index fund or any equity investment, there is always a probability in any period that the value of the assets will fall. Because the debt continues to compound, the portfolio equity is reduced and the percentage losses can be high, assuming that the leverage ratio is also high. Investments that have lost all of their equity are referred to as "underwater," but the odds would still favor these investments recovering their value over longer periods of time, assuming that the average rate of expected appreciation is still higher than the interest cost of the debt.

Leveraged portfolios can be created by using a margin account or by purchasing derivatives such as futures and options. Of the three alternatives, margin is not recommended as the interest rates are often high, not enough money can be borrowed, and the risk of a margin call rises significantly as the leverage ratio increases. Instead, combinations of futures and options can provide both high degrees of leverage, low cost access to capital, and appropriate risk management.

In this chapter, we focused on two challenges that make managing leveraged portfolios more difficult. The first is increased volatility, and we showed that it is possible to develop indexes with less volatility than the S&P 500 by blending either all of the sector indexes, or only selected ones with low correlations. Lower volatility leads to less risk when the portfolio is leveraged, and the result is higher risk-adjusted returns.

The second challenge is managing the initial and ongoing amount of investment exposure. When the level of exposure is high, investors put themselves at risk of taking a loss that can devastate the portfolio. This recommended amount of index exposure will depend upon the investor's financial situation, risk tolerance, and long-term investment goals. Dollar cost averaging of the initial investment is not recommended, as that only defers the exposure problem until the assets are fully invested.

As the portfolio accumulates capital gains, the question then becomes how to reinvest the proceeds without creating too much risk. One approach, maintaining a constant leverage ratio, is discredited, and we show that a $2\times$ leveraged portfolio that attempts to maintain such a ratio will experience shortfalls over periods of time that can make it underperform the index. In Chapter 12, we examine this problem more closely, with regard to the leveraged ETFs on the market.

Instead, an approach in which either the level of portfolio assets is kept relatively constant or it grows at a slow rate over time is recommended. This technique allows the portfolio to lower its leverage ratio and volatility whenever the underlying asset prices, thereby locking in excess gains. An intelligent reinvestment strategy can significantly increase the expected value of an investment portfolio over time.

Finally, we showed a method for creating simulations of leveraged portfolios in Excel using the NORMINV() function to generate random returns for a period. This technique opens the door to analysis of possible portfolio outcomes based upon different combinations of annual index returns, and will be used extensively throughout the remainder of the book.

CHAPTER 3

Indexing with Synthetics and Futures

I n this, the first strategy chapter, a leveraged index portfolio is constructed using options on ETFs to create synthetic positions. In order to generate higher returns, the portfolio is overweighted in both small-cap and value indexes, two categories that have historically outperformed the S&P 500 over time. The fund is designed to be a long-term, multiyear investment, although rapid short-term gains are possible in certain circumstances.

Even though this is the first strategy chapter of six, this is by no means simply an introductory or example strategy. This investment is designed to outperform the majority of the passive and actively managed equity funds in the marketplace over multiyear periods without a significant increase in long-term volatility.

This portfolio uses synthetics, which can be created by purchasing options that are available in every brokerage account. Synthetics are a proxy for owning an underlying stock or index on a leveraged basis. Synthetics can be replaced with futures contracts, and later in the chapter we make this substitution in order to lower the margin call risk and obtain higher levels of initial leverage.

ASSET ALLOCATION

This strategy uses its assets to purchase derivatives on a target asset allocation of shares of three exchange-traded funds (ETFs). We present the

ETF performance and fund characteristics in Table 3.1 for each of these funds, and also provide those of the S&P 500 (SPY) for comparison.

Fund listing and portfolio allocation:

Allocation (%)	Fund
50%	iShares Russell 2000 Value ETF (IWN)
25%	Standard & Poor's 500 Midcap (MDY)
25%	iShares Morgan Stanley Capital Index Europe and Far East (EFA)

The core of the portfolio is IWN, the small-cap value ETF. Half of the stocks in the Russell 2000 small-cap index are categorized as growth, and the other half as value, based upon their PE ratio and growth expectations. This fund has been selected for its superior Fama-French factors and its broad diversification.

The other two funds are more traditional equity indexes. MDY, the mid-cap SPDR, offers a diversified collection of U.S. equities; EFA provides international diversification, primarily Europe and Japan. The holdings are similar. There is a high concentration of financials and industrials, but these are very broad categories that have considerable diversification within them. Financials, for example, includes very different types of companies: regional banks, insurance companies, REITs, investment banks, and government-sponsored enterprises (GSEs) like Fannie Mae and Freddie Mac.

There are two other factors that make these ETFs useful for this portfolio. The first is that they pay dividends, which can reduce the interest costs associated with a leveraged portfolio. Secondly, options are available on all of these ETFs, and this permits the creation of synthetic positions. The mechanics are given later in this chapter.

Although ETF valuation ratios cannot be used as a timing signal, they do provide some indication of whether stocks are more likely to be over- or underpriced. All of the valuation ratios shown seem reasonable, as compared to, for example, the over 40 PE ratios for the pre-bubble NASDAQ or Nikkei, but of course it would be misleading to think that they could never go lower.

There are high correlations between the returns of the three ETFs and the broad index, which is to be expected with any diversified portfolio of equities. Correlations could be reduced by selecting certain sector funds, such as energy and utilities, which historically provide some independence from the movements of the broader market. However, that would also skew the sector diversification and dilute the impact of the Fama-French factors.

TABLE 3.1 ETF Summary Statistics

	IWN	MDY	EFA	SPY
Valuation				
Price/Earnings (PE)	14.73	17.28	14.2	14.95
Price/Book (PB)	1.48	2.27	2.05	2.59
Dividend Yield	1.85%	1.24%	1.86%	1.78%
Holdings				
Software	2.9%	3.4%	0.6%	3.7%
Industrial Materials	16.5%	13.8%	17.2%	12.4%
Energy	4.2%	9.7%	7.5%	10.9%
Utilities	5.0%	6.9%	5%	3.4%
Hardware	7.1%	8.4%	4.2%	10.4%
Media	2.1%	1.2%	1.8%	3.2%
Telecommunication	2.1%	1.0%	5.9%	3.7%
Healthcare	4.8%	11.8%	6.3%	11.7%
Consumer Services	6.8%	9.5%	4.6%	7.5%
Business Services	8.3%	13.2%	4.7%	4.1%
Financial Services	32.6%	14.5%	27.8%	20.0%
Consumer Goods	5.6%	6.02%	13%	8.4%
Avg. Return				
1999	NA	16.9%	NA	11.5%
2000	NA	24.9%	NA	0.5%
2001	13.2%	−1.0%	NA	−15.2%
2002	−13.2%	−15.3%	−12.7%	−21.3%
2003	56.6%	42.9%	49.4%	34.6%
2004	14.6%	11.3%	16.0%	6.4%
2005	18.2%	22.2%	22.8%	10.1%
2006	16.0%	8.1%	21.0%	14.3%
Total	16.8%	12.6%	16.6%	3.9%
Avg. Volatility				
1999	NA	15.1%	NA	14.2%
2000	NA	18.7%	NA	17.0%
2001	17.0%	22.5%	NA	19.4%
2002	21.6%	18.9%	18.3%	20.2%
2003	14.0%	12.4%	13.5%	10.3%
2004	14.5%	10.8%	11.0%	7.9%
2005	15.1%	12.0%	10.6%	8.1%
2006	8.8%	8.9%	8.5%	5.5%
Total	15.8%	15.6%	13.4%	14.1%

(Continued)

TABLE 3.1   ETF Summary Statistics   *(Continued)*

	IWN	MDY	EFA	SPY
SPY Correlation				
1999	NA	0.84	NA	
2000	NA	0.71	NA	
2001	0.71	0.92	NA	
2002	0.72	0.91	0.84	
2003	0.88	0.83	0.89	
2004	0.89	0.96	0.96	
2005	0.87	0.95	0.48	
2006	0.82	0.83	0.73	
Total	0.73	0.86	0.81	

One last but important point: *Never use daily prices to calculate correlations when including indexes with foreign stocks.* The differences in time zones and closing prices will greatly reduce the correlations between the two securities, providing misleading results. Instead, use weekly or monthly correlations to get a clearer picture of the risks involved. In Table 3.1, monthly correlations are calculated for each fund.

INDEX PORTFOLIO RETURNS

During the past five years (2002 to 2006), a portfolio with the above asset allocation would have returned 17.5 percent annually, an extremely high return. However, this period avoids the bear market of 2001 and includes a falling dollar that helped propel EFA's returns, so it's not prudent to rely too much on recent history.

Instead, it is better to develop conservative long-term estimates for these three funds. There are eleven years of market data for MDY with an average annualized return of 15 percent, so we can be more confident that the returns are relatively high. This model uses 13 percent as an estimate for MDY's long-term returns.

There is not as much pricing data on the IWN ETF specifically, but there is the long-term historic return data from the Fama-French portfolios, which shows that small-cap value stocks have returned at least 16 percent on average since the 1950s. Fourteen percent is used here to be somewhat conservative.

For EFA, the foreign index, it would be tempting to extrapolate the excellent recent performance of these stocks, especially given the global growth consensus. However, these are still large-cap growth stocks primarily, which historically have lower returns. Also, the U.S. dollar could conceivably rebound and create a headwind for foreign assets. Let's be conservative and use 10 percent.

When we blend these three estimates in the proposed proportions, we get a long-term return of 12.75 percent, which is very reasonable and well above an expected cost of debt. If leveraged portfolio assets can compound at this rate for several years, a significant amount of equity can be created.

In 2004, 2005, and 2006, a portfolio based upon the above asset allocation would have had an annualized volatility of 10.7 percent, which is extremely low. This suggests that the proposed portfolio would have very high risk-adjusted returns and could be leveraged to very high levels.

However, we are going to reevaluate this volatility figure. Three years is just not enough data to assume that in the long-term, volatility will be that low. During the late 1997 to 2002 period, volatility was much higher, and it is only reasonable to assume that the index is capable of returning to those levels. Thus, we're going to raise the expected volatility to 21.4 percent—double the previous three-year average.

Applying Leverage

This portfolio uses a relatively low level of leverage to complement the security selection and achieve higher long-term returns (see Table 3.2). The leverage ratio is 1.6×, which indicates that for every $100,000 of equity, the investment will have $60,000 of debt and $160,000 of combined assets.

The basic leverage formula tells us that a portfolio with these characteristics—that is, 1.6× leverage, 12.75 percent underlying, and 5 percent cost of debt—will have an average return of 17.4 percent. This is an extremely high return that, when compounded for five or ten years, provides expected total returns of +123 percent and +397 percent, respectively.

TABLE 3.2 Projected Growth of $10,000 Invested in the Leveraged Portfolio

	Rate of Return	$10,000 Invested for		
		5 Years	10 Years	20 Years
S&P 500	10%	16,105	25,937	67,275
Portfolio, No Leverage	12.75%	18,221	33,202	110,238
Portfolio, Leveraged	17.40%	22,302	49,737	247,378

However, we plan to reduce the leverage ratio somewhat over the life of the investment, resulting in lower returns but less risk.

On average, the assets in the portfolio pay a dividend yield of 1.70 percent, and we are initially assuming a cost of debt of 5 percent. One thousand dollars of equity supports $1,600 of assets, which pays $27.20 a year in dividends, and $600 of debt, which requires $30 a year in interest costs. Dividend payments are expected to grow over time.

Because there is relative parity between income and expenses, the portfolio is unlikely to find itself in a position in which it has to sell a significant amount of assets to pay the ongoing interest costs. This is part of the reason that the initial leverage ratio of 1.6× was selected.

The low leverage ratio also helps minimize the risk of a portfolio collapse—we'll explore that possibility more in the section on margin requirements.

For reinvestment, the portfolio will use a very simple strategy in which both assets and the interest on the debt accumulate at their relative rates. As the assets are expected to grow at an average rate of 12.75 percent, and the debt at 4.67 percent (the current broker rate, slightly lower than the 5 percent estimate), the portfolio's leverage ratio should fall over time, reducing both the risk and expected returns.

In addition, the portfolio will be rebalanced periodically by adjusting the number of synthetics owned. Rebalancing a leveraged portfolio of synthetics is difficult because of the transaction costs and the minimum contract size, so some tracking error is expected.

HOLDING SYNTHETIC POSITIONS

The last chapter explained the basics of creating a synthetic position using options on stocks, ETFs, or indexes. In Table 3.3 we apply the practice to the three ETFs that constitute the portfolio, purchasing three in-the-money call options and selling three put options at the same strike price. Initially, options with fourteen months to expiration will be used, and after that, new options will be purchased every year.

The target $160,000 portfolio can be created through the purchase of only $9,757 of debit, or cash outlay. This is the capital efficiency of derivatives at work. This purchase leaves the remaining $90,243 of equity in cash, available for both margin requirements and additional interest accumulation.

The synthetic will capture the majority of the appreciation in the underlying over the period until expiry; however, it has a slightly higher breakeven point due to its cost of capital, which is a function of the interest rate and the ETF's dividend payments.

TABLE 3.3 Initial Synthetic Purchases and Margin Requirements

	Allocation	Price	Shares	Strike	Long Call	Short Put	Debit	Total	Margin
IWN	$80,000	72.59	1102.1	@ 70 exp 1/09	11.20	6.60	4.60	$5,070	$20,419
MDY	$40,000	159.13	251.4	@ 155 exp 1/09	22.60	12.90	9.70	$2,438	$10,204
EFA	$40,000	83.57	478.6	@ 80 exp 6/08	10.80	6.10	4.70	$2,250	$9,211

For the option pricing, the model uses today's ask price quotes for the long option and the bid quotes for the short option. We also use fractional shares, but in practice we would have to settle for having an asset allocation that is slightly off, as each option contract is set at 100 shares.

When the synthetic option expires, the portfolio will either sell the call or buy back the put and then open a new synthetic position at a different strike price. Any gain is then deposited into the cash account and accrues interest over the next year.

Let's review a specific synthetic on the security IWN for the initial option, which has exactly 437 days to expiry. As is shown in Table 3.4, this synthetic has a strike price of 70 and a cost of 4.60 resulting in a breakeven point of 74.60 for the security. Anything higher than that will be profitable, and anything lower will lose money.

This breakeven point represents a price level that's 2.77 percent higher than the current pricing level. This is a result of the 4.67 percent cost of capital used to price the option (this value can be found in any option calculator) and the expected five dividend payments that the seller will receive over the life of the option.

We will assume that IWN appreciates at 14.71 percent in the period before expiry. We arrive at that figure by using 12.15 percent annual appreciation, which is the expected appreciation of 14 percent minus the 1.85 percent dividend, and then extrapolating from 365 to 437 days.

$$14.71\% = (14\% - 1.85\%) \wedge (437/365)$$

Assuming IWN appreciates at this rate over the life of the option, each share will be worth $83.27, a level $8.67 above breakeven, which translates to a total gain of $9,557 on the $80,000 IWN position over the 14 months.

What's missing? To properly estimate the value of a synthetic leveraged position as compared to owning the underlying security, be sure to include both the value of the interest received and the cost of margin. Note that volatility doesn't drive the pricing of synthetics, but does enter into the margin requirements.

The IWN position costs $5,070 to initiate, which leaves $44,930 in cash available for margin and to accumulate interest. If we assume 4.67 percent interest (equal to the cost of capital on options) for 437 days, this cash

TABLE 3.4   IWN Synthetic Position

Market	Strike	Debit	Breakeven	Premium
72.59	70	4.6	74.6	2.77%

account provides another $2,523 for the period, for a total of $12,080 before margin. (Margin requirements are addressed later in this chapter.)

An expected return of $12,080 on a $50,000 investment over 437 days is a 19.8 percent annualized return. Synthetics should provide results that are very close to the leveraged investment formula, and in this case it does: 14 percent return on IWN with a 1.6 leverage ratio and 4.67 percent cost of capital comes to 19.6 percent, which is very close to the above analysis.

$$19.6\% = (14\% \times 1.6) - (4.67\% \times 0.6)$$

TRANSACTION COSTS

Transaction costs associated with this strategy include the bid-ask spread and the commission costs of buying and selling options. In this strategy, the portfolio can use long-term equity anticipation securities (LEAPS), which helps minimize the ongoing transaction costs and allows it to hold the position longer. LEAPS are options that have a year or more to expiry. LEAPS are available on many, but not all, securities, and have been increasing in popularity since their introduction in the 1990s.

Different customers and different brokers will have very different transaction costs, so it's impossible to create a model that applies to everyone. A multimillion dollar account is likely to be able to get better prices on its options and pay less for its trades, due to its importance as a customer. A retail investor at a more traditional broker that uses market orders would pay more.

We can estimate expenses at roughly 1 percent of the underlying per year. To more precisely calculate this, divide half the option bid-ask spread by the cost of the underlying security, and then add the average commission cost to create a per-transaction cost. IWN is the most costly, and MDY is the least.

Note that when using synthetics, either the call option or the put option expires worthless, eliminating one transaction. Also, sometimes it is a little cheaper to have an in-the-money option exercised and then sell the shares rather than buy back the option. This is called a same-day sale, and for most brokers this requires no additional margin for the stock.

There are other ETFs and indexes with extremely low bid/ask spreads, such as the SPY, an S&P 500 tracker ETF, or IWM, a Russell 2000 tracker. However, those ETFs don't have the value tilt that this portfolio requires. The value tilt is worth at least two or three points of additional appreciation per year, which more than makes up for any increase in costs.

Transaction expenses always need to be placed in the proper perspective. While its helpful to try to minimize them, over the long term an investor's success is almost certainly going to be the result of allocating sufficient capital to appreciating securities rather than simply avoiding cost.

EXPECTED RETURNS AND REINVESTMENT

This model estimates the value of the underlying portfolio annually for seven years and then applies leverage. By starting with a "base case" of expected returns and then moving to a Monte Carlo approach, we can compare the ranges of possible returns for both the unleveraged assets and the leveraged portfolio.

Given average returns, after seven years the $160,000 of underlying assets increases to $370,626. When modeling the returns of the underlying portfolio, the model assumes precise rebalancing to simplify the calculations, with the understanding that this is not likely possible for synthetics and some limited tracking error will occur.

Dividends are sometimes double-counted in these types of analyses, throwing off the results. The correct approach is to either include dividends in the investment gains and remove them from the interest payments, or vice versa, generally depending on whether the focus of the model is total return or cash flow. In Table 3.5, we include them in the investment gains.

After applying the relatively simple leverage model in which the portfolio makes no additional investments but just allows the assets and debt to compound, we subtract the $82,586 of debt (which grew from the original level of $60,000) and are left with $288,040 of equity, a 16.3 percent annual return on the initial investment.

As the portfolio gains equity, the leverage ratio falls, which reduces the expected annual percentage returns for the next year, but makes the overall investment less risky. This risk reduction can help to lock in prior investment gains.

ADDING PORTFOLIO VOLATILITY

On a daily or weekly basis, a leveraged portfolio will provide returns that are equivalent to the daily or weekly return on the underlying portfolio

TABLE 3.5 Portfolio Growth with Expected Appreciation

	Underlying Portfolio (rebalanced annually)				
Year	IWN	MDY	EFA	Total	Returns
0 (start)	80,000	40,000	40,000	160,000	12.75%
1	90,200	45,100	45,100	180,400	12.75%
2	101,701	50,850	50,850	203,401	12.75%
3	114,667	57,334	57,334	229,335	12.75%
4	129,287	64,644	64,644	258,575	12.75%
5	145,772	72,886	72,886	291,543	12.75%
6	164,357	82,179	82,179	328,715	12.75%
7	185,313	92,656	92,656	370,626	12.75%

	Leveraged Portfolio (compounding assets and debt)				
Year	Assets	Debt	Equity	Leverage	% Return
0 (start)	160,000	60,000	100,000	1.60	
1	180,400	62,802	117,598	1.53	17.6%
2	203,401	65,735	137,666	1.48	17.1%
3	229,335	68,805	160,530	1.43	16.6%
4	258,575	72,018	186,557	1.39	16.2%
5	291,543	75,381	216,162	1.35	15.9%
6	328,715	78,901	249,813	1.32	15.6%
7	370,626	82,586	288,040	1.29	15.3%

multiplied by the leverage ratio. For example, if we estimate that weekly price movements of 3 percent upward or downward are commonplace in the unleveraged portfolio, and the leverage ratio is 1.6×, then the leveraged investment should expect to have weekly fluctuations in the equity portion of the investment of about 4.8 percent.

Of course when asset prices change, the leverage ratio also changes, as the ratio of total assets to equity would be affected. As an example, if the market value of assets declines 3 percent, then the leverage ratio rises from 1.60 to 1.63, and the expected return and volatility of the portfolio would rise accordingly.

Long-term volatility of the underlying portfolio is estimated at 21.4 percent, which is well above recent averages, but equivalent to long-term averages. Given these expectations, the estimated return and volatility can be used to develop an expected percentile table of returns (see Table 3.6). Each of the lines in the table would represent an equally likely outcome.

TABLE 3.6 Percentile Distribution

Expected Return (Underlying)	12.75%
Expected Annual Volatility	21.40%
Starting Leverage Ratio	1.6

Percentile	Underlying	Leveraged	Leverage Ratio
5%	−22.4%	−38.7%	1.94
10%	−14.7%	−26.3%	1.78
15%	−9.4%	−17.9%	1.71
20%	−5.3%	−11.2%	1.66
25%	−1.7%	−5.5%	1.62
30%	+1.5%	−0.4%	1.59
35%	+4.5%	+4.4%	1.56
40%	+7.3%	+8.9%	1.54
45%	+10.1%	+13.3%	1.52
50%	+12.8%	+17.6%	1.50
55%	+15.4%	+21.9%	1.48
60%	+18.2%	+26.3%	1.46
65%	+21.0%	+30.8%	1.45
70%	+24.0%	+35.6%	1.43
75%	+27.2%	+40.7%	1.42
80%	+30.8%	+46.4%	1.40
85%	+34.9%	+53.1%	1.38
90%	+40.2%	+61.5%	1.37
95%	+47.9%	+73.9%	1.34

Estimates are based upon a normalized distribution, although, as we studied in the index chapter, models like this tend to underestimate the downside risk over shorter time periods such as weeks or months.

The model shows that the underlying portfolio is capable of generating annual returns below the cost of capital about 32 percent of the time, and negative returns about 27 percent of the time, making it a riskier portfolio, at least on a one-year basis. More optimistically, it is also capable of delivering returns in the 20s and 30s for the underlying, which when leveraged becomes 30 percent to 50 percent.

We can monitor the results at a single random run, as provided in Table 3.7. This run almost triples the initial equity in seven years, providing an annual 17.3 percent return, but with plenty of ups and downs, as is typical for any equity investment, but particularly those that are leveraged.

The first year provides an above-average return, 53 percent, generating an equity windfall and significantly increasing the amount of invested

TABLE 3.7 Random Sequence of Index Returns

	Index		Start				Performance		Ending			
Year (start)	Rand()	% Return	Assets	Debt	Equity	Leverage	Gains	Interest	Assets	Debt	Equity	% Return
1	0.85	35.2%	160,000	60,000	100,000	1.60	56,361	2,802	216,361	62,802	153,559	53.6%
2	0.12	−12.4%	216,361	62,802	153,559	1.41	−26,838	2,933	189,523	65,735	123,788	−19.4%
3	0.34	4.0%	189,523	65,735	123,788	1.53	7,489	3,070	197,013	68,805	128,208	3.6%
4	0.53	14.3%	197,013	68,805	128,208	1.54	28,249	3,213	225,262	72,018	153,244	19.5%
5	0.90	40.1%	225,262	72,018	153,244	1.47	90,260	3,363	315,522	75,381	240,141	56.7%
6	0.46	10.4%	315,522	75,381	240,141	1.31	32,703	3,520	348,225	78,901	269,323	12.2%
7	0.47	11.3%	348,225	78,901	269,323	1.29	39,254	3,685	387,479	82,586	304,893	13.2%

assets, but also pushing down the leverage ratio. This helps reduce the impact of the poor returns in the second and third years. At the end of the third year, the annualized return is under 10 percent, but the assets are still almost three times higher than the amount of debt. Still, a skittish investor could consider selling out after the two bad years.

But then the market improves significantly in the fourth and fifth years, creating more than $100,000 of equity. The gain in equity reduces the leverage ratio to 1.3, and years six and seven are more typical, just slightly below average but well above the cost of capital, and the portfolio ends the seven-year period with low leverage and just over $300,000 in equity.

RANDOM SCENARIOS WITH MONTE CARLO

Single runs can be illustrative, but are not particularly indicative of the range of possible returns. A better approach is to simulate large numbers of portfolios—for example 800—and analyze both the leveraged and unleveraged results. The summary is provided in Table 3.8.

This is called a Monte Carlo analysis, and is easy to do with Excel or a procedural programming language. Monte Carlo analysis is inaccurate by definition, but the most accurate approach—calculating the effects of every possible series of returns—would be incredibly expensive computationally as the potential combinations soon run into the hundreds of billions.

Readers should be aware that there are reports of bugs in the random number generator algorithms used in specific versions of Excel, so before attempting Monte Carlo analysis using this software package, be sure that this isn't an issue.

After seven years, the 800 portfolios have accumulated $276,815 of equity on average from the original $100,000 investment. This is about $50,000 more than would be expected from an unleveraged portfolio, that is, the same $100,000 invested without leverage or reinvestment, so we can precisely calculate the extent to which the leverage and reinvestment strategy adds value.

The average annualized seven-year return for a portfolio in this analysis is 15.65 percent. With leveraged portfolios, note that there is often a large gap between the median and the mean equity, and the median and mean percentage returns. The high potential returns from leveraged portfolios tend to skew the average equity upward, while the potential negative equity can push the average percentage returns downward. We can use the

TABLE 3.8 Percentile Rankings of Portfolio Returns

	Unleveraged	Leveraged	Return	Diff
Avg.	224,626	276,815	+10.6%	52,189
Std.	110,823	177,317	+23.1%	66,494
Min.	28,269	−37,356	−186.9%	−65,625
Max.	794,140	1,188,037	+42.4%	393,898

Distribution	Unleveraged	Leveraged	Return	
5%	84,635	52,830	−8.7%	−31,805
10%	106,940	88,518	−1.7%	−18,422
15%	117,606	105,583	+0.8%	−12,023
20%	127,892	122,041	+2.9%	−5,851
25%	139,755	141,021	+5.0%	1,267
30%	154,351	164,376	+7.4%	10,025
35%	164,937	181,314	+8.9%	16,376
40%	177,652	201,658	+10.5%	24,005
45%	190,210	221,750	+12.0%	31,540
50%	204,526	244,656	+13.6%	40,130
55%	218,038	266,274	+15.0%	48,236
60%	230,544	286,284	+16.2%	55,740
65%	247,066	312,719	+17.7%	65,653
70%	263,985	339,790	+19.1%	75,805
75%	284,485	372,590	+20.7%	88,105
80%	307,181	408,904	+22.3%	101,723
85%	338,135	458,430	+24.3%	120,295
90%	372,083	512,747	+26.3%	140,664
95%	437,944	618,125	+29.7%	180,181

following formula to calculate the annualized percentage return based on the starting and ending equity.

$$\text{RoE} = (P1/P0) \wedge (1/Y) - 1$$
$$P1 = \text{final price}$$
$$P0 = \text{starting price}$$
$$Y = \text{number of years}$$

The 15 percent to 85 percent range in the percentile rankings is approximately the "one standard deviation" result, with two-thirds of the portfolios falling within this range. Even here, there is still a very high variability for both the leveraged and unleveraged portfolio. Given the estimated volatility of 21.4 percent, the underlying blended index simply isn't very predictable over the seven-year period.

At the high end, this investment is capable of generating $300,000 or more of equity in the seven years, resulting in cumulative annual returns in the low to midtwenties. The high returns in the best performing portfolios help to skew the overall average final equity figures upward.

One hundred and seven of the 800 leveraged portfolios have negative returns, and 60 portfolios have losses in excess of 25 percent. This unfortunate result generally occurs when the underlying fails to appreciate over the seven-year period—for example, because of multiple years of double-digit losses.

MARGIN CALLS

One of the disadvantages of a synthetic is that the structure of the investment requires margin, and thus leaves it vulnerable to margin calls. This is usually the case for unhedged investments, and can be overcome by using options or similar hedging instruments, as we will explore in detail in later chapters.

The margin requirement can be viewed as a maximum leverage ratio, and we can use current synthetic prices and margin requirements to back out this maximum. Every broker has slightly different margin requirements for put options, although the exchange generally sets the minimum levels. High net worth customers are sometimes allowed to use portfolio margin, which reduces requirements.

For this analysis, we'll use the standard short put requirements of a typical online broker, which states that the initial and maintenance margin is:

> ...the greater of the current marked-to-market value of the option plus 20% of the underlying less any amount the option is out-of-the-money; or the current marked-to-market value of the option plus 10% of the value of the strike price.

The first portion of this requirement applies to at or near the money put options, which is what most synthetics are.

This formula was used to calculate the margin requirements for each of the synthetics shown in Table 3.3, and the result was that the $160,000 portfolio required $49,592 of capital for both the purchase and margin requirements combined. This suggests that a $320,000 portfolio could be created with approximately $100,000 of equity, which gives us a maximum leverage ratio of a little over 3.2.

While beyond the scope of this chapter, we did check that result using options with different strike prices and implied volatilities using the Black-Scholes formula and were able to find some combinations that allowed a maximum initial leverage ratio of about 3.4 or so; therefore, the estimate is very close. A leverage ratio ceiling of 3.3 is examined in the following analysis.

There are two formulas that are useful in these circumstances. The first helps to find the minimum level of assets required to avoid a margin call, given a specific amount of debt and maximum estimated leverage ratio. This formula is:

$$A = (L \times D)/(L - 1)$$
$$A = \text{Assets}, D = \text{Debt}, L = \text{Leverage Ratio}$$

For example, if the portfolio has $100,000 in debt, and the maximum leverage ratio is 3.3, then it needs, at minimum, $143,478 in assets to hold the position.

Second, if we know the portfolio's starting leverage ratio and the maximum leverage ratio, we can find the level of negative return that would trigger a margin call by using this formula, which is simply a derivation of the previous formula, but substituting assets and debt based on the starting leverage ratio.

$$R = Lo - (Lm \times (Lo - 1))/(Lm - 1))/Lo$$
$$R = \text{Rate of Return (a negative number)}$$
$$Lo = \text{Leverage, original}$$
$$Lm = \text{Leverage, maximum}$$

This formula has been adjusted slightly to include the increase in debt based upon the accrued interest cost. Table 3.9 shows the return required to trigger a margin call, the probability of this annual return based upon the average return and volatility estimates, and the normal distribution of annual returns.

From the table we find that once a synthetic portfolio's leverage ratio climbs above 2.5, we begin to face a low but significant risk of a margin call occurring within the next year. The risk is also somewhat understated, as it only captures the probability of a margin call once a year at the ending dates, rather than on a daily basis.

In the Monte Carlo analysis, 54 of the 800 portfolios, or a little less than 7 percent, faced a margin call during the seven years, and 85 percent of the

TABLE 3.9	Probability of Margin Call Next Year at Selected Leverage Ratios	
Initial Margin	Min. Index Return	Probability of Breach (3.3)
1.10	−86.16%	0.000%
1.20	−74.63%	0.001%
1.30	−64.87%	0.004%
1.40	−56.50%	0.021%
1.50	−49.25%	0.074%
1.60	−42.91%	0.201%
1.70	−37.31%	0.453%
1.80	−32.33%	0.882%
1.90	−27.88%	1.534%
2.00	−23.88%	2.440%
2.10	−20.25%	3.611%
2.20	−16.96%	5.042%
2.30	−13.95%	6.713%
2.40	−11.19%	8.595%
2.50	−8.65%	10.651%
2.60	−6.31%	12.844%
2.70	−4.14%	15.139%
2.80	−2.13%	17.500%
2.90	−0.25%	19.897%
3.00	+1.50%	22.303%
3.10	+3.14%	24.698%
3.20	+4.67%	27.062%

margin calls occurred in the poorest performing 10 percent of portfolios. Generally it takes two years of double-digit negative returns in the first three or four years to trigger a margin call.

Margin calls start out minor and typically get worse. Meeting the margin call might have helped the portfolio recover, but also may lead to another margin call in a few months. In the analysis, only a small fraction of portfolios that received a margin call would have gone on to generate positive returns for the seven-year period, although many would have gained some equity after meeting the margin call.

A large turnaround after a margin call is possible but statistically unlikely—unfortunately, the odds favor another margin call within the next one or two years. While excessive leverage is often blamed for margin calls, actually it is a symptom of an underperforming underlying investment that has fallen far short of expectations.

SUBSTITUTING FUTURES

While this portfolio has very high average returns and provides better performance in the majority of cases to either its unleveraged counterpart or a conventional index fund, there is a way to improve upon this overall strategy by substituting futures contracts. Futures behave identically to synthetics, but are generally more liquid and use less margin, resulting in better capital efficiency, lower transaction costs, and a lower likelihood of a margin call.

Russell 2000 Value index futures are available on the Intercontinental Exchange (ICE) with the ticker VV. This would comprise the core of the portfolio, which would then be rounded out with other futures products, such as an MSCI EAFE index and an S&P Midcap index. This results in significantly lower transaction costs than the ETF options listed above.

One drawback of futures contracts is that they are typically larger than options contracts, and this may make it difficult to get the exact asset allocation of $160,000 of small-cap value, $80,000 of midcap, and $80,000 of foreign stocks. The minimum size of the Russell 2000 Value contract is 500× the index, which is currently around $400,000. Smaller contracts, known as minis, are available on the Russell 2000, but this doesn't have the value tilt required.

Index futures expire, but can be rolled over to later and later expiration dates, which makes it easy to hold a long-term position. During a rollover, a portfolio may be rebalanced by adjusting the number of futures contracts held.

Index positions using futures require only 5 percent to 10 percent margin in order to hold a position, which allows a 10 or 20 to 1 leverage ratio. This means that for a $160,000 portfolio, an investor could initially hold the position with only $8,000 to $16,000 of margin, which allows the remainder of the $100,000 of original equity to earn interest and compound. Of course, if the portfolio loses value, additional cash would need to be contributed immediately in order to hold the position.

By using futures contracts instead of synthetics, this portfolio can survive much larger losses in its first few years without getting a margin call, allowing the investor to continue to hold a position, even if it takes initial losses. Table 3.10 shows the improved probabilities, and even at 4× or 5× leverage, the probabilities are low.

However, it's important not to overstate the benefit. An investment that suffers large declines is always going to have a difficult time recovering its equity, and could still certainly get a margin call in the future if the future

TABLE 3.10 Probability of Position Liquidation
Next Year at Selected Leverage Ratios

Initial Margin	Min. Index Return	Probability of Breach (20)
1.60	−58.68%	0.014%
2.00	−44.91%	0.148%
2.50	−33.89%	0.720%
3.00	−26.55%	1.797%
4.00	−17.37%	4.843%
5.00	−11.86%	8.106%
10.00	−0.84%	19.125%

returns continue to fall short of the cost of debt. A leverage ratio can climb from 5× to 50× very quickly.

In the above Monte Carlo simulation using synthetics, we ignored the cost of transactions and margin calls. Because using futures contracts largely eliminates these two items, the average return and payoff is exactly the same as in Table 3.10.

The next question: Given the high level of leverage available with futures contracts, should we take advantage of that and get even higher returns? Rerunning the analysis using higher levels of leverage provides the results shown in Table 3.11.

Compare the 50 percent line, which is the median portfolio, to the 85 percent line beneath it. Higher leverage does improve the median return, but also creates an opportunity for extremely high returns. A starting leverage ratio of 4 provides a 10 percent chance of turning $100,000 of equity into $1 million within the seven-year period, almost a 40 percent annual return.

Still, at the higher leverage ratios, margin calls and losses in excess of starting capital become much more likely, and the investor should be prepared for this. The median portfolio concept at these levels is also somewhat meaningless as the dispersion is so wide, and the mean is only useful if the investor can invest in multiple leveraged portfolios over time.

Ultimately, the right starting leverage ratio depends on the investor's financial situation and overall risk profile. If this were the primary retirement vehicle for an investor, then 1.6× seems like a relatively conservative leverage ratio. On the other hand, if an investor can make new investments every year and is well capitalized and diversified, a higher leverage ratio may be a better option.

TABLE 3.11 Portfolio Returns Using Higher Initial Leverage

Leverage	1.6	2.0	2.5	3.0	4.0	5.0
Avg.	287,015	319,403	372,198	380,947	433,107	584,074
Stdev	202,126	235,533	325,592	317,422	361,348	614,906
Return (ann.)	16.3%	18.0%	20.7%	21.1%	23.3%	28.7%
Min.	−37,303	−85,779	−150,051	−108,361	−193,819	−334,999
15%	98,664	106,552	91,405	92,825	86,125	25,031
50%	245,999	269,002	304,862	313,360	360,669	448,328
85%	474,701	532,973	663,399	646,741	805,207	1,139,441
Max.	1,309,753	1,580,482	2,616,811	2,850,885	2,186,278	4,551,993
Margin Call	1.4%	6.0%	12.3%	18.3%	25.3%	32.0%

SUMMARY

In this chapter, we constructed a relatively low-risk leveraged portfolio using both synthetic positions and futures contracts. The portfolio has average long-term returns exceeding 15.6 percent before transaction costs and is only a little more risky than an average index fund.

Simple models are easy to create, understand, and share—the challenge is then to make sure that the model reflects reality. In this strategy, we define reasonable assumptions for the model—for example, the concept of tracking debt and equity with synthetics or futures and the average return and volatility for the blended funds in the unleveraged portfolio—and then use those concepts to build a model that tracks only eight variables but gives us exactly the results we need.

It is necessary to make certain assumptions about the underlying fund's return and risk based upon both recent returns and long-term historic averages. Although six to eight years of pricing data for each fund is available, we only used it as a starting point, and in most cases adjusted the numbers to reflect more conservative estimates. The greatest change was raising the expected volatility to reflect long-term historical averages.

The portfolio initially has a 1.6 leverage ratio and then continues to accumulate and compound both its assets and debt, and this results in a leverage ratio of about 1.3 after seven years. The chosen initial leverage ratio and reinvestment strategy was selected to balance both relative safety of principal and the opportunity for increased returns. On average, the reinvestment strategy generates $50,000 of additional equity on the $100,000 starting portfolio within the seven-year period, and in 75 percent of cases, the leveraged portfolio is worth more than an unleveraged portfolio would be.

The portfolio is capable of a very wide range of returns and a single standard deviation is quite high. This creates a "lottery ticket" effect where a few leveraged investments can generate extremely high returns that help pay for the losses in other investments, and explains why the mean ending equity is generally higher than the median.

Depending upon the investment structure used and the margin requirements, margin calls are possible but statistically unlikely for this portfolio. The likelihood of a margin call can be recalculated periodically using the current leverage ratio, the maximum leverage ratio, the average rate of return, and the overall volatility.

When the synthetic positions are replaced with futures, the probability of a margin call declines significantly. Futures have low transaction costs and are simpler to manage than synthetics, but their high minimum contract sizes restrict their use to investors with deeper pockets.

Margin calls are always a potential issue with leveraged investments, and in the upcoming chapters, we will show how to use option positions to create hedged positions and thereby obtain much higher levels of leverage and capital efficiency.

CHAPTER 4

Capturing Index Appreciation with Calls

T his chapter shows how to use various call options to capture index appreciation. The first step is to develop an understanding of how call options are priced. While most finance professionals are familiar with the Black-Scholes model, this chapter presents a simple alternative explanation that can help investors better appreciate option pricing in the context of hedging, sharing, and transferring risk.

The bulk of the chapter is devoted to comparing the expected profitability of various options by applying the Black-Scholes model to the appreciation expected over the life of the option for both short-term and long-term and in-the-money and out-of-the-money options. The analysis shows that some options are very good at capturing appreciation with low risk, while others are expected to have negative value.

The pricing and expected value of call options is very dependent upon volatility, both implied and realized, and throughout this chapter the relationship is examined in depth. An approach is also modeled in which out-of-the-money options are held until they are at the money in order to show the pitfalls of predefined price targets and related trading strategies.

INTUITIVE OPTION PRICING

The Black-Scholes option pricing model allows investors and financial professionals to quickly price any option by providing just five inputs: the price of the underlying security, the volatility, the days to expiry, the expected dividends, and the interest rate. There is no question that it is extraordinarily useful and worthy of the Nobel Prize in economics.

But perhaps the formula is too easy to use. Its speed and precision can rob finance students and professionals of the principles and intuition behind option pricing. They fail to understand why some options are priced differently than others or the reasons behind rapid price changes when the price of the security or the volatility changes.

In this section and the next, we will approach option pricing from a unique perspective and help explain exactly why and how call options are priced the way they are, and what specifically the price of an option represents. This awareness is critical for selecting options with high profitability and subsequently managing the associated risk.

Options as Potential Liabilities

Life is full of decisions that require us to estimate potential liabilities with very little information. Taking a new job, buying or renting a new house, and even getting married and having children compels us to try to define the risks inherent in those actions and make a decision as to whether the action is worth the potential reward, based upon what little we know.

Similarly, the seller of a call option faces a potential liability that is difficult to quantify. If they are long the underlying security, it could decline in value during the time the option is held. Or if they don't own it at all, it could appreciate rapidly, requiring them to buy it on the open market and immediately sell it for a lower price.

Both scenarios create losses, and the existence of these scenrios represents a potential liability. The net present value of this liability is the price of the option, and the Black-Scholes formula can be seen as an attempt to quantify this liability.

For simplification, let's assume that the seller owns shares of the security, either directly or through a derivative (that is, futures or another option), and is therefore concerned about decline in its value at the time of expiry. Pricing the option properly requires the seller to estimate this potential loss and set a premium that compensates them for both this loss and the cost of capital.

Table 4.1 calculates the expected loss of a one-month at the money call option by applying a normal distribution to the index returns in order to calculate the probability that the stock will be priced at a specific level at expiry. The market and strike price is set to 100 for simplicity.

Notice that the table contains some low probabilities of very high losses, for example the odds of a 5 percent or more loss are only 12 percent.

TABLE 4.1 Loss Calculation Using Probability Weighting

Annual Volatility	15.00%
Monthly Volatility	4.33%
Strike Price	100
Market Price	100

% Loss	Cumulative Probability	Weight	Loss	Cumulative Loss
−20%	0.00%	0.00%	−20.00	0.00
−15%	0.03%	0.03%	−15.00	0.00
−12%	0.28%	0.25%	−12.00	−0.03
−10%	1.05%	0.77%	−10.00	−0.11
−9%	1.88%	0.84%	−9.00	−0.19
−8%	3.23%	1.35%	−8.00	−0.29
−7%	5.30%	2.06%	−7.00	−0.44
−6%	8.29%	2.99%	−6.00	−0.62
−5%	12.41%	4.12%	−5.00	−0.82
−4%	17.78%	5.37%	−4.00	−1.04
−3%	24.42%	6.64%	−3.00	−1.24
−2%	32.21%	7.79%	−2.00	−1.39
−1%	40.87%	8.66%	−1.00	−1.48
0%	50.00%	9.13%	0.00	−1.48

While the underlying security is very unlikely to decline by that amount in the next thirty days, if that event occurs, the associated losses would be extremely high and would have to be weighted accordingly. More than half of the expected loss is due to the potentially high losses that could occur as a result of improbable scenarios.

The final result, 1.48, is only the starting point for the price of the call option, and adjustments would have to be made for the cost of capital, any dividends, and any other market assumptions about the volatility of the stock at various levels. Also, dozens of potential price targets would be used rather than the one-point intervals that we present here in order to obtain higher precision.

Regardless of how accurate we are with our projections and calculations, if the actual volatility of the security is lower than our initial estimate, then our option will be sold too cheaply and will not compensate us for our expected loss. If this were to occur systematically and we continued to sell options at an insufficient level, we would burn through all of our capital. Thus, as a seller of options, it is to our advantage to keep expected volatility high in order to maintain a decent profit margin.

Strike Prices

If an at-the-money call option (as call options with strike prices equal to market price are referred to) is sold on a security, all of the upside during the period until expiry or exercise will be given to the buyer of the option, and all of the downside goes to the seller. This requires the seller to estimate this potential downside along with the cost of capital in order to effectively price the option and make an acceptable profit on the transaction.

The strike price of an option is the determinant of how exactly capital gains and losses will be apportioned at the expiry of the option. It can be seen as the division of risk and reward in the underlying security.

In-the-money call options give the buyer all of the gains, but only a portion of the losses. These options are less risky for the seller because both the threshold required in order to take losses, and the losses themselves, are lower. Although these options will initially be expensive due to the intrinsic value, the time value is inexpensive and may be just barely above the cost of capital.

Some beginning investors believe that selling out-of-the-money call options is a "can't lose" proposition, because even if the option is exercised, profits are generated. But the often-overlooked danger, of course, is that the option isn't exercised because the price of the underlying security plummets and the seller takes the loss. Thus, the same analysis of potential gains and losses has to be performed for these options.

In the last chapter, we combined two options to create synthetic positions that allowed an investor to capture all of the gains and losses for the period. However, as we saw, synthetics are inefficient and are better replaced with futures.

Time and Volatility

In Table 4.1 we calculated our monthly volatility by dividing our annualized volatility by the square root of twelve. As time increases, the expected range of returns widens, but not at a linear rate. The result is that the expected loss for the seller on an at-the-money two-month option is not twice as high as that of an at-the-money, one-month option. It is only 1.41 times as high (1.41 is the square root of 2).

Of course, if the seller has to hold the security for two months rather than one month, there would be an additional cost of capital. But typically, in option pricing, especially with high volatilities and low interest rates, it is risk rather than the cost of capital that drives the pricing.

A reduction in volatility is good news for a seller because it reduces the range of possible returns for the security in the time period, which helps reduce the probabilities of extreme price movements and consequently the expected loss. The passage of time accomplishes the same thing. Both effects reduce the liability associated with call options, which also reduces their expected value.

By the time an option is close to expiry, the closing price of the underlying security is generally predictable within a few dollars, barring any very unlikely circumstances. At this point, the option should be trading very close to the expected liability at expiry, which, if it's out-of-the-money, is almost zero.

The nonlinear relationship between time and price helps make longer-term options a good value, as we will see in our comparisons of various options, and is the basis for the many profitable spread positions that are presented in future chapters.

Dividends and Interest Rates

Aside from the risk associated with losses, the seller of an option also has to determine the cost of capital for holding a security. The cost of capital is determined by the broker interest rate minus any expected dividends. This can be low or even negative for stocks with high dividend yields, and can sometimes create situations in which options are exercised just to collect a dividend or avoid paying one.

Investors and traders new to options sometimes believe that buying stock is a better deal than buying a call option because the owner of a stock collects dividends. Of course, this simplified analysis ignores the reduction in the cost of capital from the dividend, the greater capital efficiency of derivatives, and the benefit of avoiding losses in the event that prices decline significantly.

A better comparison would be one between a call option and a futures contract. Both are leveraged positions with high capital efficiency. The difference is that call options are hedged positions, and the expense of this hedge comes directly out of investment profits.

Following an Option

Now we can apply these principles to the sale of a single option. For example, let's assume that a seller buys futures contracts on 100 shares of the index at $100, the current market price, and then sells in-the-money calls on 100 shares at a strike price of $99 for thirty days. How should these call options be initially priced?

The seller first needs to be compensated for the expenses of the futures contracts. This expense includes a cost of capital of about 3 percent to 4 percent annually that is built into the price of the futures. For one month it comes to about thirty cents per share.

Next, the seller has to estimate their potential loss. Even if index volatility is low, the chance of the price falling more than $1 is relatively high, and there is always the potential for catastrophic losses. Using the analysis in Table 4.2 (similar to the methodology in Table 4.1), the seller calculates his or her estimated loss at $1.07.

Finally, because the shares are being sold for a price $1 below the current market, we add in this intrinsic value. The total, $0.30 + $1.07 + $1, or $2.37, is the price of the one-month option.

Then suppose that the market price of the index immediately declines to $98 in the first week. If prices remain static, the seller is now facing a potential loss on their security, but a gain on their options sale, so the position is still profitable, but not quite as much as it previously was.

In terms of market position, the seller has lost money on the futures contract but made money on the short option, as its value declines because it has lost intrinsic value and is now out-of-the-money.

Then, a week before expiry, the market price of the index moves up to $103. The risk inherent in this position for the seller has declined dramatically, as there is very little chance that the index could move down below $99 within only one week, and the profit is just about locked in. The price

TABLE 4.2   Loss Calculation of an ITM (In-the-Money) Option

Annual Vol.	15.00%
Monthly Vol.	4.33%
Strike	99

% Loss	Probability Cumulative	Weight	Loss	Accum. Weighted Loss
−20%	0.00%	0.00%	−19.00	0.00
−15%	0.03%	0.03%	−14.00	0.00
−12%	0.28%	0.25%	−11.00	−0.03
−10%	1.05%	0.77%	−9.00	−0.10
−9%	1.88%	0.84%	−8.00	−0.17
−8%	3.23%	1.35%	−7.00	−0.26
−7%	5.30%	2.06%	−6.00	−0.39
−6%	8.29%	2.99%	−5.00	−0.54
−5%	12.41%	4.12%	−4.00	−0.70
−4%	17.78%	5.37%	−3.00	−0.86
−3%	24.42%	6.64%	−2.00	−0.99
−2%	32.21%	7.79%	−1.00	−1.07
−1%	40.87%	8.66%	0.00	−1.07
0%	50.00%	9.13%	0.00	−1.07

of the option rises to reflect the increased intrinsic value, but the time value becomes negligible.

Finally, the buyer exercises the option just before expiry with a market price of $102.80. The seller has a profit, because they own the futures contract and can deliver the shares and still keep the premium. And, the buyer has a profit, as an option was purchased at $2.37 and then sold for $2.80, an 18.1 percent profit in thirty days.

Many investors who are new to options often believe that an option price reflects some belief about the future appreciation of the security, but here we show that at every point in time, the price of the call option represents the intrinsic value, the cost of a futures contract, and a hedge against the market price falling below the strike price, but not any future expectations about appreciation—only volatility.

This is a good time to mention that sometimes buying and selling options is presented as a zero-sum game in which only one party can profit, but here we show that rising prices benefit all of the parties involved. This is partly because the seller also owns futures contracts as a hedge for delivery, and partly simply the nature of derivative securities. There is no loser in this transaction, unless we include the fate of some other trader who sold their futures contract a month too early.

Risk Components of Various Options

Now let's look at a handful of options, again from the seller's perspective. In Table 4.3, we've listed the days to expiry, market price, strike price, interest rate, and volatility for various options as a comparison. We will assume no dividends for these options in order to simplify the calculations and set the market price at 100.

The last three columns perform the following calculations as part of the Black-Scholes formula. These calculations can be embedded in any spreadsheet to quickly price an option based upon changing inputs.

$$A1 = (LN(B5/C5) + (D5 + E5 \wedge 2/2)^*(A5/365))/(E5^*SQRT((A5/365)))$$
$$A2 = F5 - E5^*SQRT((A5/365))$$
$$Price = B5^*NORMSDIST(F5) - C5^*EXP(-D5^*(A5/365))^*NORMSDIST(G5)$$

Let's examine the first four, at-the-money options. As we increase the number of days to expiry, the price increases, but not at a linear rate. This is because the expected loss for the seller of the call option increases at the square root of time to expiry. A 180-day option provides 200 percent more time than a 60-day option, but costs only 92 percent more.

TABLE 4.3   Comparison of the Intrinsic and Time Value of Selected Options

Option	Days	Market	Strike	Rate	Vol.	A1	A2	Price	Intrinsic	Time
#1	30	100.00	100.00	5.0%	15.0%	0.12	0.07	1.92	0.00	1.92
#2	60	100.00	100.00	5.0%	15.0%	0.17	0.10	2.85	0.00	2.85
#3	90	100.00	100.00	5.0%	15.0%	0.20	0.13	3.61	0.00	3.61
#4	180	100.00	100.00	5.0%	15.0%	0.29	0.18	5.48	0.00	5.48
#5	30	100.00	85.00	5.0%	15.0%	3.90	3.85	15.35	15.00	0.35
#6	30	100.00	90.00	5.0%	15.0%	2.57	2.52	10.38	10.00	0.38
#7	30	100.00	95.00	5.0%	15.0%	1.31	1.27	5.58	5.00	0.58
#8	30	100.00	101.00	5.0%	15.0%	−0.11	−0.16	1.44	0.00	1.44
#9	30	100.00	102.00	5.0%	15.0%	−0.34	−0.39	1.05	0.00	1.05
#10	30	100.00	103.00	5.0%	15.0%	−0.57	−0.61	0.74	0.00	0.74
#11	30	100.00	100.00	5.0%	20.0%	0.10	0.04	2.49	0.00	2.49
#12	30	100.00	95.00	5.0%	20.0%	0.99	0.94	5.88	5.00	0.88

The next three options—#5, #6, and #7—are thirty-day options that are in-the-money by various amounts. Each option has an intrinsic value equal to its discount to the strike price, and a very low time value. The expected loss for each option for the seller is very low, as the buyer is putting up what could be considered $5 to $15 of collateral to hold the position.

Options #8, #9, and #10 are all out-of-the-money. Notice how little the price declines for each additional $1 of strike price, because the seller still carries a large amount of the downside risk for the security, and the relatively small premium provides little compensation.

The next option, #11, has increased volatility, which increases the expected loss for the seller and raises the prices. This option is priced about 25 percent higher than #1. But in option #12 the strike is well below market, and volatility is less of a factor. This option is only 30 cents more than #7.

Notice that in all of these options, either the intrinsic value is high, or the time value is high, but not both. High intrinsic values are generally a sign that the buyer of the option is taking on most of the downside risk, rather than the seller, and that helps keep both the risk and the value of the time low.

CAPTURING APPRECIATION WITH OPTIONS

Viewing call options from the seller's perspective is useful for understanding how options are priced, but from this point on we will approach call options from the perspective of a buyer and investor that has the goal of capturing index appreciation over a specific period of time.

We start with measuring time decay, the effect that makes options a wasting asset, and then compare this expense with the income from both steady appreciation of the underlying asset and then the outsize returns that are possible with options. We will find that some options have much higher expected profitability than others.

Daily Cost of Options

As a rule, short-term, at-the-money options lose value extremely quickly, while the decay of longer-term options is much slower. If we compare this uneven rate of decay with a regular 9 percent rate of appreciation for the index, we can find some surprising results.

Table 4.4 examines six at-the-money call options, and then six in-the-money options. In this and most other examples, we set the market price at 100 to make comparisons easier, and no dividends are assumed. Each option is priced using Black-Scholes, and then a daily rate of decay is calculated by dividing the time value by the number of days until expiry.

For the at-the-money options, the daily rate of decay for a 30- or 60-day call option is much higher than that of a 360- or 720-day option. When going from 360 days to 720 days, $5 buys twelve extra months, or 360 days, at only 0.014 dollars per day.

However, when we buy our options at a lower strike price of 90, or 10 percent in-the-money, all of the rates of decay for our call options fall

TABLE 4.4 Comparison of Short- and Longer-Term Call Options

Option	Days	Market	Strike	Tate	Vol.	A1	A2	Price	Cost/Day
#1	30	100.00	100.00	5.0%	15.0%	0.12	0.07	1.92	0.064
#2	60	100.00	100.00	5.0%	15.0%	0.17	0.10	2.85	0.047
#3	90	100.00	100.00	5.0%	15.0%	0.20	0.13	3.61	0.040
#4	180	100.00	100.00	5.0%	15.0%	0.29	0.18	5.48	0.030
#5	360	100.00	100.00	5.0%	15.0%	0.41	0.26	8.51	0.024
#6	720	100.00	100.00	5.0%	15.0%	0.57	0.36	13.55	0.019
#7	30	100.00	90.00	5.0%	15.0%	2.57	2.52	10.38	0.013
#8	60	100.00	90.00	5.0%	15.0%	1.90	1.84	10.81	0.013
#9	90	100.00	90.00	5.0%	15.0%	1.62	1.54	11.27	0.014
#10	180	100.00	90.00	5.0%	15.0%	1.29	1.18	12.71	0.015
#11	360	100.00	90.00	5.0%	15.0%	1.11	0.96	15.40	0.015
#12	720	100.00	90.00	5.0%	15.0%	1.07	0.86	20.13	0.014

dramatically. The $10 of intrinsic value reduces the cost of the time value to approximately 1.3 or 1.4 cents a day, which is roughly the cost of capital.

A low daily cost allows the investor to cost-effectively capture the index appreciation over time. As a comparison, at 10 percent annualized appreciation, the average daily appreciation is 2.73 cents, which would make only options #5 through #12 profitable. Options #1 through #4 are not expected to appreciate faster than their decay, given average appreciation.

The lower strike-prices transfer the downside risk from the seller of the option to the buyer, and as a result are more expensive initially, but cost less over time. In a later section we'll more closely examine the risk of losses with in-the-money call options.

Table 4.5 directly compares the daily cost of these selected options with the expected appreciation over the same period. Ten percent appreciation and 15 percent volatility are assumed, which is the approximate historical average for the S&P 500 index.

Again, only the long-term at-the-money options, #5 and #6, are profitable. The one-year option has an expected return of 17.4 percent, while the two-year option has an expected return of 55 percent, or 24.5 percent annualized.

All of the in-the-money options are profitable, as the lower strike price buys down the cost of the hedge. The short-term in-the-money option is expected to appreciate 4.1 percent in one month, which, when reinvested and annualized, compounds to 61.2 percent annually. The longer-term options have higher percentage returns, but lower annualized returns, because the gains can't be reinvested as rapidly.

Higher volatility reduces the percentage returns of the short-term and at-the-money options more than the in-the-money options, as they are more sensitive to volatility changes. Options #11 and #12 are still marginally profitable even if we double implied volatility from 15 percent to 30 percent, while the returns of other options all become negative.

Like our leveraged funds in previous chapters, when in-the-money options appreciate, they build equity, which lowers their leverage ratio, volatility, and expected returns. However, the reduction of returns is offset by the lower cost of the hedge, and this can actually reverse the situation, creating an environment where returns increase and accelerate.

In Table 4.6, a two-year, in-the-money option on an index growing at an annualized rate of 10 percent is analyzed month-by-month. In the first three months, the option appreciates at about 1.6 percent in each month, but this increases to almost 2 percent as the option moves in the money.

After the option is very deep in-the-money, the return no longer benefits from a reduction in the cost of the hedge and thus falls, as we would expect from a leveraged investment. We can see this effect in the last few months.

TABLE 4.5 Call Option Price Compared to Expected Appreciation

Option	Days	Market	Strike	Rate	Vol.	Price	Index Appreciation	Final Price	Option Gain ($)	Option Gain (%)	Annualized Gain (%)
#1	30	100.00	100.00	5.0%	15.0%	1.92	0.80%	100.80	-1.13	-58.6%	-100.0%
#2	60	100.00	100.00	5.0%	15.0%	2.85	1.60%	101.60	-1.25	-43.8%	-96.8%
#3	90	100.00	100.00	5.0%	15.0%	3.61	2.41%	102.41	-1.19	-33.1%	-80.0%
#4	180	100.00	100.00	5.0%	15.0%	5.48	4.88%	104.88	-0.60	-10.9%	-20.7%
#5	360	100.00	100.00	5.0%	15.0%	8.51	10.00%	110.00	1.49	17.4%	17.4%
#6	720	100.00	100.00	5.0%	15.0%	13.55	21.00%	121.00	7.45	55.0%	24.5%
#7	30	100.00	90.00	5.0%	15.0%	10.38	0.80%	100.80	0.42	4.1%	61.2%
#8	60	100.00	90.00	5.0%	15.0%	10.81	1.60%	101.60	0.80	7.4%	53.1%
#9	90	100.00	90.00	5.0%	15.0%	11.27	2.41%	102.41	1.14	10.1%	46.9%
#10	180	100.00	90.00	5.0%	15.0%	12.71	4.88%	104.88	2.17	17.1%	37.1%
#11	360	100.00	90.00	5.0%	15.0%	15.40	10.00%	110.00	4.60	29.9%	29.9%
#12	720	100.00	90.00	5.0%	15.0%	20.13	21.00%	121.00	10.87	54.0%	24.1%

TABLE 4.6 Month-by-Month Growth of a Two-Year Call Option

Month	Days	Market	Strike	Rate	Vol.	Price	Gain
0	720	100.00	90.00	5.0%	15.0%	20.13	
1	690	100.80	90.00	5.0%	15.0%	20.45	1.58%
2	660	101.60	90.00	5.0%	15.0%	20.77	1.59%
3	630	102.41	90.00	5.0%	15.0%	21.11	1.61%
4	600	103.23	90.00	5.0%	15.0%	21.45	1.63%
5	570	104.05	90.00	5.0%	15.0%	21.81	1.65%
6	540	104.88	90.00	5.0%	15.0%	22.17	1.67%
7	510	105.72	90.00	5.0%	15.0%	22.55	1.69%
8	480	106.56	90.00	5.0%	15.0%	22.93	1.72%
9	450	107.41	90.00	5.0%	15.0%	23.33	1.74%
10	420	108.27	90.00	5.0%	15.0%	23.74	1.77%
11	390	109.13	90.00	5.0%	15.0%	24.17	1.79%
12	360	110.00	90.00	5.0%	15.0%	24.61	1.82%
13	330	110.88	90.00	5.0%	15.0%	25.06	1.85%
14	300	111.76	90.00	5.0%	15.0%	25.53	1.88%
15	270	112.65	90.00	5.0%	15.0%	26.02	1.91%
16	240	113.55	90.00	5.0%	15.0%	26.52	1.93%
17	210	114.46	90.00	5.0%	15.0%	27.04	1.96%
18	180	115.37	90.00	5.0%	15.0%	27.58	1.98%
19	150	116.29	90.00	5.0%	15.0%	28.13	1.99%
20	120	117.22	90.00	5.0%	15.0%	28.68	1.99%
21	90	118.15	90.00	5.0%	15.0%	29.25	1.98%
22	60	119.09	90.00	5.0%	15.0%	29.83	1.97%
23	30	120.04	90.00	5.0%	15.0%	30.41	1.95%
24	0	121.00	90.00	5.0%	15.0%	31.00	1.93%

Volatility Skew

These potential returns from held call options are extremely high. Compounding a two-percent-a-month return allows an investment to double every three years. However, this analysis is incomplete because it uses average returns and doesn't take into account the implied volatility differences of various call options, and the potential high positive and negative returns from large price movements.

In our previous tables, all of our options had the same volatility regardless of their strike price. However, the markets price options on the same security but with different strike prices and different expiration dates, using different implied volatilities. This adjustment is usually known as the volatility skew.

In Table 4.7, captured after a market decline during a very high volatility period, at-the-money options are priced with an implied volatility of

TABLE 4.7 Current Implied Volatilities of S&P 500 ETF Options

Current Price: 140.95
Current Date: 11/26/2007

Strike	Dec. 07	Jan. 08	Mar. 08	Sep. 08	Dec. 09
			Implied Volatility		
125	37.4%	33.5%	33.1%	30.6%	28.9%
130	34.4%	31.6%	31.0%	29.4%	28.2%
135	31.7%	29.4%	29.4%	28.1%	26.9%
140	29.0%	27.2%	27.7%	26.9%	26.4%
145	26.1%	24.9%	25.7%	25.6%	25.8%
150	23.6%	22.5%	23.9%	24.5%	25.2%
155	21.2%	20.3%	22.2%	23.5%	24.4%

Strike	Dec. 07	Jan. 08	Mar. 08	Sep. 08	Dec. 09
			Required Index Return for Breakeven		
125	0.8%	1.7%	3.8%	8.0%	15.5%
130	1.2%	2.3%	4.5%	8.9%	16.8%
135	1.8%	3.1%	5.5%	10.0%	17.9%
140	2.9%	4.2%	6.7%	11.3%	19.4%
145	4.6%	5.8%	8.1%	12.6%	20.9%
150	7.0%	7.8%	9.9%	14.3%	22.6%
155	10.1%	10.5%	12.1%	16.1%	24.2%

28.99 percent, almost identical to the level of the VIX, which closed for the day at 28.91. The in-the-money options then have higher implied volatilities, and the out-of-the-money options have lower volatilities. The IV (implied volatility) of the deepest in-the-money option is almost 80 percent higher than the IV of the most out-of-the-money option.

As we move further out in time, the market assumes that volatility will revert to a long-term average, and the difference between the IVs for in-the-money and out-of-the-money options shrinks. Typically the IV of longer-term options is higher than short-term options, but sometimes when volatility is high, as in this example, the IVs of the short-term options are higher.

The standard explanation for the volatility skew is that it helps to model the observed distribution of market returns, as opposed to the log-normal distribution that the Black-Scholes model assumes. The actual observed distribution of market returns has more downside risk than upside, and thus the implied volatilities have to be adjusted higher as we move down in strike price, and lower as we move up.

In-the-money options are not as sensitive to implied volatility, so the effect is somewhat muted, but an eight-point difference in volatility is still significant. It is the market's way of telling investors that protection against extreme downside risk is in high demand and, consequently, very expensive.

At these high implied volatilities, can any options be profitable? Absolutely. All of them have the potential to deliver gains if index appreciation is high enough during the period, and there have been many months in the past with gains of 5 percent or better. But the hurdle imposed by these volatilities can be extreme.

In the bottom half of Table 4.7, the breakeven point for each of these options was calculated. Of course the out-of-the-money options have high breakeven points, but what is surprising is how high the at-the-money and especially the in-the-money breakeven points are. Index appreciation will have to be much higher than historical averages to make even the deep-in-the-money calls purchased for December, January, or even March profitable.

However, index appreciation is always uneven, and purchasing calls may allow an investor to take gains but avoid losses. When the market falls, the owner of a call has a hedge in place that limits their loss to their initial investment, but when the index rises, they may be able to make several times their initial investment, offsetting many losing investments. This asymmetry is the final piece of the puzzle.

Uneven Appreciation

Let's take a one-year look at the money option as an example and assume that, from historical analysis, we are confident the underlying index will return 10 percent a year with a standard deviation of 15 percent. We'll use 20 percent implied volatility for the option, a level that reflects a typical premium over the average historic volatility.

Our best guess for the value of the index at the same time next year is 10 percent higher than today's value, and we could use that prediction to forecast expected call option returns. However, a better approach is to consider all of the possible potential returns of the index and then calculate the expected value of our call option given that distribution. With a call option, extremely high returns and corresponding gains are always possible, but the strike price transfers some of the loss potential to the seller.

In Table 4.8, one thousand potential one-year returns of the underlying are generated using a normal distribution. Our index starting point is 100, and as expected, most of the ending prices are between 100 and 120, with some outliers in the 80s and 90s and the 130s and 140s. Our median, at the

TABLE 4.8 Percentile Distribution of Index Returns and Call Option Prices

Days	Market	Strike	Rate	Vol.	A1	A2	Price
360	100.00	100.00	5.0%	20.0%	0.35	0.15	10.36

Percentile	Underlying	Call	% Return
2%	79.45	0.00	−100.0%
5%	85.07	0.00	−100.0%
10%	90.69	0.00	−100.0%
25%	99.68	0.00	−100.0%
50%	110.53	10.53	1.6%
75%	119.75	19.75	90.6%
90%	129.95	29.95	189.0%
95%	134.80	34.80	235.8%
98%	141.37	41.37	299.3%
Avg.		12.37	
Stdev		12.05	
Min.		0.00	
Max.		64.47	

50 percentile rank, is 110.53, a +10.53 percent index return. (It should be 10 percent, but Monte Carlo is inexact by definition.)

But even though our median value for the call at expiration is 10.53, which would make for an anemic 1.6 percent return on our initial investment, our mean return is 12.37, which is 19 percent higher than the initial purchase price of our call. As in other leveraged investments, the high potential upside drives the average return.

The distribution of call option returns also has a very high standard deviation, 12, which is not much lower than the average return itself. This reflects both the relatively high likelihood that the option will expire worthless (about 25 percent probability), and the outside chance that it will deliver a huge windfall, such as a 300 percent or 400 percent return.

The outcome of purchasing a single call on the index is unpredictable, but if we turned this into a repeated strategy in which every month we purchased a one-year, at-the-money call on the index, and if the volatility levels remained consistent, then the call option purchases would be expected to generate 19 percent average annual returns on invested capital.

Also, in this model, the average annual return is set at 10 percent, and the annualized volatility is set at 15 percent. However, the implied volatility of the call option is 20 percent. Even with the implied volatility premium, this investment is still profitable.

OPTION ANALYSIS

We can repeat this same analysis for other options to calculate the average expected return for each option. In Table 4.9, we compare the returns of 91-day, 182-day, 365-day, and 730-day options with three different strike prices. We use a 20 percent implied volatility for the at-the-money options, and then raise the IV a little for the in-the-money options, and lower it for the out-of-the-money options.

For each option, we calculate the price and the expected payoff to determine the percentage return. The payoffs are based on the value of the call after a random series of quarterly returns. Note that all of the payoffs are positive—every option has value based upon the potential for an extreme price change to make the option profitable.

For example, call option #9, which is the 91-day 105 strike (that is, 5 percent out of the money) call option, has a payoff of 2.00, but an estimated cost of 2.28. While the option has value, given these underlying assumptions about volatility, it is not a good investment and is expected to result in a −12.4 percent return on the initial investment. In contrast, option #1, the same option but 5 percent in-the-money, has an expected payoff of 4.5 percent after 91 days, which if compounded quarterly, results in a 19 percent annual return.

In this example, options that are deeper in-the-money generate higher average returns, as the buyer is compensated for the risk associated with selecting a lower strike price. However, this is partly because of the volatilities assumed—if we had a reason to believe that the actual volatility of

TABLE 4.9 Percentage Return of Selected Options

Option	Days	Market	Strike	Rate	Vol.	Cost	Payoff	Stdev	% Return
#1	91	100.00	95.00	5.0%	21.0%	7.87	8.22	6.37	4.5%
#2	182	100.00	95.00	5.0%	21.0%	10.10	11.11	9.34	10.1%
#3	365	100.00	95.00	5.0%	21.0%	13.68	16.95	14.09	23.9%
#4	730	100.00	95.00	5.0%	21.0%	19.38	28.11	23.18	45.1%
#5	91	100.00	100.00	5.0%	20.0%	4.61	4.52	5.07	−1.8%
#6	182	100.00	100.00	5.0%	20.0%	6.88	7.39	8.04	7.4%
#7	365	100.00	100.00	5.0%	20.0%	10.45	13.06	12.94	24.9%
#8	730	100.00	100.00	5.0%	20.0%	16.13	23.97	22.20	48.7%
#9	91	100.00	105.00	5.0%	19.0%	2.28	2.00	3.40	−12.4%
#10	182	100.00	105.00	5.0%	19.0%	4.29	4.47	6.40	4.1%
#11	365	100.00	105.00	5.0%	19.0%	7.62	9.69	11.48	27.0%
#12	730	100.00	105.00	5.0%	19.0%	13.10	20.16	21.02	53.9%

the index would be higher than the implied volatilities, then the out-of-the-money options would provide higher percentage returns.

For the two-year options, it doesn't really matter which strike prices are selected—the average returns all cluster around 50 percent. As the time to expiry lengthens, the strike price has less of an affect on the total return.

While these call option returns are relatively high, the problem an investor would have is that the standard deviation of the payoff is also extremely high, often equaling the payoff itself. As a result, the ending value of an option is essentially a coin flip, in which the investor is as equally likely to lose all their money as to double it. In these situations, a string of bad luck can be very destructive for an investment portfolio.

Let's look at one option specifically: #4, a two-year option with a strike price of 95, that is, 5 percent in-the-money. This is a typical option that could be used to capture long-term index appreciation. This option costs 19.38, and has an expected payoff of 28.11, a 45.1 percent average return.

However, the standard deviation of the payoff is 23.18, which means that using a normal distribution of returns, the call option would be expected to take a 50 percent or greater loss about 25 percent of the time. On the other hand, there's roughly a 10 percent chance that the option could double in value during the two-year period.

Investments with payoffs in this variable require very careful asset allocation—we want to invest enough to make a difference in the event that there is a substantial payoff, but not so much that we risk going broke. We will focus on money management strategies more in later chapters, but the principle at work is that this investment is not predictable unless we are able to repeat it dozens of times, thereby reducing the random element.

Marginal Returns—Extending Time or Lowering Strike

There are two ways to make a call option more valuable—lower the strike price, or extend the time. Each action will statistically result in a higher payoff at expiry in exchange for a higher purchase price. We can use the previous table and analysis to decide which is the better alternative.

An at-the-money, 91-day option has a cost of 4.61 and an estimated payoff of 4.52, resulting in a return close to zero. Lowering the strike price by five points will cost an additional 3.26, but is expected to add 3.70 to the payoff. This represents an opportunity to make a 13.40 percent return on the initial investment of lowering the strike price.

If we extend the option for 91 more days, but leave the strike price unchanged, the cost of the option rises 2.27, but the potential payoff increases 2.86, a 26.06 percent return on the additional cost of this call option. This is the better choice from a payoff perspective, although of course it does require the investor to wait 91 more days for their money.

What if we do both? When we lower the strike price and extend the option ninety-one more days, the additional cost is 5.49, and the additional expected return is 6.59, a +20.01 percent return on the additional capital required.

Lowering the strike price provides higher average returns in higher volatility environments, because risk is transferred from the seller to the buyer, and the buyer is compensated for this risk. In lower volatility environments, extending the remaining time left on the option usually provides the better return.

This analysis helps to show why long-term, deep-in-the-money options are so valuable. In situations where at-the-money 30-day or 90-day options may not be profitable, adding extra months and lowering the strike price can change the payoff significantly, and, given average appreciation, will provide extremely high average returns.

Out-of-the-Money

Earlier we showed that out-of-the-money calls have a very difficult time capturing any index appreciation before expiry because their decay is so high. However, that doesn't mean that these options can't be profitable. Their degree of leverage is often so high that a rise in the underlying index can sometimes transform them into at-the-money options that are much more valuable.

In Table 4.10, we analyze the index appreciation and the option decay of an out-of-the-money call option. The strike price is 5 percent higher than market, and the index is appreciating at an annual rate of 10 percent. Every month the underlying security gains in value, but the option loses value, and the result is a 0 to 3 percent loss in the value of the option every month until just before expiry. The result is that the option loses about 16 percent of its value as an investment.

But as we've seen before, even though the average appreciation for an option may be insufficient to build value, there is still the likelihood of excess gain during the life of the option.

Table 4.11 calculates the value of the out-of-the-money call option after one month, given potential index returns. Small percentage returns have large effects on this option, and a 3 percent drop in the index can wipe out 30 percent of its value.

If the underlying index moves up 5 percent, then the call option is now at the money. It has no intrinsic value, but due to the 330 days left until expiry, has a significant time value, resulting in a +42 percent return on our investment in just 30 days.

TABLE 4.10 Change in Value of an Out-of-the-Money Index Option over Time

Month	Days	Market	Strike	Rate	Vol.	Price	Gain
0	360	100.00	105.00	5.0%	15.0%	5.96	
1	330	100.80	105.00	5.0%	15.1%	5.98	0.26%
2	300	101.60	105.00	5.0%	15.2%	5.98	0.08%
3	270	102.41	105.00	5.0%	15.3%	5.97	−0.13%
4	240	103.23	105.00	5.0%	15.4%	5.95	−0.38%
5	210	104.05	105.00	5.0%	15.5%	5.91	−0.67%
6	180	104.88	105.00	5.0%	15.6%	5.85	−1.03%
7	150	105.72	105.00	5.0%	15.7%	5.77	−1.46%
8	120	106.56	105.00	5.0%	15.8%	5.65	−2.02%
9	90	107.41	105.00	5.0%	15.9%	5.49	−2.75%
10	60	108.27	105.00	5.0%	16.0%	5.29	−3.72%
11	30	109.13	105.00	5.0%	16.1%	5.03	−4.84%
12	0	110.00	105.00	5.0%	16.2%	5.00	−0.66%

TABLE 4.11 Potential One-Month Change in Value of an Out-of-the-Money Option

Return	Days	Market	Strike	Rate	Vol.	Price	Return
−5%	330	95.00	105.00	5.0%	16.0%	3.62	−39.2%
−4%	330	96.00	105.00	5.0%	15.9%	3.99	−33.1%
−3%	330	97.00	105.00	5.0%	15.8%	4.38	−26.5%
−2%	330	98.00	105.00	5.0%	15.7%	4.80	−19.5%
−1%	330	99.00	105.00	5.0%	15.6%	5.24	−12.1%
0%	330	100.00	105.00	5.0%	15.5%	5.71	−4.2%
1%	330	101.00	105.00	5.0%	15.4%	6.20	4.1%
2%	330	102.00	105.00	5.0%	15.3%	6.72	12.8%
3%	330	103.00	105.00	5.0%	15.2%	7.27	22.0%
4%	330	104.00	105.00	5.0%	15.1%	7.85	31.7%
5%	330	105.00	105.00	5.0%	15.0%	8.45	41.7%

Because of the random, fluctuating nature of index returns, it is possible to hold an out-of-the-money option, wait for an increase in the value of the index, and then sell it immediately, locking in profits. On the other hand, we could be waiting for an increase that never comes, and the option could expire worthless.

We can simulate this strategy using random scenarios. In each scenario, we will purchase and hold the same one-year, 5 percent out-of-the-money call option for up to 40 weeks, or until it is at-the-money, whichever comes first. If the index doesn't reach the price target by the end of 40 weeks, we will sell the option while it still has some value.

We will check the index price weekly to simplify the model, which may result in some missed sales or perhaps selling at a higher price level. We'll also assume that the implied volatility remains constant at a long-term average value (15 percent), which is likely true in the aggregate, but of course false in specific scenarios.

To generate weekly returns, we can use an average appreciation of 0.18 percent with a standard deviation of 2.08 percent. To convert annual appreciation to weekly, we use the following formulas:

$$10\% \text{ average annual appreciation} = 1.10 \wedge (1/52) - 1 = 0.18\%$$
$$\text{weekly appreciation}$$
$$15\% \text{ average annual volatility} = 15\%/\text{sqrt}(52) = 2.08\%$$

In 1,000 random scenarios, the index hit the price target 79 percent of the time and the investor was able to sell the call option before the 40-week deadline. However, not all of these sales resulted in gains. Generally, sales in the first 26 weeks were profitable, but after that, the time remaining on the option was too low to generate any gains.

In other words, this strategy only made money if the index went up 5 percent in the first six months. Still, 73 percent of the scenarios resulted in selling at a profit, and the median scenario generated a 39.2 percent profit in sixteen weeks.

But the downside of this strategy is stark. While only 16 of the 1,000 scenarios had a gain higher than 90 percent, 144 scenarios had a loss larger than 90 percent. This is an asymmetric payoff, in which an investor risks a large amount of money to make a comparatively small amount. This downside also pushes down the mean return, which is only 14 percent with a 58 percent standard deviation.

Would this strategy generate profits? Certainly. But there are two lessons here. The first is that out-of-the-money call options are best held for a period and then sold early to someone else, while they still have value at an at-the-money option. However, because of their decay, we shouldn't assume that they will appreciate any faster or slower than an in-the-money option on a percentage basis.

Second, holding an at-the-money option, or any option, until it hits a predetermined price target and then selling it can appear like a no-lose proposition; however, in many cases the investor is either selling too early or holding on too long. This leads to payoffs that look high on average, but can hide potential catastrophic losses when the index fails to deliver and the option's decay continues to accelerate.

Another scenario was created where the same call option was simply held for 40 weeks and then sold. The result: a 40 percent mean return with a 156 percent standard deviation. Holding the option for the full 40 weeks provides greater opportunities for the underlying security to deliver outsize returns, and more than 10 percent of the scenarios have returns in excess of 250 percent, which helps raise the average considerably, and helps compensate for the low median return: −19 percent.

Monthly Returns of Calls

A final experiment we can do is to select a variety of calls, generate 1,000 potential monthly returns for the index, and then revalue the calls, given the difference in the market price and the time remaining to expiry. This helps us determine which calls are better at capturing appreciation in a month, assuming that volatility remains unchanged. In a repeated strategy, volatility would be expected to increase in some months and fall in others, so this is a simplifying assumption.

In this case, we won't use a Monte Carlo simulation, but rather a 999-line normal distribution. In Excel, the monthly return is calculated as follows, with zscore stepping from .001 to .999 in increments of .001.

$$= \text{NORMINV}(\text{zscore}, (1.1 \wedge (1/12)) - 1, 0.15/\text{SQRT}(12))$$

This captures a reasonable distribution of index return and option valuation scenarios and weights them according to 0.1 percent probabilities. Calculations using this method are quick and precise, in comparison to Monte Carlo simulations, which sometimes have to be run repeatedly to get consistent results.

Table 4.12 shows the expected return and standard deviations of a number of call options over a one-month period. Overall, we assume 10 percent average annual return with a 15 percent standard deviation. On the left side, volatility is low (IV = 15 percent), but on the right, volatility is high (IV = 25 percent). We keep the volatility constant during the transaction, so that if an investor buys a call option at a high volatility, we assume that they will also sell it at the same high volatility.

The highest returns come from short-term, out-of-the-money call options in low-volatility environments. The one-month, out-of-the-money option provides a 17 percent return in a single month, on average, with an extremely high standard deviation.

However, this return is only dependent upon the investor's ability to correctly guess the index volatility in the next month and find options that are at or below that volatility, which is difficult to do consistently. This

TABLE 4.12 Monthly Returns of Selected Options (sorted from highest to lowest, held in low and high volatility environments)

Short-Term Options, Low Volatility vs. High Volatility Environments

Months	Strike	% Return	Stdev	Months	Strike	% Return	Stdev
1	105	17.12%	336%	1	90	2.49%	41%
1	100	13.50%	144%	2	90	0.79%	35%
2	105	10.03%	147%	3	90	0.56%	31%
3	105	8.22%	103%	3	95	−1.74%	38%
2	100	8.15%	93%	2	95	−3.04%	46%
1	95	7.37%	71%	1	95	−4.03%	63%
3	100	6.65%	73%	3	100	−5.64%	45%
2	95	5.73%	59%	2	100	−10.63%	57%
3	95	5.01%	51%	3	105	−11.25%	52%
1	90	4.25%	41%	2	105	−22.15%	65%
2	90	3.92%	39%	1	100	−27.08%	89%
3	90	3.69%	36%	1	105	−63.62%	96%

Long-Term Options, Low Volatility vs. High Volatility Environments

Months	Strike	% Return	Stdev	Months	Strike	% Return	Stdev
9	105	4.48%	47%	24	90	1.07%	34%
9	100	3.89%	40%	18	90	1.04%	39%
12	105	3.83%	39%	24	95	1.00%	27%
12	100	3.39%	34%	12	90	0.95%	40%
9	95	3.33%	33%	18	95	0.90%	29%
18	105	3.09%	30%	24	100	0.90%	24%
12	95	2.97%	29%	9	90	0.86%	47%
9	90	2.82%	27%	24	105	0.79%	18%
18	100	2.80%	27%	18	100	0.73%	24%
24	105	2.66%	25%	12	95	0.67%	30%
12	90	2.59%	24%	18	105	0.52%	21%
18	95	2.53%	24%	9	95	0.40%	33%
24	100	2.45%	23%	12	100	0.30%	25%
18	90	2.27%	21%	12	105	−0.15%	21%
24	95	2.25%	21%	9	100	−0.21%	27%
24	90	2.06%	18%	9	105	−0.98%	23%

strategy would be considered volatility speculation, as the call options are extremely unprofitable if volatility comes in lower than expected, as we can see from the right side.

Short-term, deep-in-the-money options provide high returns in low-volatility environments and can still hold their value in high-volatility environments. A 3 percent monthly return may sound low, but compounded over two years this doubles the original investment.

Longer-term in-the-money call options can still build value in high-volatility environments, but, like any option, these perform better in low-volatility environments. The 24-month 90 strike price (that is, 10 percent in-the-money) options deliver 2.06 percent a month in a low-volatility environment, which translates to a 27.7 percent return annualized. Their 18 percent standard deviation means the value will fluctuate a lot, but not nearly as much as a short-term in-the-money option.

When we see standard deviations of returns that are ten times higher than the average return, that's generally an indication that the investment is unpredictable except in vast amounts of transactions and over long periods of time. If we simply purchased a single call option and held it for one or two months, it would be impossible to try to guess the results with any accuracy. Our 2 percent average monthly return would be swamped by the random factor.

But repeated strategies can still work, and provide some predictability due to the law of large numbers. Later chapters focus on how to build these repeated investment strategies and manage that type of portfolio.

More about Volatility

When implied volatility is high, are call options a good deal or a bad deal? Or, putting the question another way, if implied volatility is high, can we count on the actual returns and volatility of the index to be higher during the life of the option?

The answer is no for returns and yes for volatility, with some caveats. We took a sample of weekly closing prices for the S&P 500 and the VIX for the period from January 1990 to August 2007. The VIX is published by the Chicago Board of Exchange (CBOE). It is a weighted average estimate for implied volatility on the S&P 500, and is a widely used measure of index volatility.

Next, we sorted the weekly data using the closing price of the VIX and divided the target weeks into six groups, A through F, with the first group consisting of the weeks in which the VIX was the lowest, the next group containing the next highest VIX closing prices, and so on. Then, for each group, we calculated the average VIX, the average return for the next week and for the next thirteen weeks, and the standard deviation of weekly returns for the next thirteen weeks. This volatility is then annualized, and the Diff IV HV column is the average percentage premium of the VIX IV over HV.

TABLE 4.13 Relationship between the VIX and Future Return and Volatility

Group	Rows	AVG VIX	% Ret, 1 Week	% Ret, 13 Weeks	St. Dev, 13 Weeks	Annua- lized	% Diff IV HV	>5% Loss
A	1 to 153	11.51	0.19%	2.59%	1.26%	9.08	+26.8%	18%
B	154 to 307	13.58	0.02%	2.56%	1.36%	9.8	+38.6%	19%
C	308 to 460	16.04	0.19%	1.81%	1.58%	11.42	+40.5%	18%
D	461 to 614	18.9	0.07%	1.02%	2.05%	14.76	+28.1%	22%
E	615 to 768	22.37	0.20%	1.55%	2.52%	18.2	+22.9%	22%
F	769 to 921	29.71	0.38%	4.63%	2.66%	19.15	+55.1%	32%
	All Rows	18.68	0.18%	2.36%	1.90%	13.74	+36.0%	22%
	Stdev	6.35	2.05%	6.71%	0.81%	5.82		

Incidentally, this is exactly the approach used by Fama and French to develop the three-factor model: Divide a sample set into groups based on a factor, and then compare the averages. It is a very useful method for finding relationships within data sets, assuming that there is enough data to draw conclusions.

As can be seen in Table 4.13, there is no significant relationship between the current level of volatility and the future returns, except perhaps at the highest levels of the VIX (group F). This means that we can consider index drift as a constant for most of the time and that it is, as usual, swamped by random noise in the short term.

But call option profitability is also determined by future volatility, and that is related to the current level of the VIX. When the VIX is higher, on average we can expect volatility to be higher in the weekly returns for the next thirteen weeks. In group F, we also see an increased chance of a 5 percent or greater price drop in the following week, according to the last column.

However, there is still a big gap between the implied volatility and the actual volatility that occurs in the ensuing weeks: for every group, implied volatility is higher, and for group F it is almost 50 percent higher. This reinforces the previous analysis that most of the time short-term at-the-money options are bad bets, as too much expected volatility is priced into the option.

Any option can always be made more profitable, on average, by extending the time or lowering the strike price. As stated previously, lowering the strike price provides the greater payoff when volatility is high, and extending the strike price is more advantageous when volatility is low. But both actions will increase the average payoff and will potentially make an unprofitable option profitable.

SUMMARY

Call options are hedging instruments that are carefully priced to compensate the seller for both the risk of loss and the cost of capital. The pricing has little to do with expected appreciation of the underlying security over the life of the option, but is instead driven primarily by volatility and time.

A volatility premium is also embedded in option pricing due to the gap between implied volatility and the actual volatility experienced by the security. Also, a volatility skew exists in the options market in order to adjust the return distribution. This skew makes in-the-money call options more expensive by raising their implied volatility, and makes out-of-the-money options less expensive.

While every option has value and the potential for gains, in many cases expected time decay makes the breakeven point of the option higher than expected appreciation, resulting in a loss. However, longer-term and in-the-money options have lower rates of decay, and this effect can make these options profitable on average, but with wide standard deviations. This means that predictable profits are only likely to be found in repeated strategies, not one-time investments.

The expected monthly return can be calculated for a call option by simulating possible monthly returns for the underlying security, revaluing the option, and weighting the outcomes. While very high profits can sometimes be made using out-of-the-money options and volatility speculation, the more consistent profits come from longer-term, in-the-money options.

When the VIX is high, the premium of implied volatility over actual volatility is still high, but the investor should be prepared for some extreme price movements. Statistical analysis of the S&P 500 and the VIX shows that sharp upward and downward moves become much more likely at these times.

In the next chapter, we apply the concepts presented in this chapter and develop a new twist on a classic profitable investment strategy: covered calls secured by futures contracts.

CHAPTER 5

Leveraged Covered Calls with Futures

C hapter 4 reviewed many different types of calls and found that, on average, long-term deep-in-the-money calls are more profitable than short-term calls. In this chapter, we'll use this knowledge to implement a classic strategy: the covered call fund.

Traditionally, covered calls are seen as low-risk, low-return strategies, but by applying leverage, we will create an investment that is capable of generating extremely high returns over short periods of time. This chapter analyzes and then backtests this strategy, both by year and in low- and high-volatility environments, in order to determine how it would have performed across a variety of market conditions.

COVERED CALLS AS A SOURCE OF INCOME

By selling an at-the-money call against a security in inventory, the owner forfeits additional appreciation for the period until expiry in exchange for the premium. This is because any appreciation will result in the exercise of the option. However, the owner will still be obligated to take any losses associated with the security, and could be left with an impaired asset.

Short-term covered calls are profitable historically because the premiums collected are, on average, higher than the losses taken on the security. This is the result of both the volatility premium, in which implied volatility is higher than historic volatility, and the rapid decay and hedging costs associated with short-term at-the-money options.

Profits are made when the underlying security remains flat or appreciates. Whether it appreciates 1 percent or 50 percent makes no difference—the option will be exercised and the seller will collect only the premium, which is generally just a small percentage of the value of the asset. But when that premium is leveraged 20×, the return can be 30 to 50 percent.

Profits are reduced when the market price of the underlying security falls, and position losses occur when the fall in the value of the security is greater than the premium collected. When the position is leveraged 20×, a one- or two-percent loss in excess of the premium translates to a 20- or 40-percent loss in the value of the investment.

This means that while 100 percent gains are extremely unlikely unless the current risk premium is sky-high, losses in excess of 100 percent are definitely possible. If the covered call premium is 3 percent of the index price, and the index loses 10 percent of its value during the period, the loss on a 20× leveraged position will be $(-10\% + 3\%) \times 20 = -140\%$ of the initial investment. For a futures contract, this will mean providing significant additional margin in order to avoid liquidating the position. One danger related to covered call strategies is that a single loss can wipe out months or years of gains. However, in practice, when the market drops, the implied volatility for short-term call options increases significantly, which can result in improved profitability in the next period or whenever the losses subside.

A more subtle danger is that the risk premium will fall sharply, reducing the profitability of covered call strategies and encouraging investors to write more and more leveraged covered calls to maintain their income level. Then, when an increased supply of calls has pushed the cost of hedging leveraged positions down to new lows, the market will drop suddenly, resulting in large losses that wipe out profits and force investors to liquidate their positions.

POSITION DETAILS

For this strategy, we will use one-month covered calls on the S&P 500 written on index futures. Not because it is the best index available or because this strategy is the best one we can find, but because we have almost two decades of data available to use for backtesting. Since 1990, the CBOE has published the VIX, a measure of implied volatility of front-month options on the S&P 500, and we can use this index to calculate the cost of a one-month at-the-money call for any point in time.

Volatility indexes are becoming more popular and prevalent, and there is another index with similar data for the Russell 2000, the RVX, but it only has been collected and published from January 2004. Still, after we complete our analysis using the S&P 500, we can use our limited data from the Russell and see if we get similar results.

This strategy assumes that a broker is willing to provide the maximum leverage for an index futures position—that is, 5 percent margin for $20\times$ leverage—and that covered calls can be written against that position with no additional margin requirement. If a broker is using portfolio margin or something similar, this should be allowed. Any potential loss on the covered call is offset by a gain on the futures contract; thus, extra margin is not required.

Not that all of our funds will be invested at maximum leverage, of course, but by calculating the returns at maximum leverage and reviewing the extreme cases, we can then lower the leverage ratio to a safer amount.

For the analysis, we've used index prices and a constant interest rate of 5 percent. As in all such calculations, we need to be careful about double counting dividends or not counting them at all—they belong in either the cost of capital or the returns, but not both.

Generally, the interest rate used in covered call calculations does not make a significant difference in return calculations. The long position of the index or future benefits from decreases in interest rates, while the covered call position benefits when interest rates rise. The effects essentially cancel each other out.

Also, for simplicity, we've assumed that each one-month option is for 30 days. Of course, some months have 31 days or 28 days, and Excel could do the calculations, but it wouldn't be able to determine which months have market holidays or extraordinary events, such as when the market was closed after the 2001 terrorist attacks.

EXPECTED STRATEGY RETURNS

The returns provided by a leveraged, covered call strategy are a combination of the returns of two strategies: an index future, and a naked short call. (A naked call is a call in which the underlying security is not owned, and therefore has the potential for unlimited losses.) We can then calculate the unleveraged returns of each of the two strategies for our historical period, and then leverage the result. See Table 5.1.

Futures contracts provide profits when the underlying security appreciates faster than the cost of capital, and this has historically been the case for the S&P 500. When we set our cost of capital to 5 percent, futures contracts provide an average of 0.49 percent per month or 6.0 percent annualized in the period from January 1990 to November 2007. If 0.49 percent

TABLE 5.1 Monthly Returns of the Index, Future, and Naked Call

	Index	Future	Naked Call	No Leverage Future + Call	20× Leverage Future + Call	20× Leverage 1 yr. Return
Avg.	0.78%	0.49%	0.35%	0.84%	16.84%	203.24%
Std.	3.93%	3.93%	2.28%	2.26%	45.29%	143.43%
Median	1.05%	0.76%	0.90%	1.40%	27.98%	106.33%
Min.	−14.58%	−14.87%	−8.70%	−11.89%	−237.78%	−209.99%
Max.	11.16%	10.87%	3.87%	4.91%	98.23%	545.16%

a month seems low, remember that this return is only the risk equity premium for the period. Adding back the interest rate (or risk-free rate, as it's called) is required to get the full index return of 0.78 percent monthly or 9.77 percent annually.

Futures contracts can be leveraged 20×, which provides a one-month return of about 10 percent. However, each month has a very high standard deviation of returns, and 19 months in our 214 month sample have declines that, when leveraged 20×, would exceed 100 percent.

The naked covered call returns, which are just the returns of writing a call option and then buying it back just before expiry, are 0.41 percent a month or 4.98 percent annualized. Of course, this is a theoretical return and doesn't include any additional margin requirement, and no broker would allow selling leveraged naked covered calls without some kind of margin. One of the benefits of using a futures contract is that it does provide collateral for a covered call strategy.

Naked call strategies have lower monthly standard deviations, 2.28 percent a month as compared to 3.93 percent for futures. This is because the income received by the premium and the avoidance of index losses helps to dampen the effect of index volatility on the strategy. Interestingly, when naked calls are combined with futures to create covered call positions, the monthly return increases, but the standard deviation remains the same, resulting in a higher average profit for the same amount of risk.

When unleveraged covered calls (i.e., short call + future + risk-free rate), are compared to the index over the eighteen-year period, the difference is stark. Historically, $1 invested in the S&P 500 index in January 1990 grew to $4.50 by November 2007. However, the same $1 invested in an unleveraged covered call fund grows to $12.11. The covered call strategy provides a 15.1 percent annualized return over the period, and has a correlation with the index of 0.87.

The 20× leveraged covered calls have a monthly return of 16.8 percent with a standard deviation of 45.3 percent. The investment delivers positive returns more than 76.6 percent of the time, and there are only 8 months out of 214 with a loss greater than 100 percent. Unlike many leveraged investments, the median is significantly higher than the mean, reflecting the greater likelihood of a sharp downward move.

ANNUAL RETURN BACKTESTS

The traditional way to calculate annual returns is to compound the monthly return twelve times. The profits from every month are reinvested to generate new months in the next month. The problem with high-risk investments is that we can't assume that we can always compound at this rate because, at any time, we could lose 100 percent of our investment or more; therefore, quoting an annualized rate as $(1 + r) \wedge 12$ is quite misleading. Still, we do want to have some indication of the profitability that an investment strategy can generate in a year.

Another approach would be to not include compounding. In this scenario, we assume that the same amount is invested twelve months in a row, and that both gains and losses are accumulated throughout the year. We'll call this the average annual return, rather than the average annualized.

Note that average annual returns assume that the investor still has the ability to continue investing even in the face of losses—for example, let's say that the investor risks $100,000 and then the investment loses 90 percent in the first month. The investor will then have to come up with another $90,000, in addition to their $10,000 remaining, in order to repeat the investment. This may require access to a line of credit or backup funds or something similar.

We can arrive at a quick estimate through simple multiplication. Our leveraged covered call investment returns 16.8 percent a month, which, multiplied by 12 months, would be 201 percent a year. The standard deviation of the return, 45.4 percent, would be multiplied by the square root of 12 to yield 157 percent. This assumes that our returns are essentially random and that prior returns do not influence the next return. We can test that assumption by checking the correlation between this month and next month's index returns, and when we do, it is −0.06, meaning an insignificant level of correlation.

The data also supports this estimate of average annual return. For the 202 rolling twelve-month periods, we get an average of 189 percent with a 149 percent standard deviation. With numbers like this, we would expect 12-month losses to be relatively rare, and in fact we find that only 25 of our rolling 12-month periods have returns less than 0 percent.

When we examine the data by calendar year, as shown in Table 5.2, we find that sixteen of the eighteen years had positive returns. Still, negative returns in individual months are common across all years, and if the worst monthly return in most years is −72 percent. The only year with sharp negative returns throughout the year (and for the year as a whole) was 2002, but it is followed by the best year by far in our sample, 2003.

Despite the two bad years, we would have to conclude that this investment rewards patience and persistence, even in the face of losses. When the market is falling and uncertainty is high, selling a covered call is risky, but as we will show, an investor can expect to be well rewarded for the risk.

VIX MODIFICATIONS

Conventional wisdom says that the best time to sell covered calls is when implied volatility is high, as the premiums collected are higher. However,

TABLE 5.2 Year-by-Year Comparison of Leveraged Covered Call Strategy

	S&P Return	Avg. VIX	Avg. Month	Best Month	Worst Month
1990	0.3%	22.9	14.3%	65.8%	−143.2%
1991	26.3%	18.4	20.6%	57.4%	−62.2%
1992	4.5%	15.2	18.1%	36.9%	−20.7%
1993	7.1%	12.5	16.8%	28.6%	−25.0%
1994	−1.5%	13.9	0.9%	43.9%	−60.3%
1995	34.1%	12.5	25.0%	28.8%	16.4%
1996	20.3%	16.3	23.2%	41.6%	−63.0%
1997	31.0%	23.0	27.3%	77.3%	−68.7%
1998	26.7%	26.2	27.7%	98.2%	−237.8%
1999	19.5%	24.5	32.5%	60.8%	−18.7%
2000	−10.1%	23.0	3.3%	64.9%	−109.0%
2001	−13.0%	25.8	−0.2%	73.8%	−137.1%
2002	−23.4%	26.2	−14.5%	87.8%	−148.4%
2003	26.4%	22.7	39.6%	64.8%	7.7%
2004	9.0%	15.6	21.5%	39.0%	−38.6%
2005	3.0%	13.0	11.2%	32.2%	−23.0%
2006	13.6%	12.6	20.8%	34.7%	−38.1%
2007	3.5%	16.8	14.9%	50.9%	−48.6%
Avg.	9.8%	19.0	16.8%	54.9%	−67.7%
Std.	16.2%	5.24	13.1%	20.8%	64.6%

clearly market risk is also higher at that point, and the potential for losses is greater. So should we adjust our strategy when the VIX is high?

We took our 214 returns and sorted them by the level of the VIX at the time the call was written, and divided the results into three groups, a low VIX group, a medium VIX group, and a high VIX group (see Table 5.3).

The low VIX group had average monthly returns of 10.9 percent, as compared to the 21.1 percent return of the high VIX group. However, the standard deviation was also much lower, 23.36 percent as compared to 64.01 percent. We can conclude that selling options when the VIX is lower is less profitable, but less risky, on average.

Also, the worst monthly returns occurred when the VIX was high. According to the historical backtest, a 100 percent or greater loss has never occurred when the VIX is low, but has occurred six times when the VIX was high. Of course, all of the highest gains only occur when the VIX is high, due to the higher premiums collected. When the VIX is low, the typical profitable month returns 20 to 25 percent, as compared to 50 percent to 60 percent when the VIX is high.

If average profits are twice as high when the VIX is high, that supports the conclusion that selling call options at those times has been a high-risk, high-reward strategy, with high-expected profitability. We could even make an argument for only selling call options when the VIX is high and putting our capital into other strategies when the VIX is low.

Or, we could increase our leverage when the VIX is low, and reduce it when the VIX is high. For example, when the VIX is low, we could invest at 20× leverage, and when the VIX is high, only 10×. This way, we can get a more consistent risk and return throughout our series.

In theory, we could even change our position on a daily basis in response to the VIX and keep the risk constant at all times. In practice, this kind of dynamic hedging, especially when practiced by many market participants, would likely lead to some kind of death spiral in which funds sell more and more futures contracts to reduce leverage in response to higher and higher volatility.

TABLE 5.3 Leveraged Covered Call Profitability in Selected VIX Scenarios

	All	Low VIX	Med. VIX	High VIX	After 5% Drop	After 5% Gain
Avg.	16.8%	12.0%	16.1%	22.4%	20.4%	22.6%
Std.	45.3%	23.4%	39.3%	63.6%	65.6%	43.3%
Min.	−237.8%	−63.0%	−143.2%	−237.8%	−109.4%	−71.3%
Max.	98.2%	30.6%	45.0%	98.2%	98.2%	90.6%
Median	28.0%	24.1%	33.5%	49.1%	42.3%	41.0%

But as a monthly strategy for a smaller investor or fund, it is certainly feasible to buy a varying amount of futures every month and then sell a corresponding number of call option contracts in order to adjust exposure without influencing the market.

When we added a very simple leverage rule to our results, which was to invest at 20× leverage normally, but at 16× leverage when the VIX is over 20, which is about 40 percent of the time, the average monthly return was reduced 9.5 percent, but our average standard deviation of returns was reduced 14.5 percent. Our worst return was also reduced from −239 percent to −178 percent. We get more return for less risk, and consequently can invest more on average.

Using a related rule set in which we invested 20 percent of our capital monthly in a 20× leveraged covered call return when the VIX was low (<20), but only 16 percent when the VIX was high over the eighteen-year period resulted in a fund turning a $10 NAV in January 1990 into $3,058 by November 2007 due to the compounding of returns. The average monthly return of the fund was 3.01 percent with a standard deviation of 7.77 percent and a max loss of −38.04 percent (see Figure 5.1).

The above thresholds and leverage ratios are arbitrary and could be improved, but we don't want to go too far down the path of making a complex VIX-return model to fit historical data. We've identified the influence of the VIX that fits our intuition—risk increases as the VIX increases—and have

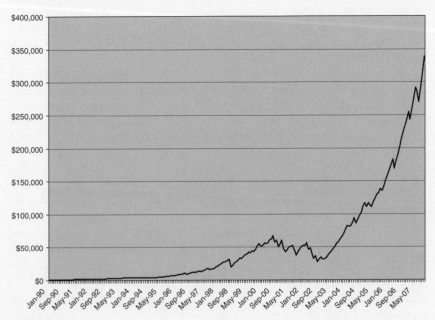

FIGURE 5.1 Growth of $10 NAV over 18 Years, Adjusted Leverage

a modification in place that should help reduce the volatility and maintain a relatively consistent level of risk and return over time.

There is one caveat. If we examine the historical returns, we see that in down markets, covered call strategies tend to become profitable before the index hits bottom, as the worst of the declines have already occurred, but a tremendous amount of volatility is still built into the index.

Thus, if we're willing to time the market to a certain extent, higher profits can be achieved—although, of course, it could be very difficult to determine when the majority of the losses have emerged and to develop a rules-based strategy around this. In our own analysis, we found that leveraged covered call returns were still extremely risky in the next month after either a 5 percent drop, but much less so after a 5 percent gain, which suggests that there is less risk in being aggressive during good market conditions rather than trying to avoid negative ones.

ASSET ALLOCATION

With high-reward, high-risk investment strategies, asset allocation is critical. Success is contingent upon the ability to continue to invest, and if we lose all of our funds, we have no way to get them back.

Although we can calculate individual investments using 20× leverage, to invest all of our funds this way would be suicide. One approach is to define a maximum monthly loss, say 35 percent for example, and then use the worst unleveraged monthly return in our series, which is −9.6 percent after the high-VIX position adjustment, and then set a leverage ratio that corresponds to this one-time loss, which in this case would be 4.

A covered call fund with a leverage ratio of 3 and the VIX modification should return 2.8 percent a month (3×0.71 percent), which comes to 39.8 percent annualized. This kind of return will multiply an investment 4.3× in five years, which is an excellent return. Of course, it assumes that a severe drop in the index won't wipe out the fund at some point.

But perhaps we can do better. If we desire higher leverage but are concerned about one-time losses, we could set up a line of credit specifically for that eventuality. This line of credit would allow us to keep investing in the face of losses until we return to profitability. We could then size our investment according to both our equity and the size of the line of credit.

Suppose that we have $100,000 in equity and $100,000 from a line of credit. We could then be comfortable investing $50,000 at maximum leverage (with high-VIX modifications), knowing that even in the historical worst case we would have enough for at least two more investments, as the max loss is 191 percent × $50,000, which leaves $105,000 in combined equity and credit.

The danger here is that if we have rapid gains, there may be a temptation to overinvest, even though our line of credit hasn't increased. Regardless of initial profitability, we should remain conservative and keep the level of investment, $50,000, relatively constant and grow it only at the rate of inflation, no matter how rapidly the account increases. We'll assume that the majority of today's gains are needed to pay for tomorrow's potential losses.

We can use our annual average return tables above to calculate the expected ending balances at the end of the first year, depending upon which year we started the strategy. On average, we would make more than $90,000 in the first year, but in some years, such as 2003, we would have garnered a +$246,000 gain. Starting at the beginning of the worst year, 2002, would have resulted in a $100,000 loss, with both the equity and the line of credit being lost by the end of the year, so there is certainly some risk.

If this strategy were repeated for four years, the average return would be almost $375,000 on our initial $100,000 of equity and $100,000 of credit, with a $157,000 standard deviation. The first year of the four has the most risk, as the fund hasn't yet built up enough equity to cushion against severe losses.

Then, over time, both the percentage returns and the risk decreases as the overall leverage gets lower. In the later years, a significant amount of equity would be built up, but only a small amount would be at risk. Consider that for the last month, more than $550,000 of equity and credit would be available, but only $50,000 would be at risk. This equals a small amount of portfolio risk overall, but also a small return.

ADDITIONAL ANALYSIS

As stated before, the interest rate and cost of capital have little effect on the profitability of a covered call strategy. Increasing the cost of capital by one percentage point reduces the unleveraged monthly return of a covered call strategy by about 0.05%, a relatively insignificant decline given the level of noise in returns.

The reason for this is that rising interest rates in effect reduce the profitability of the futures contracts, but raise the average premium of the covered calls. Thus, a covered call strategy actually has a built-in hedge against interest rate fluctuations. Even when rates are raised to 1979 levels of 15 percent, the monthly returns are still almost 10 percent.

When we applied the same analysis to the Russell 2000 using the index returns and the ∧RVX historical data, the analysis was similar, and the futures covered call strategy provided average returns of approximately

19 percent per month when leveraged 20x. Because the ∧RVX has only been collected for four years, there wasn't enough data to do sensitivity analysis on the level of volatility, but, on an annual basis, the returns were very similar to the S&P 500, which is expected because the two indices are highly correlated.

SUMMARY

A covered call strategy using index futures is, when fully leveraged, a high-risk, high-return strategy that can generate extremely high returns over a short period of time, but can also potentially result in a loss greater than 100 percent of invested capital. This makes risk management and asset allocation critical, as overinvesting will almost certainly lead to a significant loss of principal that would be very difficult to recover from.

While covered calls were advocated during the 2002 S&P downturn, the strategy's returns was still negative, and highly leveraging the position would have been a mistake.

However, when unleveraged, the strategy generates higher returns over time than the S&P 500, and with lower risk. This suggests that there is an appropriate level of risk for the strategy, but, as we determined in the low/high VIX analysis, this level likely changes on a monthly basis.

Later chapters will address asset allocation and risk management in further detail, and also will discuss the use of puts in the above strategy. Using hedging tactics would allow an investor to invest more aggressively, although at some points the portfolio insurance would become prohibitively expensive.

CHAPTER 6

Rolling LEAPS Call Options Explained

I n Chapter 4 we showed that longer-term call options are, on average, a better value than shorter-term options because of their ability to capture more appreciation for only a marginal increase in cost.
As a result, any call option can be made more valuable by extending its
life; that is, selling the option and replacing it with an identical one, but
with a later expiration date. This technique is called rolling an option
forward.

This chapter applies this technique to extend both the lifetime and
the potential value of LEAPS call options. This practice can allow an investor to maintain a leveraged, hedged position on an index for a period
of years. Like every strategy in this book, this one is presented both as a
viable method for benefiting from long-term index appreciation and a foun-
dational strategy for learning advanced concepts in indexing and options.
Again, we advise against assuming that later strategies are better, as each
has its own merits.

Rolling LEAPS Call Options is a simple strategy to execute, has a high
degree of predictability in cash outflows, is relatively low risk, and has low
transaction costs. However, it also has significant hidden complexity, and
because of its long-term nature may trap investors into low returns or unexpected losses several years later.

For these reasons, we devote both a concept chapter and a strategy
chapter to this strategy, as much of what we learn can be applied to both
spread-based strategies and higher-risk strategies, which are discussed in
later chapters.

UNDERSTANDING LEAPS CALLS

"LEAPS" is simply a name given to an option that has more than nine months to expiry. The name is an acronym for "Long-Term Equity Anticipation Securities." Other than the expiration date, there is no difference between LEAPS options and traditional shorter-term options, and in fact, a LEAPS will eventually become a short-term option if it is held for a long time.

LEAPS options are available for many, but not all, large-cap stocks and ETFs, and coverage continues to expand as the instruments become more popular. Indexes also have options with more than nine months to expiry, but as these are technically not equity options, they are usually referred to as "long-dated options" (or some similar term).

The long-term nature of LEAPS affects the characteristics of the option in several ways. LEAPS options decay very slowly, and as a result the change in the price of a LEAPS is primarily dependent upon the appreciation of the underlying security and any changes in long-term volatility. Time decay is present of course, but may not be noticeable on a weekly or even monthly basis.

Long-term volatility is related to short-term volatility, but generally doesn't rise or fall nearly as fast. If the VIX spikes from 15 to 25, the long-term volatility of the same security may rise only from 22 to 27. This indicates that the market generally believes that volatility will revert to a long-term mean value at some point.

Both LEAPS call and put options are available, and both are long-term hedging instruments that allow buyers to transfer risk to sellers for a long period of time. LEAPS calls are often seen in spreads or as stock substitutes, as it is cheaper to buy an in-the-money LEAPS call than the stock.

For example, an investor could buy a LEAPS call, and then sell one-month calls on the same security to implement a covered call strategy. As a result, this strategy would have much higher capital efficiency than simply using the stock itself as the underlying security. Sometimes owning a LEAPS is known as "renting a stock."

Of course, the LEAPS has volatility risk in the period before expiry, and these securities are still quite expensive when compared to short-term options, as the creation of a LEAPS option requires a long-term commitment of capital.

In Table 6.1, the effects of a decline in volatility were calculated for an at-the-money LEAPS call and two in-the-money LEAPS calls. All options are negatively affected, but the impact on the in-the-money options is significantly lower. The deep-in-the-money LEAPS call (that is, 80 strike price) costs less than a third of the price of the stock, and is fairly resistant to even large changes in the long-term volatility.

TABLE 6.1 At-the-Money LEAPS Call Option vs. In-the-Money LEAPS Call Options: Effect of a Decline in Volatility on Prices

Days	Market	Strike	Rate	Vol.	Price	% Loss
720	100	100	5%	25%	18.49	
720	100	100	5%	20%	15.99	−13.6%
720	100	90	5%	20%	23.92	
720	100	90	5%	20%	21.90	−8.5%
720	100	80	5%	25%	30.40	
720	100	80	5%	25%	29.00	−4.6%

Because LEAPS options tend to be more thinly traded, the bid-ask spread is usually wider than that of shorter-term options. This cost may not be a factor for an investor who is planning on holding the option for a year or more, but if an investor is buying and selling LEAPS regularly, this could create both high transaction costs and, occasionally, liquidity risk (that is, wider bid-ask spreads) during certain periods.

LEAPS—by the Greeks

This is a good place to mention "the Greeks." The Greeks are a set of variables associated with any option that measures its sensitivity to changes in the underlying security or in the market environment. They can be used to compare the pricing parameters of various options and identify shared risk characteristics.

The Greeks can be intimidating mathematically, but any online brokerage or option calculator should provide access to these variables, and we won't spend any time learning how to calculate them. Many traders and investors develop a familiarity with them by plugging sample dates and strike prices into an option calculator and viewing the effects on the Greeks and specifically the option's price.

Also, some traders consider the Greeks unreliable because they only are accurate for a specific instant in time, and will immediately change as soon as the price or implied volatility of the option changes. The Greeks also don't effectively capture the effect of volatility changes due to price changes alone, that is, the volatility skew.

We start with an in-depth analysis of the at-the-money option and then compare it with the other options, shown in Table 6.2. Call option A is in-the-money, B is at-the-money, and C is out-of-the-money. Option B, the

TABLE 6.2   Greek Comparison of Three LEAPS Call Options on the SPY ETF

Market Price = 149.02

	A	B	C
Days	726	726	726
Strike Price	130	150	170
Implied Volatility	27.19%	23.66%	20.66%
Interest Rate	3.89%	3.89%	3.89%
Dividends	0.78	0.78	0.78
Delta	0.745	0.606	0.434
Gamma	0.001	0.001	0.009
Theta	−0.020	−0.020	−0.017
Vega	0.662	0.779	0.805
Price	33.91	21.28	11.46

at-the-money two-year LEAPS call, has a delta of .606, which indicates that for every $1 the underlying security rises in price, this option will be expected to gain 0.606 in value, which is about 2.9 percent of the original option price.

Where does the other forty cents of appreciation go? The LEAPS option has more than twenty dollars of time value, and for every increase in the price of the underlying, the time value will decrease to some extent. For this option, every increase in the intrinsic value by $1 will reduce the time value by almost 40 cents, resulting in a delta of .606.

The gamma, which is the amount that the delta changes for every $1 increase in the underlying, is almost zero, and time decay, as measured by a theta of −0.0190, is extremely low. Theta is the specific amount of value that the option loses every day if none of the other parameters change, and is always low for LEAPS or longer-term options, especially if they are in-the-money.

The sensitivity of the option to volatility is measured by vega, which is the amount of value that the option gains for every 1 percent increase in the implied volatility of the underlying security. For example, 0.77 would be considered high, but the implied volatility of LEAPS options doesn't change as quickly as that of shorter-term options, so this can be somewhat misleading.

If we compare our ATM (at-the-money) option B to option A, an option more than 20 points in-the-money and with a higher implied volatility because of the skew, we see immediately that the in-the-money option is about 50 percent more expensive, and consequently requires a larger commitment of capital.

However, it is not $20 more expensive, only about $12.60 more, and that has to be seen as a positive tradeoff. The delta of the in-the-money option is significantly higher: .745 versus .606. This represents the lower cost of hedging and the higher appreciation expected over the life of the option. Less time value is lost as intrinsic value is gained.

The theta, or time decay, appears the same, but because the in-the-money option has a much higher price, as a percentage the value is relatively low. The vega is also lower, reflecting the reduced impact of volatility on an in-the-money option, but is still a significant factor in pricing.

The in-the-money option is the better purchase if we expect an average amount of index ETF appreciation over the two years—for example, about 25 points. It would provide a 30 percent return over two years, as compared to only 12.8 percent for the at-the-money option. The in-the-money option also has a narrower range of returns and is somewhat more predictable.

An out-of-the-money option, C, is also included in the analysis for the sake of completeness. This option has a delta of only 0.43 because of the high strike price; however, the gamma is high, which indicates that the delta would increase significantly as it moves in the money. The theta is low, but the option is very sensitive to volatility; that is, it has a 0.8 vega, which is why out-of-the-money options are sometimes referred to as volatility speculation.

One Year Later

During the life of any call option, there is on ongoing race between delta and theta, or appreciation and time decay. As the underlying appreciates and a call option moves into the money, intrinsic value is gained, but time value is lost. However, if the option fails to appreciate at all, value is still lost with the passage of time.

While the Greeks can provide useful information as to how the value of an option will change over time, a simpler and potentially more accurate approach is to revalue the option using new inputs. In Table 6.3, we show the results of a two-year LEAPS call option after it is held for one year, based upon the appreciation of the underlying. For the sake of simplicity, we've assumed the same volatility and simulated a skew, and the initial market price of the index is scaled at 100.

Holding a two-year LEAPS option for one year is a viable way to capture appreciation. The LEAPS option acts as a leveraged instrument, increasing or decreasing in value according to the appreciation in the underlying security.

As Table 6.3 shows, even if the underlying security appreciates, it still may not be enough to offset time decay. At +5 percent annual index appreciation, the call option has still lost almost 5 percent of its value after one

TABLE 6.3   Value of a Two-Year LEAPS Call Option after One Year (given selected index returns)

	Days	Market	Strike	Rate	Vol.	Price
Original	730	100.00	85	0.05	0.27	27.93

Index Gain/Loss	Days	Market	Strike	Rate	Vol.	Price	% Return
−15%	365	85	85	0.05	0.24	10.16	−63.6%
−10%	365	90	85	0.05	0.25	13.83	−50.5%
−5%	365	95	85	0.05	0.26	17.85	−36.1%
0	365	100	85	0.05	0.27	22.11	−20.8%
+5%	365	105	85	0.05	0.28	26.57	−4.9%
+10%	365	110	85	0.05	0.29	31.16	+11.6%
+15%	365	115	85	0.05	0.30	35.84	+28.4%
+20%	365	120	85	0.05	0.31	40.60	+45.4%
+25%	365	125	85	0.05	0.32	45.42	+62.6%

year due to time decay. Breakeven for the above option is at about +6.5 percent appreciation for the year. This reflects both the hedging cost and the cost of capital built into the LEAPS.

If volatility has changed during the year, then the price of the option will be affected, but the effect may be minimal if the option is significantly in-the-money. Table 6.4 simulates a 5 percent drop in implied volatility for the base option, from .27 to .22.

TABLE 6.4   Value of a Two-Year LEAPS Call after One Year (selected index returns plus a decline in volatility)

	Days	Market	Strike	Years	Rate	Vol.	Price
Original	730	100.00	85	2.00	0.05	0.27	27.93

Lower Volatility (−5%)							

Gain/Loss	Days	Market	Strike	Years	Rate	Vol.	Price	% Return
−15	365	85	85	1.00	0.05	0.19	8.56	−69.3%
−10	365	90	85	1.00	0.05	0.20	12.33	−55.9%
−5	365	95	85	1.00	0.05	0.21	16.48	−41.0%
0	365	100	85	1.00	0.05	0.22	20.90	−25.2%
5	365	105	85	1.00	0.05	0.23	25.49	−8.7%
10	365	110	85	1.00	0.05	0.24	30.21	8.2%
15	365	115	85	1.00	0.05	0.25	35.01	25.4%
20	365	120	85	1.00	0.05	0.26	39.86	42.7%
25	365	125	85	1.00	0.05	0.27	44.75	60.3%

When the underlying security declines in value and the option is at the money, such as in the −15 percent scenario, then the lower volatility can have an impact—in this case, the option is worth about $1.60 less. But for the +25 percent scenario, the loss is only about $0.75, because the option is significantly in-the-money.

Because volatility is a mean-reverting variable, in general we should expect the effects to even out somewhat over time. Conceptually, it would be more or less impossible for volatility to increase by 20 percent every year or decrease by 20 percent every year for several years in a row. Instead, we would expect that in some years, volatility would increase, and in others it would decrease.

Tables 6.3 and 6.4 also show that the volatility skew has an effect on the price of the option and will provide a small amount of additional profitability as the underlying security appreciates, or an additional loss in the event the security declines. The volatility skew may be seen as additional delta.

ROLLING LEAPS FORWARD

LEAPS options are available with expiration dates as much as three years into the future, which creates a tremendous opportunity for the underlying security to appreciate. However, an option position can be held even longer if the LEAPS option is repeatedly rolled forward, a process that involves periodically selling the option and then purchasing a new one with the same strike price but a later expiry.

For example, if the S&P 500 index is trading at 1480, and we initially purchased a two-year call option on the index with a strike price of 1400, after one year we could sell the option and then replace it with another two-year option. This could be done over and over, regardless of market conditions, and would not need to be done on any specific date.

LEAPS calls can be rolled over for many years, and although there is a cost associated with the roll-forward transactions, the objective is that the underlying security and the associated option will appreciate at a higher rate, creating a profit. While profits are unlikely every year, as in some years the security will decline, the roll-forward costs can be budgeted with some precision and over the long term, returns are relatively predictable.

Rolling a LEAPS allows the underlying security to compound, and as the option builds equity, the cost of maintaining the hedge decreases. Using our example, if the next year the S&P 500 is trading at 1600 and volatility is low, then the LEAPS will be 200 points in-the-money, and additional time can be purchased relatively cheaply. When the option is very deep-in-the-money, the cost of holding the position is equivalent to the cost of capital; that is, broker rate on debt minus dividends.

ROLL COST PREDICTION

The roll-forward cost of a call option at a specific strike price can be estimated with fair precision by calculating the cost differential between two-year and one-year options at the same strike price. For example, if a two-year call option on a security sells for $15 and a one-year call option with the same strike sells for $10, then next year's roll-forward cost will be about $5.

We can develop better precision by analyzing the factors that influence this differential. First is the cost of capital, which is the broker rate minus the expected dividends. For most call options on indexes this will be around three or four percent a year.

When the option is near-the-money, the current-level volatility will tend to have more influence on the pricing. This is because the expected losses on a two-year at-the-money option are higher than those of a one-year option—but not twice as high, just somewhat higher. These increased losses result in a higher hedging expense, and this raises the roll-forward cost.

The exact roll-forward cost will be dependent upon the strike price, the remaining time on the option, the additional amount of required time, the market price, and the volatility. We know three of these variables in advance, and thus need to account for the other two—the market price, and the volatility—in order to forecast the range of potential roll-forward costs.

Note that estimating the roll-forward cost is critical because if this payment isn't made, the option will expire, resulting in a total loss if the market price is lower than the strike price. This could potentially wipe out years of investment profits.

Like many situations in leveraged investing, it is essential not only to select the right amount to invest initially, but also to carefully budget for the future expenses required to maintain the investment. Overinvesting will lead to a cash crunch and potentially catastrophic short-term losses that could be avoided if a position could have been held a little longer.

In Table 6.5, we show eighteen possible roll-forward prices for a LEAPS option based upon potential market prices and changes in volatility. While there is a range of values, we can see that it is somewhat predictable, and that it is very likely that next year's roll-forward cost will be somewhere between $4.50 and $5.90 per share. Dividends would also reduce this amount.

Volatility has a small, but relatively insignificant impact on the roll-forward cost because one call option is being sold at the same time another is being bought. If volatility is high for the sold option, it will also be high for the purchased option, and this offsets the roll-forward cost. In the example

TABLE 6.5 Potential LEAPS Call Option Roll-Forward Prices Given Possible Appreciation and Volatility

Days	Market	Strike	Years	Rate	Vol.	Price	Days	Market	Strike	Years	Rate	Vol.	Price	Diff
Same Volatility														
365	80	85	1.00	0.05	0.23	6.94	730	80	85	2.00	0.05	0.23	11.75	4.81
365	90	85	1.00	0.05	0.24	13.53	730	90	85	2.00	0.05	0.24	18.96	5.43
365	100	85	1.00	0.05	0.25	21.61	730	100	85	2.00	0.05	0.25	27.17	5.57
365	110	85	1.00	0.05	0.26	30.56	730	110	85	2.00	0.05	0.26	36.02	5.46
365	120	85	1.00	0.05	0.27	39.99	730	120	85	2.00	0.05	0.27	45.27	5.28
Lower Volatility														
365	80	85	1.00	0.05	0.19	5.67	730	80	85	2.00	0.05	0.19	10.02	4.35
365	90	85	1.00	0.05	0.20	12.33	730	90	85	2.00	0.05	0.20	17.33	5.00
365	100	85	1.00	0.05	0.21	20.68	730	100	85	2.00	0.05	0.21	25.76	5.09
365	110	85	1.00	0.05	0.22	29.90	730	110	85	2.00	0.05	0.22	34.85	4.95
365	120	85	1.00	0.05	0.23	39.54	730	120	85	2.00	0.05	0.23	44.31	4.77
Higher Volatility														
365	80	85	1.00	0.05	0.26	7.90	730	80	85	2.00	0.05	0.26	13.05	5.15
365	90	85	1.00	0.05	0.27	14.45	730	90	85	2.00	0.05	0.27	20.22	5.77
365	100	85	1.00	0.05	0.28	22.38	730	100	85	2.00	0.05	0.28	28.31	5.93
365	110	85	1.00	0.05	0.29	31.16	730	110	85	2.00	0.05	0.29	37.02	5.87
365	120	85	1.00	0.05	0.30	40.44	730	120	85	2.00	0.05	0.30	46.14	5.70

just shown, higher or lower volatility adds or subtracts about 50 cents from the roll-forward cost.

ESTIMATING AVERAGE RETURNS

We can model a LEAPS roll-forward strategy for ten years by simulating an initial purchase of a two-year LEAPS call option, rolling it forward eight times, and then holding it for the remaining two years (see Table 6.6). To simplify our analysis initially, a steady annual appreciation and average volatility can be used. The annual rate of return for the options is calculated on the right side.

The average return is 13.70 percent for the ten years, which is significantly above the 10 percent annual appreciation of the index. This may seem like a small increase, but over the ten-year period it results in 38 percent more invested capital.

The annual return is highest in years 3, 4, and 5, when leverage is high, but hedging costs are low. In the first year, hedging costs reduce the return somewhat to only 14.2 percent, and in later years, the option is so deep-in-the-money that the leverage is low, and this pushes returns closer to the level of the index. During that period, however, the risk would also be reduced, as is the case with lower-leverage investments.

The average level of volatility over the ten years has an effect on the profitability, and as we raise the estimated average volatility, the return declines, especially in the early years, because the hedge provided by the LEAPS call is relatively expensive. Later, when the option is deep-in-the-money, volatility is less of a factor (see Table 6.7).

Regardless, a little appreciation goes a long way. If we model a higher performance and higher volatility index with a higher expected return, such as a mid-cap or small-cap, and assign it a higher initial volatility, it still comes out ahead, as shown in Table 6.8.

As a rule, rolled LEAPS calls are only profitable in the long-term when the cumulative index appreciation is higher than the cost of capital built into the options. If appreciation falls below the cost of capital, the LEAPS calls decline in value, but can still be rolled over. However, hedging costs will increase if the option is close to the money.

One of the greatest advantages of using rolled LEAPS call options is that the strategy is relatively predictable. Cash outflows can be forecast with some precision and within a certain range, and index returns are relatively predictable over long periods of time. The combination of these two factors reduces the uncertainty inherent in the strategy.

TABLE 6.6 Two-Year LEAPS Call Option Held and Rolled for a Ten-Year Period

Year	Index	Cash Flow	% Gain	Long Days	Market	Strike	Years	Rate	Vol.	Price	Days	Market	Strike	Years	Rate	Vol.	Price
0	100.00	−26.45		730	100	85	2.00	0.05	0.23	26.45	365	110	85	1.00	0.05	0.24	30.21
1	110.00	−5.20	14.2%	730	110	85	2.00	0.05	0.24	35.41	365	121	85	1.00	0.05	0.25	40.70
2	121.00	−4.99	14.9%	730	121	85	2.00	0.05	0.25	45.69	365	133	85	1.00	0.05	0.26	52.53
3	133.10	−4.76	15.0%	730	133	85	2.00	0.05	0.26	57.29	365	146	85	1.00	0.05	0.27	65.70
4	146.41	−4.56	14.7%	730	146	85	2.00	0.05	0.27	70.26	365	161	85	1.00	0.05	0.28	80.27
5	161.05	−4.40	14.3%	730	161	85	2.00	0.05	0.28	84.66	365	177	85	1.00	0.05	0.29	96.34
6	177.16	−4.27	13.8%	730	177	85	2.00	0.05	0.29	100.61	365	195	85	1.00	0.05	0.30	114.04
7	194.87	−4.18	13.3%	730	195	85	2.00	0.05	0.30	118.22	365	214	85	1.00	0.05	0.31	133.51
8	214.36	−4.11	12.9%	730	214	85	2.00	0.05	0.31	137.63	365	236	85	1.00	0.05	0.32	154.94
9	235.79	0.00	12.6%	730	236	85	2.00	0.05	0.32	159.01							
10	259.37	174.37	9.7%														

IRR	13.70%

TABLE 6.7	Effect of Average Volatility on the Average Return of a Rolled LEAPS Call Strategy

IV	% Return
0.19	14.70%
0.20	14.44%
0.21	14.17%
0.22	13.90%
0.23	13.62%
0.24	13.33%
0.25	13.05%
0.26	12.76%

If we know the planned holding period, then we can use either statistics or Monte Carlo analysis to calculate estimated index returns for that period, and then apply those returns to the LEAPS call strategy with an estimated volatility.

Table 6.9 calculates 1,000 ten-year returns, with each year having an estimated 10 percent return and 15 percent volatility, which is similar to the S&P 500 historical data. We then plugged our ten-year index return into the rolling LEAPS call model to determine the overall strategy return.

Based on the table, we can see that there is approximately a 35 to 40 percent chance of having a strategy return that is below the index return, but on average the strategy return would provide an extra $0.60 per dollar invested, and could provide as much as $2 or $3 of additional returns over the ten years.

Also, rolled LEAPS call options are not susceptible to margin calls or early exercise, due to the hedge inherent in call options, and the strategy avoids high transaction costs because option purchases and sales are made only once a year.

INVESTING CASH FLOW

Because a rolled LEAPS call consumes cash, in the form of the roll-forward payments, and accumulates appreciation, it can be used to invest regular cash flow. The proceeds of an annuity or a dividend-paying stock could be used to make regular roll-forward payments on an index call option.

For example, we could take an income stream of $10,000 a month and match it to a portfolio of in-the-money call options. We could assume that the roll-forward cost will be 5 percent of the value of the underlying

TABLE 6.8 Ten-Year Strategy Returns for a LEAPS Call Option on a Higher Performance Index

Year	Index	Cash Flow	% Gain	Long Days	Market	Strike	Years	Rate	Vol.	Price	Days	Market	Strike	Years	Rate	Vol.	Price
0	100.00	−25.80		730	100	90	2.00	0.05	0.29	25.80							
1	112.00	−6.46	13.7%	730	112	90	2.00	0.05	0.30	35.80	365	112	90	1.00	0.05	0.30	29.34
2	125.44	−6.24	15.9%	730	125	90	2.00	0.05	0.31	47.74	365	125	90	1.00	0.05	0.31	41.50
3	140.49	−5.90	16.9%	730	140	90	2.00	0.05	0.32	61.70	365	140	90	1.00	0.05	0.32	55.79
4	157.35	−5.54	17.1%	730	157	90	2.00	0.05	0.33	77.77	365	157	90	1.00	0.05	0.33	72.22
5	176.23	−5.22	16.8%	730	176	90	2.00	0.05	0.34	96.09	365	176	90	1.00	0.05	0.34	90.87
6	197.38	−4.95	16.4%	730	197	90	2.00	0.05	0.35	116.85	365	197	90	1.00	0.05	0.35	111.90
7	221.07	−4.74	16.0%	730	221	90	2.00	0.05	0.36	140.26	365	221	90	1.00	0.05	0.36	135.52
8	247.60	−4.58	15.5%	730	248	90	2.00	0.05	0.37	166.60	365	248	90	1.00	0.05	0.37	162.02
9	277.31	0.00	15.1%	730	277	90	2.00	0.05	0.38	196.18	365	277	90	1.00	0.05	0.38	191.71
10	310.58	220.58	12.4%														
IRR		15.88%															

TABLE 6.9   Summary of Random Rolling LEAPS Call Option Strategy Returns

Percentile	Index % Return	LEAPS % Return	Index in 10 Years	LEAPS in 10 Years	Diff.
10%	2.99%	−6.98%	$1.34	$0.49	−$0.86
25%	5.96%	3.78%	$1.78	$1.45	−$0.34
50%	9.00%	11.47%	$2.37	$2.96	$0.60
75%	12.49%	18.44%	$3.25	$5.43	$2.19
90%	15.25%	23.21%	$4.14	$8.06	$3.93

portfolio, on average, which means that the income stream will support the costs of a $200,000 roll-forward portfolio. That still leaves the initial cost of the LEAPS options, of course.

This budgeting exercise also helps us determine how large a portfolio we can manage. If we find ourselves trying to manage a $500,000 portfolio with $10,000 of expected annual income, then obviously we would be very likely to have difficulties maintaining this position over time, especially if volatility increases and the underlying security declines in value—a common situation in a downturn or recession that could trigger a cash crunch.

CAPTURING APPRECIATION

The delta of an option is a critical variable that corresponds to both the expected price of the option given a $1 change in the underlying security, and the increased cost required to reduce the strike price by $1. Delta can be found in most option price quotes or calculators.

All call options have a delta somewhere between zero and one, depending upon the volatility and the strike price. At-the-money options with a long time to expiry typically have a delta of about .5 or .6, and this rises to .8 or .9 once the option is significantly in-the-money. An option that is far out-of-the-money may have a delta of only .2 or .3.

The delta is a direct result of the constant trade-off between an option's time value and the intrinsic value. As we showed in Chapter 4, call options will usually have either a high call value or intrinsic value, but not both at the same time. An at-the-money call option with a high time value will increase in value when the underlying security appreciates, but as it gains in intrinsic value, it will also lose some of its time value.

This presents a problem for LEAPS call options when they are used to capture appreciation over long periods of time. LEAPS call options that are at-the-money or out-of-the-money tend to have low deltas and thus don't capture as much appreciation. This can create a situation where the underlying security appreciates, but an at-the-money option simply treads water or even declines in value over time.

Still, if this option is rolled over for several years, even if the first year's returns are anemic, over time it should gain more intrinsic value and have a higher delta. Thus, the decision to buy deep-in-the-money is a financing decision—should we pay more now in order to have more appreciation later?—and also a risk management decision, because an in-the-money option can lose its intrinsic value quickly if the underlying security declines.

Another approach is to purchase an out-of-the-money option cheaply, and wait for appreciation to push the option deep-in-the-money. This approach will often result in a high amount of value lost to maintaining the hedge, but if appreciation comes in higher than expected, it could result in a huge windfall if a low-cost option grows in value and then is used to capture more appreciation for several years (see Table 6.10).

The delta of the option also influences how the investment position is exited. If the call option is deep-in-the-money, then time decay is minimal and the call option can be sold at any time to receive its full intrinsic value.

On the other hand, if the option is at-the-money or out-of-the-money, then holding the option is risky, because there is no guarantee that expected appreciation will compensate for the current time value. In this case, it's better to either sell the option or continue to roll it forward rather than hold it to expiry.

ROLLING UP

During the annual roll-forward transaction, a LEAPS option can also be rolled up to a higher strike price in order to generate cash. For example, an investor sells a one-year option on SPY, the S&P index ETF, with a strike price of 140, and buys a two-year option with a strike price of 150. The cash generated by rolling up the option to a higher strike price helps to compensate for the roll-forward costs.

When the SPY call option is rolled up 10 points, it is likely that only 7 to 9 dollars of cash per share will be received, even if the option is on-the-money. This is related to the delta of the option and is dependent upon both the volatility and the relationship of the strike price versus the market price. Thus the benefit of receiving a smaller payment now has to be weighed against both the future payoff and the possibility that the value of the security could decline.

In principle, a LEAPS option could be held for many years and rolled up periodically, and the proceeds reinvested in new LEAPS options. This allows the investor to rapidly reinvest the proceeds and maintain a high leverage ratio, allowing gains to compound quickly.

TABLE 6.10 Out-of-the-Money LEAPS Call Option Rolled for Ten Years (12% index appreciation assumed)

Year	Index	Cash Flow	% Gain	Long Days	Market	Strike	Years	Rate	Vol.	Price	Days	Market	Strike	Years	Rate	Vol.	Price
0	100.00	−13.12		730	100	110	2.00	0.05	0.23	13.12	365	112	110	1.00	0.05	0.24	14.44
1	112.00	−6.89	10.0%	730	112	110	2.00	0.05	0.24	21.33	365	125	110	1.00	0.05	0.25	24.71
2	125.44	−7.24	15.8%	730	125	110	2.00	0.05	0.25	31.95	365	140	110	1.00	0.05	0.26	37.87
3	140.49	−7.12	18.5%	730	140	110	2.00	0.05	0.26	44.99	365	157	110	1.00	0.05	0.27	53.70
4	157.35	−6.77	19.4%	730	157	110	2.00	0.05	0.27	60.47	365	176	110	1.00	0.05	0.28	72.06
5	176.23	−6.37	19.2%	730	176	110	2.00	0.05	0.28	78.43	365	197	110	1.00	0.05	0.29	92.96
6	197.38	−6.01	18.5%	730	197	110	2.00	0.05	0.29	98.96	365	221	110	1.00	0.05	0.30	116.53
7	221.07	−5.73	17.7%	730	221	110	2.00	0.05	0.30	122.25	365	248	110	1.00	0.05	0.31	143.00
8	247.60	−5.53	17.0%	730	248	110	2.00	0.05	0.31	148.53	365	277	110	1.00	0.05	0.32	172.69
9	277.31	0.00	16.3%	730	277	110	2.00	0.05	0.32	178.08							
10	310.58	200.58	12.6%														

IRR	17.24%

136

For example, if the index is expected to appreciate 10 percent a year, in theory, we could roll up our strike price 10 percent a year and maintain the same level of leverage. Our LEAPS options could be held for many years, and the cash generated from roll-ups would more than pay for the roll-forward costs. The excess profits could be invested in additional LEAPS, simulating an ever-growing portfolio of assets, debt, and equity.

In Table 6.11, a $20 roll-up is done after three years and after seven years. The result is a higher internal rate of return (IRR) due to receiving cash earlier in the life of investment, and the LEAPS having a higher degree of leverage later in the life of the investment. However, the higher leverage would also make the investment more volatile in the later years.

In practice, roll-ups are difficult to plan for, because both the timing of future appreciation and the level of volatility are unknown. Ideally, a roll-up should be done after a period of above-average appreciation and low volatility, and these are, of course, unpredictable. This means that we can't count on using roll-ups to pay roll-forward costs or to generate income.

SELECTING INDEXES AND STRIKE PRICES

Many higher performance indexes also have higher volatility, which can create a complex trade-off when the index is used as the underlying security in a rolled LEAPS call strategy. Higher performance indexes offer higher appreciation on average, but the high volatility will raise both the cost of rolling over a LEAPS option and the risk associated with the investment strategy.

How to proceed? The first step, of course, is to ensure that the portfolio's diversification has been met. Blending multiple indexes will reduce the long-term volatility of the investment portfolio. A LEAPS can be considered a portfolio of debt and equity, and the proportion of equity in each security can be kept constant in order to maintain an equal weight portfolio. This is easier if all of the LEAPS are in-the-money by the same percentage amount.

For example, the following portfolio would be balanced:

ETF	Price	Options Position
SPY	145	500 shares, 15% in-the-money
MDY	155	500 shares, 15% in-the-money
IWM	70	1000 shares, 15% in-the-money
EFA	80	1000 shares, 15% in-the-money

Periodically rebalancing the portfolio can become complex if the securities appreciate at different amounts, but could be handled during the annual roll-ups by purchasing new LEAPS call options with similar

TABLE 6.11 10-Year Rolled LEAPS Call Option with Rollups

Year	Index	Cash Flow	% Gain	Long Days	Market	Strike	Years	Rate	Vol.	Price	Days	Market	Strike	Years	Rate	Vol.	Price
0	100.00	−26.45		730	100	85	2.00	0.05	0.23	26.45	365	110	85	1.00	0.05	0.24	30.21
1	110.00	−5.20	14.2%	730	110	85	2.00	0.05	0.24	35.41	365	121	85	1.00	0.05	0.25	40.70
2	121.00	−4.99	14.9%	730	121	85	2.00	0.05	0.25	45.69	365	133	85	1.00	0.05	0.26	52.53
3	133.10	10.45	15.0%	730	133	105	2.00	0.05	0.26	42.08	365	146	105	1.00	0.05	0.27	47.68
4	146.41	−6.59	13.3%	730	146	105	2.00	0.05	0.27	54.26	365	161	105	1.00	0.05	0.28	61.81
5	161.05	−6.29	13.9%	730	161	105	2.00	0.05	0.28	68.09	365	177	105	1.00	0.05	0.29	77.62
6	177.16	9.60	14.0%	730	177	125	2.00	0.05	0.29	68.03	365	195	125	1.00	0.05	0.30	76.91
7	194.87	−7.79	13.1%	730	195	125	2.00	0.05	0.30	84.70	365	214	125	1.00	0.05	0.31	96.00
8	214.36	−7.42	13.3%	730	214	125	2.00	0.05	0.31	103.42	365	236	125	1.00	0.05	0.31	117.20
9	235.79	0.00	13.3%	730	236	125	2.00	0.05	0.32	124.28							
10	259.37	134.37	8.1%														
IRR		13.98%															

proportions of equity and with strike prices that are a similar amount in-the-money.

Next, we can compare the long-term volatilities for various LEAPS call options. This is a snapshot of the current volatilities for two-year options:

S&P 500 (large-cap)	SPY	24.57
S&P 600 (mid-cap)	MDY	26.69
Russell 2000 (small-cap)	IWM	25.45
Russell 2000 Value	IWN	27.88
MSCI EAFA	EFA	21.51
NASDAQ	QQQQ	26.96

While there are some differences between implied volatilities, they are all relatively high and at about the same level, reflecting the market's uncertainty about volatility trends over the next two years, but are not so high that buying in-the-money options would make capturing appreciation cost-prohibitive.

If we use our initial model from earlier in the chapter, higher volatilities reduce the initial returns of the strategy significantly—for example, each one-percentage-point increase in the initial volatility decreases the first-year's returns by 0.9 percent. However, a one-percentage-point increase in the performance of the underlying will raise the first-year's returns by 3.5 percent. Thus, in the first year, one point of additional appreciation is worth about four points of volatility.

However, once the option is deep-in-the-money by years three and four, the impact of higher volatility is reduced and appreciation in the underlying becomes more important. In year four, one point of volatility reduces the return by −0.3 percent, but one point of appreciation raises the return by +2.2 percent.

This analysis would support the conclusion that, if the portfolio is held for the long-term, it is preferable to build a higher performing portfolio of indexes, even if the implied volatilities are higher. However, trade-offs still exist that may make it preferable to include lower volatility indexes if they provide reasonable diversification.

MARKET DROPS AND VOLATILITY SPIKES

LEAPS call options are a form of stock substitution, and deep-in-the-money calls are functionally equivalent to synthetics. Like most stock substitution strategies, the viability of rolling LEAPS calls is dependent upon the volatility of the underlying investment. When volatility is high, it becomes harder for LEAPS buyers to capture appreciation because of the seller's higher hedging expenses.

This can present a problem for investors who use call options to capture appreciation after a market decline. When the market drops, volatility also spikes, making it more expensive to take a position in a security and benefit from the potential rebound, because when volatility returns to normal, the call will then decline in price and some of the recovery will have been wasted.

This situation is partly because the market does expect rebounds, and partly because of put-call parity. The prices of put options have to be similar to the price of calls or an arbitrage opportunity would be created.

In any event, this means that it probably won't be to an investor's advantage to buy immediately after a drop when volatility is still high, because little or no additional profits would be realized. It would be better to wait instead until volatility subsided, which could happen after an upward move, or perhaps also because the market's fears subside and investors accept that the current price level is relatively stable.

However, volatilities on LEAPS call options don't change quite as quickly as those of short-term options. It is common to see the implied volatility on a one- or two-month call jump from 18 percent to 35 percent, but the volatility on the two-year LEAPS only jumps from 23 percent to 28 percent. This increase in volatility would not necessarily erase the profitability of a significant rebound, and the long time to expiry would provide more security than owning a shorter-term option.

To help select the appropriate strike price, an investor would review the price differential between at-the-money and out-of-the-money options and also forecast the price of the option with lower volatility. But, as a rule, if a rebound is expected, the best approach would be to buy the option deep-in-the-money so that it has a high delta and captures as much of the appreciation as possible, and accept the fact that leverage will be lower during this period.

Of course the classic solution to capture appreciation in a high volatility situation would be to sell a put option, but this can backfire if another market decline occurs and the option expires or is exercised in the worst possible market conditions.

In addition to our two possible courses of action, waiting for volatility to subside, or buying deeper in-the-money, we could also sell options to take advantage of the high volatility. One modification to a rolled LEAPS call strategy is to sell a short-term, at-the-money or out-of-the-money call option at the same time, and then buy the short call back at expiry.

LEAPS COVERED CALLS

Chapter 5 presented a covered-call strategy that used a futures contract as the underlying security, but another option is to use a LEAPS call. An in-the-money two-year LEAPS call is purchased on the underlying security, and one-month calls are written repeatedly for twelve months, at which point the LEAPS call is then rolled forward and more calls are written.

For example:

SPY, the S&P 500 ETF is trading at 145

Buy SPY two-year LEAPS @ 130 for 28.80

Sell SPY one-month call @ 145 for 3.20

Note that the LEAPS covered-call strategy requires the strike price of the LEAPS to be below the level of the strike price of the short call, otherwise cash margin is required to hold the position.

At the end of the month, if the price of the underlying security remains the same or declines, the short-call option will expire worthless, and the LEAPS call will also likely have lost value due to the effect of time decay and any loss on the underlying. The goal is that the premium provides enough profitability to offset the loss.

But if the value of the SPY increases, the short call will expire in the money and will need to be bought back before expiry. Additionally, there is some exercise risk if the price moves much higher and the seller wants to capture the dividend. The value of the LEAPS would also increase, but typically not at the same rate, due to the lower delta.

This strategy has a similar payoff to the Futures covered-call except that the level of leverage is much lower because the LEAPS is more expensive, and the profitability is somewhat lower due to the time decay of the LEAPS. Also, some vega risk is introduced into the position, as the implied volatility of the LEAPS may increase or decrease.

Still, this strategy is expected to be profitable on a monthly basis, or at least the value of the LEAPS is expected to increase faster than any required cash outflow, and in a sluggish market the investor may collect an amount equal to the value of the initial cost of the LEAPS in premiums. Also, even if the market climbs much higher, the position is net long, as the delta of the LEAPS is higher than the delta of the short call.

However, a worst-case scenario is possible in which calls are written repeatedly in a rising market to capture premiums, cash is paid out to buy back the covered calls, and then the market drops significantly and the value of the LEAPS is wiped out, leaving the investor with no cash, a depreciated security, a roll-forward payment due, and the possibility that the next call written will require both cash margin and another large cash outflow.

Thus, risk has to be carefully managed, because there's always the possibility that the next quarter's index returns could be a correction or worse, while implied volatility doubles, and again we would see the impact of not being able to control cash outflows in an option strategy. The rolled-LEAPS-call strategy is certainly much more manageable by comparison.

SUMMARY

In this chapter we illustrated how LEAPS calls can be used to maintain leverage on an underlying security for a period of many years or even decades. Although these options decay and expire, like any other option, they can also be rolled forward to future expiration dates repeatedly, which allows an investor to continue to benefit from the long-term appreciation in the underlying asset.

By comparing the Greeks of in-the-money and at-the-money LEAPS options, we can determine that the best approach is to purchase a LEAPS option deep-in-the-money. When strike prices are lower, the option has low time decay and high delta, and this allows the call option to appreciate at close to the same level of the underlying security.

Options that are at-the-money or out-of-the-money have much higher hedging costs as a result of the seller being forced to maintain a long-term position with significant risk. This translates into an expensive option with high decay and low delta, which typically isn't profitable unless the underlying security appreciates very quickly.

Call options are rolled forward by selling the first option and buying a second on the same security with the same strike price, but an expiration date farther into the future. This roll-forward transaction needs to be planned for carefully, because if cash is not available to roll the option forward at the necessary time, the option could expire worthless, wiping out the initial investment.

The roll-forward cost can be quickly estimated by taking the difference between a one-year and two-year option at the same strike price; however, the exact cost a year from now will be a result of the actual appreciation of the underlying security, the level of long-term volatility in the market, and, to some extent, long-term interest rates.

When a call option is rolled forward, it can also be rolled up by purchasing the option at a higher strike price. This allows the investor to buy a less expensive option and as a result take cash out of the position. Roll-ups can allow an investor to buy more LEAPS options and make additional investments, and LEAPS call options on several different indexes could be combined into a diversified portfolio.

The primary benefit of a rolled LEAPS call option strategy is that it is predictable. Initial costs and cash outflows for the next several years can be forecast to a reasonable level of precision, and thus payments can be budgeted. While nobody knows the eventual payoff for the various indexes with any certainty, if an investor is able to ensure that they are capable of holding and maintaining an investment for several years, then that provides some level of safety and security.

LEAPS calls can also be used to write covered calls, but this strategy, while profitable, requires a high degree of risk management. On average, the practice will deliver reasonable returns, but often cash must be paid out to buy back positions. If this happens repeatedly and is then followed by both a decline in the index and the need to roll the LEAPS forward, then a cash crunch could ensue, forcing the investor to liquidate the position at a loss and potentially abandon the strategy.

CHAPTER 7

Long-Term Returns Using Rolled LEAPS

T he last chapter introduced the technique of rolling LEAPS call options in order to maintain permanent leverage on the index. Rolled LEAPS call options have predictable cash outflows, and this can reduce some of the risk involved in managing a leveraged portfolio, while still delivering high returns.

In this chapter, we analyze the returns of various sector- and index-based LEAPS portfolios using recent market data in order to further understand the behavior of these investments in different market conditions. Also, results are analyzed with and without rebalancing to determine the effect of that technique on the portfolio returns and draw some conclusions about the nature of leverage with a permanent hedge.

LEAPS call options can be used as the basis for a covered-call writing strategy, and we do this with two indexes to see the results. Selling calls can help pay for the interest and roll-forward costs, but definitely has an effect on the predictability of the cash flows, as will be seen.

STRIKE PRICE SELECTION

LEAPS call options can be viewed as composed of three distinct components: intrinsic value, interest costs, and a hedge. The intrinsic value is simply the difference between the current market price and the original strike price. The time value includes both the interest costs and the hedging costs. The interest costs can be backed out by using the cost of capital (prevailing interest rate minus dividends), and then the hedging costs are what remain.

As shown in Table 7.1, a two-year LEAPS call option with a strike price of 80 has an intrinsic value of $20, and the time value, $10.10, is split between the interest rate and the hedge. The interest rate is equal to 5 percent of the strike price, or approximately $7.44, and the $2.66 is the hedging cost for the two years. (Note: The interest costs are under $8 because the interest is prepaid for two years.)

The 90-strike option has an intrinsic value of $10 and an interest cost of $8.37. The remainder, $4.73, is the two-year hedging cost. The higher strike price makes it more expensive to hedge, and this expense cuts into profitability. The one-year roll-forward cost is a reasonable approximation of the minimum level of appreciation required to be profitable, and 5.69 percent is relatively high.

While all of these options have high average returns, the 80-strike price option appears to provide a good combination of capital efficiency and return under normal and above-average conditions, and can still hold its value when the index is flat. This is the initial level we will use in this strategy.

Note that we could certainly track the performance of the hedging component on a daily basis if we needed to—that is, separate the portfolio into a basket of a futures plus a hedge. The hedge would gain or lose value inversely to the underlying security, and would also lose value over time due to time, only to be replenished through the annual roll-forward transactions.

SECTOR PERFORMANCE: 1999 TO 2006

In most discussions of investment strategies, the backtested data and strategy mechanics are carefully selected in order to show the strategy in the most favorable light. For example, a proponent of leveraged emerging market index investing would be sure to include 2005 and 2006, years in which China surged and the index posted huge gains.

In this backtest, instead of chasing performance, we will follow the data. In January 1999, nine sector ETFs were introduced to track the performance of individual sectors of the U.S. S&P 500. These ETFs, referred to as the Sector SPDRs (S&P Depository Receipt), are market-cap weighted and have relatively low expense ratios, with an average of just 0.23 percent. LEAPS are available on all of these ETFs.

The period used in the analysis, January 1999 to 2006, was not a good one for the stock market, as shown in Table 7.2. During this period, the

TABLE 7.1 Returns of Selected LEAPS

	Days	Market	Strike	Rate	Vol.	Price	Intrinsic	Time	Interest	Hedge
Current Prices										
70% Strike LEAPS	720	100.00	70.00	0.05	0.25	37.84	30.00	7.84	6.51	1.34
80% Strike LEAPS	720	100.00	80.00	0.05	0.24	30.10	20.00	10.10	7.44	2.66
90% Strike LEAPS	720	100.00	90.00	0.05	0.23	23.09	10.00	13.09	8.37	4.73
Roll-Forward Cost							Diff. (2yr-1yr)			
70% Strike LEAPS	365	100.00	70.00	0.05	0.25	33.86	3.99			
80% Strike LEAPS	365	100.00	80.00	0.05	0.24	25.23	4.87			
90% Strike LEAPS	365	100.00	90.00	0.05	0.23	17.55	5.55			
In One Year +5% Return							% Return			
70% Strike LEAPS	365	105.00	70.00	0.05	0.25	38.69	2.3%			
80% Strike LEAPS	365	105.00	80.00	0.05	0.24	29.79	−1.0%			
90% Strike LEAPS	365	105.00	90.00	0.05	0.23	21.62	−6.4%			
In One Year +10% Return							% Return			
70% Strike LEAPS	365	110.00	70.00	0.05	0.25	43.59	15.2%			
80% Strike LEAPS	365	110.00	80.00	0.05	0.24	34.49	14.6%			
90% Strike LEAPS	365	110.00	90.00	0.05	0.23	25.95	12.4%			
In One Year +15% return							% Return			
70% Strike LEAPS	365	115.00	70.00	0.05	0.25	48.52	28.2%			
80% Strike LEAPS	365	115.00	80.00	0.05	0.24	39.29	30.6%			
90% Strike LEAPS	365	115.00	90.00	0.05	0.23	30.46	31.9%			

TABLE 7.2 Returns for Sector by Year

Returns (ETFs)	SPY	XLB Materials	XLE Energy	XLF Financial	XLI Industrials	XLP C. Staples	XLU Utilities	XLK Tech	XLY C. Disc	XLV Health	Avg
1999	14.1%	10.0%	27.8%	3.9%	12.2%	−11.6%	−1.1%	48.4%	−0.1%	11.0%	10.3%
2000	−0.8%	−9.1%	19.1%	28.8%	16.4%	15.0%	16.8%	−26.2%	5.7%	−2.7%	7.1%
2001	−16.6%	6.7%	−18.8%	−10.6%	−16.5%	−3.8%	−11.8%	−36.4%	4.1%	−8.4%	−10.6%
2002	−22.8%	−12.1%	−13.8%	−14.9%	−23.8%	−22.3%	−27.9%	−38.9%	−23.9%	−0.4%	−19.8%
2003	34.0%	38.2%	32.0%	36.5%	40.8%	15.1%	32.2%	48.0%	41.1%	18.5%	33.6%
2004	6.1%	15.1%	35.4%	5.0%	13.3%	8.9%	23.6%	−4.0%	8.7%	−4.5%	11.3%
2005	7.2%	7.3%	35.6%	8.6%	5.7%	1.7%	14.0%	5.6%	−2.4%	9.9%	9.5%
2006	15.2%	17.1%	17.3%	18.0%	12.6%	13.9%	19.8%	11.5%	18.0%	6.7%	15.0%
Total	30.0%	95.1%	200.2%	74.4%	61.0%	12.4%	63.4%	−27.4%	52.0%	34.8%	64.4%
Return (Annualized)	3.3%	8.7%	14.7%	7.2%	6.1%	1.5%	6.3%	−3.9%	5.4%	3.8%	6.4%
Volatility (Annualized)	14.1	21.6	20.7	17.1	17.4	12.5	16.1	29.9	18.3	13.9	13.5

S&P returned an average of 3.33 percent, well below the cost of capital. This is a dividend-adjusted return, and capital gains during the period were extremely low. The only sector that performed well was energy, which returned almost 15 percent annualized for the period, just about tripling over the eight years because of higher energy prices that fueled both rising dividend yields and significant capital gains.

Most of the other sectors returned between 5 percent and 9 percent annualized, gaining 40 to 70 percent over the eight-year period. Consumer goods performed poorly, and tech fared the worst, losing 28 percent of its value over the eight-year period; but the midpoints are even lower, and in 2000 to 2002 the tech sector had lost more than three-quarters of its value.

In every year, there were some relationships between sector performances; for example, eight of the nine sectors had double-digit losses in 2002 and all had double-digit gains in 2003. Still, wide variations between sectors in a single year are common. For example, in 2004 sector returns ranged from −4.52 percent for the health care sector to +35.40 percent for the energy sector.

SECTOR PORTFOLIO RETURNS

The ETF prices are scaled to 100, and then adjusted each year based upon returns and dividends. Two-year LEAPS call options are initially purchased on 2,000 shares of each ETF, and the strike price used at purchase is 80, or 80 percent of the original market price.

At the beginning of each year, all of the call options are rolled over by selling the one-year option and buying another two-year option at the same strike price. This transaction exchanges a cash payment for an additional year of appreciation. The model doesn't address transaction costs, but for only one trade each year per security, it wouldn't be a significant factor.

Despite the simplicity, a few assumptions are needed. The first is that the long-term cost of capital is 5 percent, which is a little high, as interest rates were reduced sharply during 2001 and 2002, but is useful as a long-term average and benchmark.

The second assumption is that implied volatility for the LEAPS options of any specific sector is held constant at one-third higher than real volatility of the period as a result of the volatility skew and implied premium. Volatility is not a critical factor in the returns, but does have some effect. This estimation is necessary because of the lack of historical data on LEAPS volatility.

Table 7.3 shows the cash flows from the purchase and roll-forward of each option. The initial costs of each sector's LEAPS call options range

TABLE 7.3 Cashflows of Rolled LEAPS Calls (by sector)

Cash Flows (start of year)	XLB Materials	XLE Energy	XLF Financial	XLI Industrials	XLP C. Staples	XLU Utilities	XLK Tech	XLY C. Disc	XLV Health	Total
1999	−62,378	−61,644	−58,939	−59,160	−56,430	−58,288	−69,834	−59,772	−57,074	−543,518
2000	−10,153	−8,809	−9,571	−8,740	−8,634	−9,147	−10,558	−9,726	−7,985	−83,322
2001	−10,738	−7,959	−8,120	−7,956	−8,106	−8,245	−12,928	−9,389	−8,112	−81,552
2002	−10,362	−9,027	−8,741	−8,923	−8,292	−8,978	−11,200	−9,121	−8,568	−83,212
2003	−10,959	−10,079	−9,654	−9,686	−7,595	−8,061	−3,649	−9,941	−8,586	−78,210
2004	−8,966	−8,274	−7,965	−8,490	−8,639	−9,240	−9,711	−8,652	−7,791	−77,730
2005	−8,193	−7,529	−7,800	−7,905	−8,415	−8,058	−9,047	−8,197	−7,964	−73,107
2006	−7,932	−7,429	−7,614	−7,740	−8,340	−7,646	−9,924	−8,316	−7,659	−72,599
2007	222,905	453,836	193,388	163,245	68,189	175,743	17,275	143,421	109,357	1,547,357
All Payments	−129,680	−120,750	−118,402	−118,600	−114,452	−117,664	−136,850	−123,113	−113,739	−1,093,249
Final Portfolio Value	222,905	453,836	193,388	163,245	68,189	175,743	17,275	143,421	109,357	1,547,357
Profit/Loss	93,225	333,086	74,986	44,646	−46,263	58,079	−119,576	20,307	−4,382	454,108
Options IRR	9.05%	22.30%	8.15%	5.31%	−8.71%	6.68%	−36.55%	2.55%	−0.65%	5.77%
Sector Performance	8.72%	14.73%	7.20%	6.14%	1.47%	6.33%	−3.92%	5.38%	3.80%	6.41%

from $56,000 to $70,000, the roll-forward costs are about $8,000 to $10,000 a year, and the final value of the LEAPS call option portfolio for a sector ranges from a low of $17,000 to a high of $400,000.

By the start of 2007, the total options portfolio is worth 1.5m, which represents a significant dollar increase over the initial investment of $543,518, and the accumulated roll-forward costs of $549,731. However, on a percentage basis this is a fairly low IRR, only 5.77 percent.

The problem is that the tech sector LEAPS options become essentially worthless. After an initial purchase of $69,834, and another $67,017 in roll-forward costs, the options are out-of-the-money and only worth $17,275 at the end of the period. The lack of return from this sector alone reduces the average annual return of the portfolio by 2.1 percent.

Two other sectors, consumer staples and health care, also failed to appreciate as fast as the roll-forward costs due to their underlying annualized returns for the period being only 1.8 percent and 3.8 percent respectively, well below the 5 percent interest rate used in pricing the options.

The energy sector performed the best during the period, and for this sector the strategy provided an IRR of 22.30 percent in the period, well in excess of the 14.73 percent returned by the underlying. By 2004, the options were far in-the-money and the roll-forward costs had fallen significantly and are some of the lowest on the chart.

The sector comparison provides an illustration of how this strategy is supposed to perform, and under what conditions it can provide reasonable returns. When the underlying security delivers returns at or below the cost of capital, the LEAPS options are not able to build value. Only when the returns are significantly higher, as in the case of the energy sector, can the strategy really shine.

One of the most interesting aspects of this analysis is how reliable and predictable the roll-forward costs are. Although each of the sector funds appreciates at different rates and has a different underlying volatility, the average roll-forward cost for a sector starts out at $9,250 and drops over time to about $8,000, and the costs for all of the sectors are fairly consistent—even though in some cases we are rolling forward $250,000 worth of options, and in other cases we are rolling $50,000.

The widest variation in roll-forward costs comes from the tech sector, of course, which has both the highest implied volatility and the most extreme losses. The roll-forward payment rises from $10,558 to almost $13,000, but then falls to $3,649 as the option moves far out of the money after consecutive double-digit declines. Conversely, the least variation is in the roll-forward payments for the consumer staples and health care sectors, the two sectors with the lowest volatilities.

TABLE 7.4 LEAPS Call Option Portfolio 1-Year Returns, by Sector

	XLB	XLE	XLF	XLI	XLP	XLU	XLK	XLY	XLV	Avg
1999	11.7%	68.5%	-27.8%	23.1%	-52.4%	-19.2%	108.8%	-16.6%	22.7%	13.2%
2000	-35.4%	35.1%	83.3%	33.8%	44.6%	40.4%	-53.5%	1.3%	-17.9%	14.6%
2001	2.1%	-40.3%	-32.8%	-43.0%	-26.2%	-39.6%	-81.6%	-1.7%	-35.4%	-33.2%
2002	-44.4%	-39.7%	-50.2%	-71.1%	-82.2%	-84.6%	-96.0%	-69.9%	-16.7%	-61.7%
2003	106.6%	76.8%	115.1%	160.0%	49.2%	149.7%	112.4%	153.7%	49.6%	108.1%
2004	25.6%	66.2%	4.3%	24.7%	15.3%	65.8%	-58.3%	12.4%	-20.4%	15.1%
2005	8.8%	54.2%	12.1%	5.9%	-11.5%	26.5%	-38.1%	-12.6%	17.6%	7.0%
2006	26.6%	22.0%	30.4%	20.3%	35.5%	36.0%	-16.3%	34.1%	8.7%	21.9%
Total	46.27%	353.24%	45.44%	12.10%	-81.33%	-24.69%	-99.67%	-16.57%	-17.59%	3.92%
Annualized	4.87%	20.79%	4.79%	1.44%	-18.93%	-3.48%	-51.04%	-2.24%	-2.39%	0.48%
LT HV	21.6	20.7	17.1	17.4	12.5	16.1	29.9	18.3	13.9	13.5
IV Used	27.1	25.9	21.4	21.8	15.7	20.1	37.4	22.9	17.4	16.8

In retrospect, holding these sector portfolios for eight years may simply not be enough time to generate reasonable performance, especially given the declines in the third and fourth years. Too much time and appreciation is spent working through the interest and hedging costs of the portfolios, and not enough is left over for reinvestment and positive compounding.

REBALANCING

In the previous strategy, each LEAPS call option is treated separately, and gains in the value of one sector are not reinvested in other sectors. In investment theory, rebalancing is used to apportion risk evenly between several different securities, and this reduces the overall volatility of the portfolio.

Rebalancing doesn't always improve returns, and if one investment is falling rapidly, continuing to sell other appreciated assets and investing the proceeds in the poor performer will have a negative impact on the portfolio over that period.

But in 2003, the much-maligned tech sector delivered the highest returns of any sector in any year, so the question is, Would selling assets in 2001 and 2002 and investing them in the tech sector have helped portfolio returns enough to overcome the prior poor performance? (See Table 7.4 for sector returns by year).

Developing a successful reinvestment strategy for rolled LEAPS call options is more difficult than doing so for a portfolio of futures. By the beginning of 2003, the XLK options portfolio was only worth $4,732, as the strike price was much higher than market and the options were far out-of-the-money. How many additional options should we have bought at this point and at what strike price? And we must keep in mind, of course, that these options will have to be rolled forward in future years.

One approach for rebalancing LEAPS options portfolios with equivalent expiration dates is to use the values of the underlying shares, but this can create distortions where some options are deep-in-the-money and others are way out-of-the-money. Generally, strike prices will need to be adjusted in order to keep the market price versus strike price relationship relatively consistent—that is, a roll-up or roll-down.

Another approach is to rebalance based upon intrinsic value. In this method, strike prices of deep-in-the-money options are rolled up, and at-the-money and out-of-the-money options are rolled down. However, if the portfolio has suffered an across-the-board decline, such as in 2002 and 2003 in our historical data, this will likely result in a portfolio of at-the-money or out-of-the-money options with their associated high hedging costs.

After a significant portfolio meltdown, there really are no good choices. The safest and surest approach would be to simply sell the entire portfolio and buy as many new two-year deep-in-the-money options as we can at the current price levels. With some modifications to our existing model, we can see how this strategy performs. For example:

1. Divide funds evenly into nine sector groups.
2. Buy 2-year LEAPS options 20 percent in-the-money in each sector.
3. Hold options for one year and then sell.
4. Rebalance funds and buy more deep-in-the-money LEAPS.

This approach eliminates the roll-forward transactions—instead, at the end of each year, the entire portfolio of LEAPS options is sold and the proceeds are reinvested evenly by purchasing LEAPS options at a new strike price that's proportional (that is, 80 percent of the level) to the market price.

Because of the lack of roll-forward transactions, in order to keep the original and proposed strategies on equal footing, the strategy invests similar amounts initially and every year, that is, $543,000 at the beginning of 1999, and then $78,000 every year through 2006. This way the returns can be appropriately compared. The results are shown in Table 7.5.

What went wrong? The strategy IRR fell from 5.77 percent to 2.88 percent, meaning that the rebalancing approach did not add value. In this case, it was better to continue to roll forward options on securities that had declined in value rather than selling the LEAPS and buying new ones and simultaneously rebalancing across sectors.

The difference can be seen most readily in 2002 and 2003. In 2003, a rebalancing approach generated large returns, but not quite the triple-digit returns that were generated without rebalancing. The portfolio simply didn't have enough leverage to take advantage of the upturn after 2002's losses.

However, note that an artifact of the historical data is that the highest appreciating sector, the energy sector, in the middle years is also the highest performing sector in the last two years. This in itself makes rebalancing problematic, as any reallocation of assets away from this sector prior to those two years is guaranteed to reduce performance.

HIGHER PERFORMANCE PORTFOLIOS

Now we take a look at a higher performing index over a longer period of time. MDY, the mid-cap SPDR ETF tracker, was created in 1995, and data is available from that point. Over time, mid-cap stocks are expected to have

TABLE 7.5 Cash Flows of Rolled LEAPS Calls, by Sector (with rebalancing)

Cash Flows (start of year)	XLB	XLE	XLF	XLI	XLP	XLU	XLK	XLY	XLV	Sum
1999	−60,333	−60,333	−60,333	−60,333	−60,333	−60,333	−60,333	−60,333	−60,333	−543,000
2000	−8,667	−8,667	−8,667	−8,667	−8,667	−8,667	−8,667	−8,667	−8,667	−78,003
2001	−8,667	−8,667	−8,667	−8,667	−8,667	−8,667	−8,667	−8,667	−8,667	−78,003
2002	−8,667	−8,667	−8,667	−8,667	−8,667	−8,667	−8,667	−8,667	−8,667	−78,003
2003	−8,667	−8,667	−8,667	−8,667	−8,667	−8,667	−8,667	−8,667	−8,667	−78,003
2004	−8,667	−8,667	−8,667	−8,667	−8,667	−8,667	−8,667	−8,667	−8,667	−78,003
2005	−8,667	−8,667	−8,667	−8,667	−8,667	−8,667	−8,667	−8,667	−8,667	−78,003
2006	−8,667	−8,667	−8,667	−8,667	−8,667	−8,667	−8,667	−8,667	−8,667	−78,003
2007	146,623	148,603	156,815	136,710	147,301	165,041	120,036	154,800	118,408	1,294,336
Annualized	3.21%	3.43%	4.33%	2.04%	3.28%	5.18%	−0.13%	4.11%	−0.36%	2.88%
Compare	8.72%	14.73%	7.20%	6.14%	1.47%	6.33%	−3.92%	5.38%	3.80%	6.41%

higher returns than large-cap stocks, such as those in the S&P 500, and the historical data supports this.

Over the 1996 to 2006 period, the annualized return of this ETF was 13.38 percent, or six points per year higher than the S&P 500 during the period. The high returns as compared to the cost of the capital and the low volatility make this investment a good candidate for a rolling LEAPS call options strategy, and over 11 years the strategy returns 19.21 percent annually, based upon the IRR of the cash flows. The results are shown in Table 7.6.

We begin by purchasing two-year LEAPS call options on one thousand shares of MDY for $29,928 in the beginning of 1996. Again the market price is scaled to 100, and the initial strike price is 80 percent of this initial figure. After ten years and $37,995 of roll-forward costs, the final options are worth $321,892.

Year by year, the return of the options portfolio follows the underlying return of MDY, but with decreasing leverage as the option builds equity. In the first year, the option portfolio returns 40.38 percent, or 2.26× the underlying return of the index, but in the last year the portfolio returns 8.30 percent, or only 1.08× the underlying. This is typical of leveraged investments that build equity and suggests that a roll-up would be appropriate at some point.

For every year, we also calculate the one-year return of a theoretical option portfolio of two-year LEAPS call options. This is similar to the above strategy in which we do a roll-up or roll-down every year, as required.

TABLE 7.6 MDY Rolled LEAPS Call Option Cashflows

			Option Returns	
Year	MDY	Cash Flow	Portfolio	80-Strike
1996	17.9%	−29,928	40.4%	40.4%
1997	23.7%	−4,347	50.4%	59.6%
1998	15.9%	−3,879	26.2%	34.0%
1999	15.7%	−3,761	23.6%	33.3%
2000	23.0%	−3,723	33.5%	57.3%
2001	−3.3%	−3,712	−7.0%	−26.2%
2002	−16.7%	−3,713	−26.6%	−61.8%
2003	42.0%	−3,724	63.9%	120.2%
2004	10.7%	−3,712	12.7%	17.1%
2005	21.4%	−3,711	26.5%	52.1%
2006	7.7%	−3,711	8.3%	7.5%
2007		321,892		
Annual/IRR	13.4%	19.21%		

These call options have higher leverage, and as a result deliver a higher multiple return of the underlying.

Higher leverage should translate into higher returns over time, but in some data sets we see a sharp negative return that distorts the outcomes. If the leverage is too high at that specific point, the portfolio is simply wiped out and it becomes difficult to recover from losses. If the portfolio soon recovers, then the data set will probably favor rolling options at their current at-the-money or out-of-the-money strike prices, rather than trying to rebalance.

REINVESTMENT ISSUES

In most strategy chapters, we begin by specifying the initial portfolio amount and asset allocation. Here we do not, and this is because this strategy is designed for investing cash flow rather than managing a lump sum. In the example of the MDY options, if we know that we have $30,000 initially and approximately $4,000 a year in cash flow to invest, then we can appropriately size the investment strategy.

But if we instead had $50,000 initially, but no expectation of future cash flow, what would be the correct approach? Would we set the $20,000 aside in a low-risk account in expectation of our future liabilities? This may be prudent, but would slash our returns, especially if we happened to be in a low-interest rate environment and earned only 2 percent or 3 percent on our savings.

The difficulty faced is that it is impossible to know if even five years of roll-forward costs would be sufficient. In the original example, a portfolio of sector-diversified LEAPS call options purchased in 1999 and rolled forward annually would have declined significantly by the start of 2003, and at that point, only a single year's worth of roll-forward payments would be remaining. Would the portfolio manager have the courage to wait for another year?

With a rolling LEAPS call strategy, there are two ways to use cash: Buy more call options, or keep the cash in savings to pay future roll-forward costs. Buying more call options raises the expected return, but exposes the portfolio manager to a potential liability, as the cash may not be available later to pay roll-forward costs. But keeping cash in savings will reduce the overall return of the portfolio due to the low-yield, low-return nature of savings accounts.

This can be illustrated with a portfolio management decision. Suppose an investor has a $50,000 portfolio of LEAPS call options with an estimated one-year return of 14 percent, and the investor is considering a roll-up in which $15,000 of equity is withdrawn, and the estimated return of the remaining $35,000 of options is 18 percent, due to their higher leverage.

If the $15,000 withdrawn were invested in those higher leverage options, the portfolio would have a higher expected return, but more risk. Alternately, if the funds were placed in cash, then the portfolio would have a lower total return but more safety due to a reduction in leverage. And if no roll-up took place, the level of leverage would stay the same.

From this perspective, roll-ups can be seen as primarily an adjustment in the portfolio's leverage ratio. However, for LEAPS call options, higher leverage also increases the hedging expenses, which is the price that the portfolio pays to avoid margin calls.

These hedging expenses create an effective maximum leverage ratio of about $4\times$ to $5\times$, although it may seem lower initially due to the prepayment of interest. This $4\times$ to $5\times$ ratio corresponds to a strike price of roughly 75 to 80 percent of market.

COVERED CALLS AND MID-CAPS

Another modification to a rolling LEAPS call option strategy is to sell short-term call options during the life of the investment. This provides the opportunity to generate cash flow that can be applied to the roll-forward costs. For selling options to be profitable, we have to assume a premium of implied volatility over realized, which historically has been the case.

In Table 7.7, a single 60-day at-the-money call option was sold at the start of every year, and over the eleven years this transaction generated $65,336 of extra income based upon an assumed average implied volatility. The extra income generated reduces the roll-forward costs on average, which raises the IRR of the strategy to 25.98 percent.

The tradeoff, of course, is predictability. In both 1998 and 2000, the combination of the roll-forward payment and the loss taken on the short call option is $10,000 and $12,000 respectively, a significant cash outflow. This expense is included in the IRR, but if the cash isn't available, then some of the appreciated LEAPS options may need to be sold to meet the obligation.

Selling at-the-money options is only possible when the strike price of the LEAPS option is above the market price, and while this is the case for MDY in our historical data, it wouldn't be true for every option. If the market price has fallen below the current strike price and the LEAPS option is out-of-the-money, cash margin would have to be held in order to write a short-term call. If selling short-term call options is anticipated, it may be

TABLE 7.7	MDY Rolled LEAPS Call Option Cash Flows W/Sold 60-day Call at Start of Each Year			
Year	MDY	LEAPS Cashflow	Short Option Cashflow	Total Cashflow
1996	17.9%	−29,928	340	−29,588
1997	23.7%	−4,347	5,405	1,058
1998	15.9%	−3,879	−6,285	−10,165
1999	15.7%	−3,761	14,222	10,462
2000	23.0%	−3,723	−8,437	−12,161
2001	−3.3%	−3,712	23,328	19,616
2002	−16.7%	−3,713	8,611	4,898
2003	42.0%	−3,724	11,750	8,026
2004	10.7%	−3,712	2,950	−762
2005	21.4%	−3,711	−467	−4,178
2006	7.7%	−3,711	13,918	10,207
2007		321,892		321,892
All Years		253,969	65,336	319,305
IRR	13.4%	19.2%	N/A	26.0%

better to hold lower strike price LEAPS call options in anticipation of a possible decline.

The more short-term options that are sold, the higher the profits will likely be, assuming a premium of implied volatility over realized, but it will become harder to predict and anticipate the required cash flows, leading to more situations where LEAPS options have to be sold at inopportune times in order to raise cash and/or reduce risk.

COVERED CALLS WITH SECTORS

If selling call options can raise the multiyear IRR of MDY from 19 percent to almost 26 percent, what could it do for our stagnant sector funds that barely return more than the cost of capital? Unfortunately, it is difficult to precisely reverse-engineer the implied volatility of any of the sector funds, as the VIX addresses only the S&P 500 as a whole, but we can make some estimates.

The average annualized volatility of monthly returns for XLB, the materials sector, is 21.65 percent, and if we assume a typical premium, then a long-term estimate would be 27 percent or so. At this volatility level, selling call options generates an extra 0.37 percent of the underlying per month, or approximately 4.5 percent a year before leverage.

When the cash flows from purchasing and rolling a LEAPS call option on the security are combined with the cash flows from selling call options and buying them back, the monthly IRR rises to 1.70 percent, which is 22.36 percent annualized. This is very good for a sector that returned only 8.7 percent a year during the period, and similar results would be expected of the other sectors.

Still, the cash flows from selling calls are relatively unpredictable, and in many months the strategy has a loss of $5 per share or more, and in one severe case, $22 per share. (The materials index gained more than 25 percent in March 1999.) This is a significant and unexpected liability to face.

There's also no guarantee that call selling will generate profits, especially over shorter periods of time. Implied volatility is simply a prediction of future volatility for the specified period, and may in fact be much too low to account for the actual volatility of the index.

For example, in this estimate, we have the benefit of being able to survey the entire market data. However, in the real world, implied volatility in financial markets will often lag the realized volatility, and when regime change occurs, the option seller may be trapped in a strategy with negative expected returns.

SUMMARY

Rolling deep-in-the-money LEAPS call options on the index is a leveraged indexing strategy that can be used to invest cash flow. It requires an initial investment and then periodic roll-forward payments that must be made in order to maintain the investment. By starting with a low strike price, such as 80 percent of market, the hedging costs are reduced, and the portfolio is better able to withstand periods of poor performance.

Availability of S&P sector performance data from 1999 to 2006 provides the opportunity to see how the strategy performed in a variety of market conditions. For most sectors during this period, the historical data showed poor performance, and the rolling LEAPS call option strategy was able to maintain its value but not deliver superior returns. For example, the financials sector returned 7.2 percent a year annualized, and the LEAPS call strategy returned just slightly higher, 8.15 percent.

For the one sector that performed well, energy, the strategy excelled, returning 22.3 percent annualized, almost seven and a half points a year higher than the underlying. At the other end of the spectrum, the tech sector declined almost 30 percent during the period, and the rolled LEAPS call options were almost worthless.

The roll-forward costs required to hold a LEAPS position were very predictable, and in the case of some LEAPS call options stayed within a reasonable range for years, despite wide fluctuations in the market price of the security. This makes the strategy ideal for investing cash flow.

Many investment strategies can benefit from periodic rebalancing, but in this case the effect was shown to be negative, as moving assets from higher performing sectors to lower performing proved to be detrimental. Also, there simply wasn't enough value in the options portfolios to continue to purchase deep-in-the-money options at some points.

Perhaps eight years may be too short a period for the rolled LEAPS call strategy to shine. We then applied the technique to eleven years of historical returns for MDY, the mid-cap sector ETF. Mid-cap stocks have returned over 13 percent during the period and benefit from Fama-French factors, and the corresponding rolling LEAPS call options strategy was able to return 19.3 percent.

A significant challenge for a LEAPS call strategy is sizing the portfolio and managing roll-forwards and roll-ups. As the option portfolio builds equity, it loses leverage. Equity can be pulled from the portfolio and invested in more options, increasing the leverage ratio and increasing average returns. Or, the proceeds can be held in cash to maintain a safety margin and address future roll-forward costs.

Higher returns for both the mid-cap and sector portfolios were achievable by selling short-term calls during the period, but this carries some risks. In one month, a short call option was sold on the materials sector for just 3 percent of the value of the underlying index, but then an ensuing rally required a cash outlay equal to 28 percent—a statistically unlikely occurrence, but always a possibility. This event underscores how unpredictable call selling can be. Regardless, it may be the only way to pull profits from a low-return index.

CHAPTER 8

Long and Short Profits with Call Spreads

S uppose an investor purchased a house, and then immediately sold off the portion that they didn't want, such as the basement or the pool to help fund the initial investment. Most investments don't provide this level of granularity, but stocks with options do. At any time, investors have the ability to sell a portion of their investment that they believe has less long-term potential, but still hold on to the piece that has more value. This is accomplished by creating a call spread.

A call spread is a pair of long and short call options on the same security. The proceeds from the short option are used to fund the long option, and when the investment is successful, the long option gains value and the short option loses value, generating profits. But spread positions are complex, as the initial and the final value of the two options is dependent upon many factors, and unexpected conditions can create liabilities and make a spread worthless.

In this chapter, three different types of debit spreads are examined: the bull call (or vertical spread), the diagonal spread, and the calendar spread. Each spread can be applied to the index to generate profits, but each also has caveats and hidden dangers associated with the strategies, including the effects of the volatility skew, early exit conditions, and/or asymmetric payoffs.

Spreads are often used in shorter-term strategies and at the end of this chapter we show how to rapidly cycle gains on these types of investments. When cycling works and conditions are favorable, huge profits can be generated in short periods of time. Of course, managing risk is essential, and the last portion of the chapter is devoted to cycling reinvestment strategies.

UNDERSTANDING DEBIT SPREADS

Debit spreads are spreads in which the long option is more expensive than the short option and, as a result, a cash payment is required at the time of purchase. Debit call spreads are long positions and have a maximum loss of 100 percent of invested capital, but an unlimited upside. Debit call spreads are also known as bull call spreads or vertical spreads.

Debit spreads using shorter-term options tend to be very unstable, often losing 5 percent or 10 percent of their value every day as the underlying price and volatility changes. This creates trading opportunities, of course, but also situations in which all of the capital in an investment could be wiped out very quickly in a market decline.

The opposite of a debit spread is a credit spread, and in a credit spread, the short option is more expensive. As a result, cash is returned to the investor in the transaction. However, a potential liability is also created, and cash margin would always be required to hold the position.

Any debit or credit spread is constantly revalued based upon current market prices. For a debit spread, this revaluation may be useful for reporting purposes, but would be generally irrelevant until the time of sale. But for a credit spread, this revaluation could result in increased margin requirements, and in a worst-case scenario, a forced sell-off in the event that the available margin in the account is insufficient to hold the position.

Credit spreads using calls are short positions and could in theory be used as a hedge for a long position, but owning a put would be generally more efficient and would provide more predictable results. Hedges are discussed more in Chapter 10.

Both debit and credit spreads are susceptible to exercise risk if American-style options are involved. Although most options are held until expiry and then auto-exercised if profitable, at some points in time it may be more advantageous to exercise an option in advance of the expiration date, particularly if a dividend is involved.

When a short call option is exercised, the broker will provide notification and the short call option position in the account will be replaced with a short position in the stock or ETF. Additional cash will then be deposited in the account in accordance with the terms of the sale. Often the account will then be above margin requirements and the short stock position will have to be closed by the end of the trading day (that is, before settlement).

Early exercise can cause traders anxiety, but is a relatively uncommon occurrence unless an option is deep-in-the-money and has little time value, and is also close to an expected dividend payment. Replacing the short call option with the underlying stock has little effect on the position's payoff, and the short stock would gain or lose value at approximately the same rate as the short call would, given the same market conditions.

Only American-style options can be exercised early, as opposed to European-style options, which can only be exercised at expiry. Generally, options on stocks or ETFs are American-style and options on cash-settled indexes are European-style. Still, as exceptions to this rule exist, it is important to check before purchasing in order to be aware of the potential for early exercise.

BULL CALL SPREADS

The simplest call spread position is the bull call spread, which is created by purchasing a call on a security and then selling another call at the higher strike price but with the same expiration date. For example:

Buy SPY @ 135 expiring Feb '08 for 5.85

Sell SPY @ 140 expiring Feb '08 for 2.31

SPY is the S&P 500 index tracker ETF, and the current SPY price is 139.58. This position is a debit spread, and the cost is the difference between the two options, or 3.54 in this example. The option expires in ten days.

The payoff at expiration is then dependent upon the closing price of the security at that time. The maximum payoff occurs when SPY closes above the strike price of the short option, and is the difference between the two strike prices, or $5 per share in the example. Receiving a payoff of $5.00 on an investment of $3.54 is a +41 percent return, which is certainly good for a two-week period.

If SPY closes at 135 or lower, the payoff is zero and the position expires worthless. If SPY instead closes between the two strike prices, then the payoff is the market price of SPY at expiry minus the strike price. As a result, the position shown here has a breakeven of 138.54. (Lower strike price plus the cost of the spread.)

Most brokerages will auto-exercise a call option if it expires in the money, and if the market price is above the strike price of the short option, then both options would be auto-exercised, and the cash proceeds from the purchase and sale would be deposited in the brokerage account.

Otherwise, if the market price is above the strike of the long call, but lower than the price of the short call, then only the long call would be exercised. In the case of an equity option, shares would be deposited in the account, and the investor would then have a long position in the stock, and, if the account has insufficient margin, would need to sell the shares in the next market day.

As a rule, the position would need to be held to expiry to generate the maximum payoff, but profits could still be made if the spread is sold early. Any broker should allow the spread position to be sold in a single transaction rather than one "leg" at a time, which could create some very unpredictable results if the market is moving rapidly and one trade wasn't executed quickly.

The value of a spread position or any options position will change whenever the price or volatility of the underlying security changes. A spread position will have its own delta, gamma, and vega that can be calculated by subtracting the Greeks of the short call from those of the long call.

Typically in a vertical call spread such as the one just detailed, the in-the-money option will have a delta of close to 1, and the at-the-money option will have a delta of about 0.5, resulting in a position delta of around 0.5 (that is, $1.0 - 0.5$). But a spread with two years to expiry may have a delta of only .15 and would only change in value very slowly in response to price increases.

Long calls have positive vega, and short calls have negative vega, and when the two positions are combined into a spread, the vega is generally low enough that the position is considered vega-neutral, although in reality it would never be exactly zero.

This property also tends to make spreads more useful for capturing appreciation in highly volatile periods than simply using long calls alone. The long call will have vega risk, and if the volatility declines, the call will lose value, potentially wiping out some of the gains from a market rebound. A spread would have no vega risk and would simply increase in value.

Of course, vega risk can also help a position—if the market continues to decline, and volatility rises even further, a long call's vega could prevent the position from losing value, while a bull call spread would suffer losses and potentially get wiped out.

CALL SPREADS AND APPRECIATION

One of the challenges in using bull call spreads to capture appreciation is that of selecting the appropriate combination of strike prices and time to expiry. If out-of-the-money call spreads are selected, the implied volatilities are lower and the payoffs are higher, but the probability of our call expiring in the money is lower. These investments can feel like a lottery ticket with the majority of positions expiring worthless before one finally pays off.

On the other hand, in the money call spreads will tend to have higher implied volatilities and will be more expensive, and as a result our percentage returns are lower. But if the returns from these options are more certain, then we are better able to reinvest and compound our portfolio's gains.

To help find the best starting point, we have to return to the basic principles of call options identified in earlier chapters. First, options with high intrinsic value are better able to capture appreciation than options with high time value. This suggests that we should be buying a call option with intrinsic value, and selling an option with time value.

Second, longer-term options are a better value than shorter-term options because additional time can be purchased inexpensively, as compared to expected appreciation. And third, over time index drift tends to swamp the "noise" in returns, making returns more predictable.

Given this, we can start with a LEAPS call spread that combines a long in-the-money option with a short out-of-the-money option. The objective is that the long option gains in value while the short option loses value. This example comes from current LEAPS call option prices on the SPX, the S&P 500 index.

The current price of the SPX is 1401.02.

Buy call on SPX @ 1300 exp 12/09 for 250.70 (IV = 19.95)

Sell call on SPX @ 1500 exp 12/09 for 138.90 (IV = 18.94)

The option is 707 days to expiry, and the debit spread costs 111.80.

Max payoff after two years: 200

Max percentage payoff: +78.9%

Breakeven: 1411.80, or +0.7%

% increase in SPX required for max payoff: +7.1%

% decline in SPX required for 100% loss: −7.2%

If the index appreciates more than 7.1 percent total in that period, we will receive the max payoff of +78 percent, but if it declines 7.2 percent, we will suffer the max loss, 100 percent. As a rule, we expect the index to appreciate roughly 10 percent a year, or about 21 percent in two years, so the odds favor the max profit scenario.

We can use our average index appreciation for a two-year period, 21 percent, and our standard deviation, also about 21 percent, to determine the likelihood of getting the maximum or minimum payoff. We can create a percentile ranking using these index return probabilities and thus get more insight into the position's probability of losses or profits.

If we assume a normal distribution of returns, as shown in Table 8.1, our max loss would occur at the 7th percentile, and our max gain at the 26th percentile. These percentiles correspond to −1.3 std and −0.67 std respectively. (Max payoff occurs below the average expected appreciation.) Our breakeven point is at the 17th percentile.

Our average payoff for the bull call spread at expiry is 168.18 with a standard deviation of 65. This can be calculated through either Monte Carlo, or by averaging all of the payoffs from a normal distribution. This represents a 50 percent return over the two-year period, but with a 58 percent standard deviation.

However, the standard deviations of the investment can be misleading as it is impossible for the payoff to ever be above 200. Generally, this position will make either the max profit or take a total loss. Partial returns and breakeven will occur only rarely.

The payoff is dependent upon our assumptions concerning average return and volatility, and if the return comes in lower than expected, or if the volatility is higher, then the spread payoff would be lower and could even go negative.

In tests, reducing the average annual return of the underlying by one percentage point cost the spread five percentage points of return, and increasing the volatility by one percent reduced the spread return by three points. Given that the average return is 50 percent, this shows that the position has a fairly high degree of resiliency, and even if the investor is wrong about some of their assumptions it should still be profitable on average.

TABLE 8.1 Percentile Distribution of Returns for a Vertical Call Spread

Percentile	Index Return	Index Level	Spread Payoff
5%	−13.54%	1211.29	0.00
10%	−5.91%	1318.18	18.18
25%	6.84%	1496.79	196.79
50%	21.00%	1695.23	200.00
75%	35.16%	1893.68	200.00
90%	47.91%	2072.28	200.00
95%	55.54%	2179.17	200.00
		Avg.	168.18
		Stdev	65.52

SPREADS AND SKEWS

In our example, the implied volatility of the in-the-money call option is higher than the out-of-the-money option. This is the result of the volatility skew, and is normal and expected. But the problem is that it makes the long option significantly more expensive than the short option.

The effect is small, but because of the fixed maximum payoff of bull call spreads, small expenses such as the volatility skew, bid-ask spreads, or commissions can cut the profitability of these positions significantly. If the initial cost of the position is increased by just a few percentage points both the average percentage payoff and the maximum percentage payoff are lowered, and can quickly fall into the single digits.

For example if we have a bull call spread with a max payoff of $10, and the bid-ask spread and the volatility skew raises the initial price from $6.50 to $6.80, then the maximum percentage return has fallen from 54 percent to 47 percent. And if the average expected payoff is $7.20, then our average percentage return has fallen from 10.8 percent to 5.9 percent.

As a result, while a bull call spread would appear ideal for owning a position which has a similar payoff to a covered call but caps the max loss, the additional cost imposed by the volatility skew can make the underlying hedge very expensive and reduce the payoff dramatically. This, coupled with the relatively high likelihood of a 100 percent loss, can make bull call spreads much less profitable and more risky than expected.

Table 8.2 captures option prices for four spreads with the same long and short strike prices but varying expiration dates. The long option is in-the-money and the second option is out-of-the-money. Note the difference between the implied volatilities of the first and second call options.

A good rule of thumb is that each 1 percent difference in the implied volatility between the long option and the short option cuts the profit potential of a call spread by 25 percent; that is, an average 20 percent gain becomes an average 15 percent gain.

TABLE 8.2 Volatility Skew Comparison, Long-Term vs. Short-Term Options

Days to Expiry	Long Option Strike	IV	Short Option Strike	IV	IV-Diff
34	135	26.93	140	24.53	2.40
159	135	26.74	140	25.08	1.66
342	135	25.55	140	24.41	1.14
706	135	24.96	140	24.23	0.73

The difference in IVs ranges from 2.40 for the options expiring in roughly a month, to 0.73 for the LEAPS options. For the LEAPS and longer-dated options, the smaller implied volatility difference helps make these positions more profitable. Unfortunately, long-dated options will tend to have higher bid-ask spreads and lower liquidity, which can also make them more expensive to purchase and exit.

EARLY EXIT

As we mentioned earlier, bull call spreads can be exited at any time by buying back the short option and then selling the long option. However, there are some caveats that often make the position not nearly as profitable as expected for an investor. The first is that exiting the position will incur two commissions and two bid-ask spreads, and these transaction costs can significantly cut into profits.

The other problem is that when the underlying security increases, the short option often will increase in value at almost the same pace as the long option increases in value. This can be seen from the delta of the position, which is that of the long option minus the short option. A low delta indicates that even if the spread moves further in the money, it is likely that the position has not increased in value significantly.

In the example shown in Table 8.3, we purchase a 3-month ITM/ATM bull call spread and hold it for one month with a five point gain. When we sell the position we find that the long option has gained $4.16, but the short option has gained $2.52, resulting in only a $1.80 gain on the spread

TABLE 8.3   One-Month Return on a Diagonal Call Spread

	Days	Market	Strike	Years	Rate	Vol.	Price
Long	90	100	90	0.25	0.05	0.20	11.64
Short	90	100	100	0.25	0.05	0.20	4.58
						Spread	7.06

	Days	Market	Strike	Years	Rate	Vol.	Price
Long	60	105	90	0.16	0.05	0.20	15.80
Short	60	105	100	0.16	0.05	0.20	6.99
						Spread	8.81
						Long Gain	4.16
						Short Gain	2.42

and a rather low profit percentage, especially given the rapid move in the underlying.

This effect occurs in reverse when the underlying falls. The decline in the long option will be offset by the gain on the short option, at least to some extent. This does help to limit the losses, especially if the long option's time value increases in value.

But the result of all of this is that the position has very little leverage until it is close to expiry. A six-month spread will likely take three or four months to post a significant gain or loss, no matter what actually happens to the underlying security. The fact that the vega risk of the position, which is the potential price fluctuations due to the change in the underlying security, is minimal also serves to keep the value relatively stable.

This is why we sometimes say that spreads "fill in" over time. Even if a bull call spread is purchased in-the-money and stays in-the-money, the position will likely not reach max profitability until the last day, generally because the short option still has time value.

In the meantime, the spread will fill in, or increase in value as the time passes, or alternately will lose value if the market price is below the strike price of the long option, and that process will take place very slowly as the spread moves closer and closer to expiry.

Table 8.4 shows a ten-point spread that fills in over a period of 90 days, assuming no change in the underlying. It initially costs a little under $7, and after 60 days, our spread has gained less than one point. Then, in the next 23 days, it gains another point. Finally, in the last seven days, it gains the third point to reach its maximum value. Selling it just a week early would have lost more than a third of the profits when commissions and bid/ask spreads are considered.

Staggered Exit

Bull call spreads can also be exited by selling the short option first, and then the long option at a later date. When selling off components of the option strategy that make up the position, this is known as selling a "leg," or "legging out."

The objective of exiting the short position early would be to make a profit on both the short option and the long option if possible. If, for example, the underlying security falls in price in the short-term, it will become cheaper to purchase the short option back. Then the long option could be held until expiry, or perhaps even rolled over, generating appreciation.

Buying back the short option is essentially a market timing problem and it would be difficult to say with certainty that any specific point in time is the right time to buy that option back. After all, it could continue to increase in value or decrease in value. However, there may be some

TABLE 8.4 Fill In for Vertical Call Spread Moving Closer to Expiry (Long and Short Call Options Displayed)

	Value	Days	Market	Strike	Years	Rate	Vol.	Price
90 days	7.06	90	100	90	0.25	0.05	0.20	11.64
		90	100	100	0.25	0.05	0.20	4.58
45 days	7.60	45	100	90	0.12	0.05	0.20	10.71
		45	100	100	0.12	0.05	0.20	3.11
30 days	7.93	30	100	90	0.08	0.05	0.20	10.43
		30	100	100	0.08	0.05	0.20	2.49
15 days	8.47	15	100	90	0.04	0.05	0.20	10.19
		15	100	100	0.04	0.05	0.20	1.72
7 days	8.93	7	100	90	0.02	0.05	0.20	10.09
		7	100	100	0.02	0.05	0.20	1.15
3 days	9.29	3	100	90	0.01	0.05	0.20	10.04
		3	100	100	0.01	0.05	0.20	0.74

situations where we could make some judgments about whether it would be better off to maintain that short option position or to buy it back.

If we enter an in-the-money/at-the-money bull call spread, and then the price of the underlying security falls significantly, we would now have an out-of-the-money short option and an at-the-money long option. If volatility is not sky-high, then the short option will have significantly fallen in value, and we could buy it back for a profit and then hold the long option to expiry.

The problem is of course that our long option would now be an at-the-money option, which is not as effective at building appreciation due to its lower delta and higher time value. Unless we have a specific reason to believe that the market will rise, the better choice might simply be to sell this option, too, take the loss, and enter another options position that reflects the new reality of the market.

What if the value of the underlying security goes up? In that case, it would be somewhat expensive to buy the short option back, but if its delta is low, it might have gained in value only a small amount when compared to the total appreciation. Typically, an at-the-money option has a delta of about 0.5; therefore, if a $100 index rose $5, the short option would have risen in value only $2.50.

This would then be an opportunity to get rid of that short option, keep the gain on the larger option, and then hold that security to expiry. At expiry, we would expect to gain the entire $5, resulting in a 100 percent gain on that $2.50 we just spent. But, of course, holding that long call to expiry would put those gains at risk, and additional losses could wipe out those gains, and even the original investment.

DIAGONAL CALL SPREADS

Our goal with bull call spreads was to own a profitable option while selling an unprofitable one on the same security at the same strike price. However, our profit potential was limited to some extent because we couldn't take advantage of differences in expiration dates, and because deep-in-the-money call options have higher implied volatilities, which makes them more expensive.

Those issues can be circumvented by using diagonal call spreads, which are a long and a short option with different strike prices and different expiration dates. This allows the freedom to construct complex positions that take advantage of both the increased appreciation available from longer-term options and often a smaller variation in implied volatilities between the two positions.

Diagonal call spreads can be extremely profitable and often money can be made on both the short position and the long position. The short call has the potential to either expire worthless or to lose enough value so that it can be bought back very cheaply, and the long option has unlimited upside. In favorable conditions, returns of +100 percent are possible on many positions.

However, diagonal spreads introduce new challenges because they create mismatches in expected liabilities and future cash flows. The expiry of the short option potentially requires a cash payment; these liabilities are often unpredictable and very difficult to plan for.

As an example, an investor buys an in-the-money call on the Russell 2000, expiring in six months, and sells an at-the-money call expiring in three months, as detailed below:

Index trades for 100

Buy Call @ 95 expiring in 180 days

Sell Call @ 100 expiring in 90 days

The long call is an asset and the short call a potential liability. In three months, the liability may have to be addressed by making a cash payment, and that could require either selling the long call or pulling funds from reserve capital.

Will this position be profitable? We know how to model both of the call options and determine the average expected payoff and the range of possibilities for each. However, their performance is interrelated—if the index is lower in three months, then the probabilities favor a lower result in six months as well.

The best approach is to use Monte Carlo and model a range of returns for the six-month period and then calculate the results for our initial payment, the amount due at the expiry of the three-month option, and the payoff of our six-month option. The values will be dependent upon the assumptions used, and we will do exactly this in the next strategy chapter.

There is a shortcut for developing a simple forecast. If we assume that both call options will have average appreciation during the period, equaling about 10 percent annually, then we can assume that the six-month-long option will be worth 5 points at expiry, and the three-month option will be worth 2.5. The difference, 2.5, can be added to the 5 points of intrinsic value to create an estimated payoff of 7.5.

Of course, at the three-month mark when the short option is bought back, the investor would have no way of knowing what the index returns for the remaining three months of the original option will be, and the effect on the value of the long option. If the strategy is repeated, situations should be expected in which the short option is bought back at a loss, but then the underlying security declines in value, resulting in a loss on the long option as well.

Another alternative would be to buy back the short option at expiry and then immediately sell the long option, thereby taking a profit or incurring a loss but also freeing up capital for further investments. This could also be part of a cycling strategy in which gains are rapidly reinvested in order to build value. However, it eliminates the potential of sky-high returns from the long option.

How should this decision be made? The long option simply has to be evaluated on its merits as to whether it would be more valuable sold or used to capture appreciation. If the long option is at-the-money or out-of-the-money, implied volatility is moderate to high, and only a few months remain to expiry, then the long call is statistically unlikely to build intrinsic value significantly in excess of its current price and should probably be sold.

Of course, a low-value out-of-the-money option could be held in anticipation of either a significant rise in either the market price or the volatility of the underlying security, but this is more or less speculation, and would likely have a random and very unpredictable result—typically expiring worthless rather than generating a profit.

On the other hand, if the short option expires or is bought back, and the long call option is then in the money and volatility is relatively low, then it does have an opportunity to build value in excess of its current price and is likely a good investment with a positive expected return. There would be some risk in the investment, as the intrinsic value could be lost by a sharp downturn, but over time, repeated positions would be expected to be profitable.

LONG/SHORT PORTFOLIOS FROM DIAGONALS

Suppose that once a month for six months, an investor purchased a six-month in-the-money call option on the Russell 2000 and sold a three-month at-the-money call option. After six months, the investor would be holding a portfolio of long and short options with many more long than short.

We could model this portfolio and attempt to determine what its long-term returns would be given average, above-average, and below-average returns for the Russell for one more month (see Table 8.5).

For our portfolio, assume that the index has been rising by approximately 1 point every month, so many of the original in-the-money options are now deep-in-the-money. The portfolio also has a high delta, and the theta would be positive, indicating that value is generated by the passage of time alone.

Table 8.6 shows the monthly portfolio returns given various returns in the underlying index. The portfolio returns are about six to seven times higher than that of the underlying, representing the high level of leverage provided by the options. The long/short options portfolio also helps to reduce the interest expense that is usually associated with holding a leveraged portfolio.

With some long/short call option portfolios, we see an effect in which drops in the index price are offset by the in-the-money options moving to at-the-money and gaining time value. It's not obvious in this portfolio, but in the event of a 5 percent decline, many of the long options would lose 40 to 50 percent of their value, but the existence of the short options reduces the total portfolio loss to only 38 percent. This effect is dependent upon the average strike price of the long options and the level of volatility selected—in our example, we assumed average volatility and didn't adjust for any skew.

If the index increased significantly in value, the short call options would have to be bought back, which could mean selling some of the other long options. Early exercise is also a possibility if the options are

TABLE 8.5 Long/Short Option Portfolio Created by Repeated Diagonals

	Long Options					
Days	**Market**	**Strike**	**Years**	**Rate**	**Vol.**	**Price**
180	100	95	0.49	0.05	0.20	9.82
150	100	94	0.41	0.05	0.20	9.84
120	100	93	0.33	0.05	0.20	9.89
90	100	92	0.25	0.05	0.20	9.97
60	100	91	0.16	0.05	0.20	10.12
30	100	90	0.08	0.05	0.20	10.43
	Short Options					
Days	**Market**	**Strike**	**Years**	**Rate**	**Vol.**	**Price**
90	100	98	0.25	0.05	0.20	5.70
60	100	99	0.16	0.05	0.20	4.19
30	100	100	0.08	0.05	0.20	2.49
	Total Long		60.07			
	Total Short		12.39			
	Account Value		47.69			

Total Long	60.07
Total Short	12.39
Portfolio Value	47.69

TABLE 8.6 Long/Short Portfolio Returns as a Function of Index Returns

Index Gain	Portfolio Gain
−5%	−38.71%
−4%	−30.88%
−3%	−22.91%
−2%	−14.85%
−1%	−6.71%
0%	1.43%
1%	7.54%
2%	13.62%
3%	19.70%
4%	25.76%
5%	31.82%

American-style and a dividend payment is upcoming, and this may necessitate selling more options to maintain the positive theta.

Any portfolio that purchases longer-term in-the-money options and sells shorter-term at-the-money options on a regular basis will end up with more long options by default, as the shorter-term options will expire earlier. At the extreme, buying a 24-month LEAPS call option every month and selling a one-month option will over time result in a portfolio that has twenty-four times as many long options than short options.

In order to change this proportion, the investor could sell some of the in-the-money LEAPS before expiry, for examples, buying 18-month options and then selling them when they have only 6 months to expiry and are in-the-money. However, this may not reduce the leverage or boost the returns as much as expected, because the longer-term options have less leverage and would change in value relatively slowly in response to market conditions.

EARLY EXIT AND THETA

In a diagonal call spread, if the underlying security falls in price, it is likely that the short option will move out-of-the-money and lose value sharply. In this case, would it be better to buy the short option back early, or instead wait and hope that it expires worthless? Again, we have to analyze the expected value of the short call option and its appreciation potential.

There's no question that buying back the short option will always remove some of the uncertainty from the portfolio. The problem is that we may be more inclined to do this when we have cash or if we can make a gain rather than because of an actual analysis in the option's expected return. It's always critical to remember that the premium received for the short option is a "sunk cost" and that an investor should ignore previous purchase and sale prices and instead deal with the reality of the position as it currently stands.

When an option's strike price is close to market and volatility is high, it is experiencing the maximum rate of decay, and being short this option provides the maximum theta. As time passes and the security appreciates at a regular rate, the long option builds value while the short option merely treads water, any appreciation being eroded by time decay.

If the underlying index moves up sharply, the investor will likely take a loss on the short option that is offset by a gain on the long option. When this occurs, buying the short option back and then selling a new one at that current market price is an effective way to profit both from the increase in value and also continue to hold a position with positive delta and theta.

When the index falls, the opposite situation occurs, and both options in the spread lose value. The short option loses time value, and the long option now trades some of its intrinsic value for time value as the strike price moves closer to market. The spread has now changed to the point where the position is theta-neutral or perhaps negative, and the position is losing value.

In this case, the investor likely would hope that the underlying will increase in value and that the losses will be reversed; however, just hoping for the best is not a viable strategy as the position now has an expected negative profitability if held to expiry. If the investor wants to maintain a position with a high expected profitability, the best alternative is to sell the position and then enter a new spread, given the new market prices.

Large drops in the index are dramatic but relatively infrequent, and when they occur, options sellers will typically get compensated for the increased volatility in subsequent trades. Maintaining positive delta and positive theta on the index over time will result in the highest expected returns, although in investing, any choice can be second-guessed, and it is impossible to determine what the right action will be in every circumstance.

The level of required price movement that would make the time value and theta of the short option shrink dramatically and consequently create a spread with negative expected profitability is different for every option and depends upon the distance between strike and market, the implied volatility, and the time remaining on the short option.

If the option is a year to expiry and volatility is moderate, then the option would have to move very far off the strike price in order to lose time value and theta. But the time value and theta of front-month options can rise or fall very quickly with only small changes in the underlying.

In Table 8.7, we take a long position in a single in-the-money option with 37 days to expiry and a short position in an at-the-money option a week from expiry and hold the diagonal spread for a week. This helps to show the effect of maintaining positive delta and theta. Note that the weekly standard deviation for the index is about 2 percent, historically.

The maximum payoff, 18 percent, is achieved when the market is flat as shown in the example. But any week in which the market closes higher will result in profitability, typically 10 to 15 percent. Only when the index moves down sharply for the week would the position lose money. This is similar to a covered call position in terms of payoffs, and as most weeks the stock market is up or neutral, its clear to see how this could generate high returns over long periods of time.

In an ideal world with weekly options, no bid-ask spreads, and no transaction costs, we could sell our spread every week and replace it with a new one in order to maintain maximum delta and theta. While in some weeks our position would lose value, in most it would be profitable and the associated investment would compound quickly.

Of course, these returns also depend upon our assumptions about both implied and historic volatility. If higher volatility were to occur, then the

TABLE 8.7 One Week Diagonal Call Profitability in Flat Market

Long Option

Days	Market	Strike	Years	Rate	Vol.	Price	Days	Market	Strike	Years	Rate	Vol.	Price
37	100	95	0.10	5%	20%	6.12	30	100	95	0.08	5%	20%	5.88

Short Option

Days	Market	Strike	Years	Rate	Vol.	Price	Days	Market	Strike	Years	Rate	Vol.	Price
7	100	100	0.02	5%	20%	1.15	0	100	100	0.00	5%	20%	0.01

Total Long	6.12	Total Long	5.88
Total Short	1.15	Total Short	0.01
Position Value	4.97	Position Value	5.87

position would probably not be as profitable, or, in a worst case, average returns could become negative.

CALENDAR CALL SPREADS

Calendar call spreads are one of the most efficient yet most complex options positions available for capturing appreciation in a security. The position is created by purchasing a call option on a security at a specific strike price and then selling a second call option with the same strike price but an earlier expiration date. The two different expiration dates create both the source of risk and potential profits.

For example:

SPY is trading at 134.13

Buy SPY Call at 135 exp 6/2008 (135 days) for 8.10 (IV = 26.03)

Sell SPY Call at 135 exp 3/2008 (44 days) for 4.60 (IV = 27.19)

Debit Spread Cost: 3.50

In calendar call spreads, the long option will always be worth more than the short option because it has more time to expiry and hence more time value. As a result, a calendar call spread is a debit spread position and requires no margin, and its maximum loss is limited to the amount of the initial investment.

Profits are generated when the difference in the value of the two options increases, and this will typically occur when the market price is very close to the strike price of the two options at the time of the short options' expiry and when volatility is moderate to high.

For example, in the position shown, if the index ETF price in 44 days is exactly 135, and the short option expires worthless and out-of-the-money, then the long option would have no intrinsic value, but would still have considerable time value, especially if volatility has increased. In this case, the long call can be sold for a considerable profit.

Losses occur when the price of the underlying security moves to a point either much higher than or much lower than the strike price of the two call options. If the price is too high, then the short option has to be bought back, and the long option sold at essentially the same price, resulting in a payoff of zero or close to it. The same thing happens when the price falls too low—the short option expires worthless, but the long option is too far out-of-the-money to be worth anything.

Volatility is also a factor as the position has a high vega. Often a calendar call spread can offer limited crash protection in the event that the price of the underlying security declines but the associated volatility rises as a result. The two effects can combine to reduce or sometimes even eliminate losses on the position.

Volatility is mean-reverting, and the effects of increases and decreases would expect to be balanced out over time. However, on a monthly basis it is a source of risk, and situations will definitely occur in which a position's profits are reduced significantly due to a decline in volatility just before expiry of the short option.

Profitable calendar call spreads are like throwing a dart and trying to hit a bull's-eye. When the price is too high or too low, the position loses value. Only if the strike price is on target or close to it are profits earned. Is there any place in an indexer's toolkit for this kind of strategy?

Our historical analysis of the index can help us find this price target, and it is approximately 0.5 percent to 1.0 percent higher than the current market price, per month. If every month we forecast average appreciation for the index, some months we will be low, and some months we will be high, but many months we would be on target. If we are close enough most of the time and manage our risk carefully, it could be a profitable strategy.

When a similar strategy is applied to the S&P 500 by purchasing two-month at-the-money call options on the index and selling one-month call options, the resulting positions are very profitable on average. In the backtest, we assume that options can be purchased and sold at the current level of the VIX. See Table 8.8.

One important caveat—while commission expenses and the bid/ask spread play a role in any options strategy, the returns of a calendar call spread are extraordinarily sensitive to these expenses and this strategy would only work on highly liquid options.

For example, if the cost of a three-month at-the-money call option is $3 and the cost of a six-month option is $4.50, then the call spread should cost $1.50. But if each option has a ten-cent bid/ask spread, then the long option is purchased for $4.55 and the short option sold for $2.95, resulting in a cost of $1.60.

TABLE 8.8 Returns of a Calendar Spread Strategy

	Mean	Median	Stdev	Min.	Max.
Calendar Call Spread	21.1%	17.6%	52.2%	−68.6%	162.8%

Backtest: January 1990 to December 2007.
Two-month/one-month at-the-money calendar spread.

And if at expiry the calendar call spread is worth $2.20, but again there is a similar spread and only $2.10 is realized, then a potential +47 percent return has been cut to +31.3 percent. A ten-cent spread has cost the position almost a third of its profits.

LEAPS CALENDAR CALLS AND EARLY EXITS

Suppose an investor buys an at-the-money call option on the S&P 500 two years out and then sells an option at the same price and same security, resulting in a 24-month/12-month calendar call spread. Would this be a profitable position over time?

Table 8.9 follows the position for twelve months, given average 10 percent appreciation and a constant level of volatility (that is, no skew).

During the one-year holding period, the long call option gains value but the short option does not, as the appreciation of the underlying security is not high enough to offset the expected time decay. The result is that the spread gains 34.66 percent in value over the year, a return about 3.5× higher than the underlying index, or equivalent to a 6× to 8× leveraged position on the index if cost of capital is included.

Interestingly, the position's breakeven point at this assumed level of volatility is −9 percent to +25 percent. If the one-year index return is anywhere in that range, which is about one standard deviation, the position would be profitable. Given a normal distribution, that likelihood would be about 66 percent.

The max payoff occurs when the index is flat for the period. Index returns over 25 percent will not cause significant losses, but when the return drops below the lower breakeven point, the investment loses value quickly.

A 20 percent drop in the index over the next year results in a −67 percent loss on the position, and it's always important to understand that calendar calls can result in near total losses, as the long call could be worth just a small fraction of its original amount if it is way out-of-the-money and volatility has declined.

CYCLING INVESTMENT GAINS

Suppose that an investor is able to construct a short-term call spread such as a calendar or diagonal using the index so that the position returns 10 percent a month, but with 30 percent volatility. As a result, two-thirds

TABLE 8.9 LEAPS Calendar Call Spread Held for One Year

Month	Index	Long	Short	Spread	LONG Days	Market	Strike	Years	Rate	Vol.	Price	SHORT Days	Market	Strike	Years	Rate	Vol.	Price
0	100.00	15.99	10.36	5.62	720	100	100	1.97	0.05	0.20	15.99	360	100	100	0.99	0.05	0.20	10.36
1	100.80	16.11	10.33	5.77	690	101	100	1.89	0.05	0.20	16.11	330	101	100	0.90	0.05	0.20	10.33
2	101.60	16.23	10.30	5.93	660	102	100	1.81	0.05	0.20	16.23	300	102	100	0.82	0.05	0.20	10.30
3	102.41	16.36	10.25	6.10	630	102	100	1.73	0.05	0.20	16.36	270	102	100	0.74	0.05	0.20	10.25
4	103.23	16.48	10.20	6.29	600	103	100	1.64	0.05	0.20	16.48	240	103	100	0.66	0.05	0.20	10.20
5	104.05	16.61	10.13	6.48	570	104	100	1.56	0.05	0.20	16.61	210	104	100	0.58	0.05	0.20	10.13
6	104.88	16.74	10.06	6.68	540	105	100	1.48	0.05	0.20	16.74	180	105	100	0.49	0.05	0.20	10.06
7	105.72	16.87	9.97	6.90	510	106	100	1.40	0.05	0.20	16.87	150	106	100	0.41	0.05	0.20	9.97
8	106.56	17.01	9.87	7.13	480	107	100	1.32	0.05	0.20	17.01	120	107	100	0.33	0.05	0.20	9.87
9	107.41	17.14	9.77	7.37	450	107	100	1.23	0.05	0.20	17.14	90	107	100	0.25	0.05	0.20	9.77
10	108.27	17.28	9.68	7.60	420	108	100	1.15	0.05	0.20	17.28	60	108	100	0.16	0.05	0.20	9.68
11	109.13	17.42	9.68	7.74	390	109	100	1.07	0.05	0.20	17.42	30	109	100	0.08	0.05	0.20	9.68
12	110.00	17.57	10.00	7.57	360	110	100	0.99	0.05	0.20	17.57	0	110	100	0.00	0.05	0.20	10.00

Return 34.66%

of returns are between −20 percent and +40 percent, but plenty of returns are still outside that range, and +50 percent or −100 percent returns are possible. What kind of reinvestment strategy could be created that would allow this portfolio to grow rapidly, but, at the same time, prevent the investment from getting potentially wiped out by a few bad returns?

In conventional index investing, the initial investment is deposited in a fund and allowed to compound over time. In some periods the compounding is positive, and in some periods it is negative, but over time, the investment is expected to build in value, and thus all of the investment gains are reinvested back in the fund in order to repeatedly build value.

With highly volatile funds, we have to assume that at any point it is possible for the entire investment to get wiped out, and thus plan accordingly. This requires withholding assets from the strategy—both initial assets and gains.

When we are rapidly reinvesting gains in a risky strategy, for example on a monthly basis, we will refer to the strategy as cycling rather than compounding, as compounding refers more to slow and steady growth over time.

Although it would be tempting to cycle one's entire net worth in the monthly strategy just described for several months in anticipation of tripling the investment, over a six- or seven-month period we also have a fairly high chance of taking one or two 50-percent losses, and once we've lost that much of our assets it will be difficult to even return to our starting point, let alone generate any profits.

Let's assume that our investor decided to be conservative and cycle only one-third of their net worth in the preceding strategy. That sounds safe on the surface—after all, two-thirds of the funds are never at risk. But what action should be taken if a 100 percent loss occurs? Should the investor then take the second third of assets and put it at risk, potentially creating a situation in which that money is lost also, and only the last third is remaining?

The problem is that this strategy is relying on repeated investment gains in order to fund future investments, but if the gains aren't there, there will be no future investments.

Managing an investment strategy like this requires careful planning and thinking many steps ahead. There is always a possibility of losing money two times, three times, or five times in a row. In that case, what is the next move? It would be simple to disregard this possibility as remote, but if it were to occur, would we simply give up on our financial goals?

Also, losing money can be very emotional—studies say that it is twice as painful to lose money as to make it. And of course, pain and the fear of pain will sap confidence. Even if the strategy looks perfect on a spreadsheet, if it has generated losses five times out of six, potentially losing

50 percent of a fund in six months, it would take a tremendous amount of courage to repeat the investment once more.

Reinvestment Strategies

One potential solution is to invest in several uncorrelated positions—for example, a trader could calculate the correlations of three different industries and take positions on indexes that track all of those sectors. However, correlations can change over time, and every equity index will likely have some covariance with the S&P 500.

And it should be mentioned that a key reason that correlations can change is because leveraged investors will often have to sell appreciated investments in order to compensate for losses in others. So, for example, if both gold and energy prices have risen sharply over the past year and investors have been trading on momentum, a decline in one could suddenly trigger a fall in the other, even if both investments are unrelated.

Thus downturns are especially dangerous for strategies that rely on a lack of correlation between returns. Asset diversification should be seen as a long-term strategy rather than protection against short-term drops.

A system that is well-known to gamblers as a method for accelerating gains in risky scenarios is the Kelley criterion. In 1956, Larry Kelley Jr. of Bell Laboratories developed a formula that can be used to calculate the maximum fraction of a bankroll that can be invested without risk of total loss.

$$f = (bp - q)/b$$

f   is the fraction to wager in every iteration
b   is the odds received on the wager
p   is the probability of winning
q   is the probability of losing (i.e., $1 - p$)

For example, if a gambler has a 60 percent chance of winning $2\times$ the investment, and a 40 percent of losing everything, then the correct fraction to wager in order to maximize the rate growth with safety would be: $((2 \times .6) - .4)/2 = 40\%$.

In this case our average return on a $1 bet would be 20 cents, so if we are investing only 40 percent of our fund, 20 percent of that would be an 8 cent gain on every $1 in our fund. An 8 percent average payoff in each cycle is quite good, and indicates that we could double our fund every nine cycles, based on the rule of 72.

Still, this means that if we lose the bet $3\times$ in a row, which is a 6.4 percent probability, then we would have lost 78.4 percent of our initial investment immediately, so we may want to be more conservative, with the understanding that it would slow our rate of growth. Betting only 20 percent would leave us with slightly over 50 percent of our fund in that eventuality, but would only grow the fund by 4 percent in an average month.

We can also apply our fraction to the volatility. If we have an investment strategy that returns 20 percent every month but with 50 percent volatility, and we invest only 20 percent of our fund in the strategy, then our fund as a whole will have returns of only 4 percent with 10 percent volatility. Of course, this is still very high for monthly volatility.

From one point of view then, the total rate of return really only matters in relation to the standard deviation of returns, which is why many portfolio analysts use the Sharpe ratio. The Sharpe ratio implicitly adjusts for the use of leverage.

The real excitement starts when we use a cycling strategy based on a constant fraction with borrowed money. For example, let's assume that we have no starting equity, but only a credit line of $100,000, and when that's gone, not only are we out of money to invest, but we are also deep in debt and in dire financial straits.

If we had access to this capital at an annual interest rate of 5 percent, and then could immediately reinvest it in a risky strategy such as mentioned previously with 20 percent monthly returns and 50 percent volatility, should we? And to what extent?

As we borrow more, interest accumulates on our credit line. If we were to lose 50 percent of our assets in three months, our interest on this borrowed and then lost money would still continue to compound.

We ran a simulation for 300 portfolios using a 33 percent constant fraction of investment, and our results after one year were, on average, a gain of $114,013 after interest was paid. However, the standard deviation of returns was $121,140, and the max loss was −$69,223.

If we decided to use a more conservative fraction, only 20 percent, our average gain falls to $58,771 with a $56,838 standard deviation, and our max loss to −$54,970. Or, if we use only 10 percent, then our average payoff is $25,391 with a $21,881 standard deviation, and our max loss falls to −$23,459.

Thus, as we reduce our fraction, we don't necessarily change the percentage chance that we will lose money after repeated investments, but instead we simply change the absolute value of the amount of potential losses.

Constant Investment and Hybrid

Another way to take advantage of risky strategies is to invest a fixed amount every period. For example, if we have a $100,000 portfolio and bet

$10,000 a month into the preceding strategy, and then, regardless of the outcome, bet $10,000 next month, and $10,000 the month after that, and so on. Or alternately, we could make minor adjustments to the amount for inflation, for example, by increasing the investment by 0.4 percent a month.

Again, it is critical to plan ahead. A $10,000 bet is 10 percent of a $100,000 portfolio, but 11.1 percent of a $90,000 portfolio, and 12.5 percent of an $80,000 portfolio. Every time we have a loss, the next bet is a larger and larger fraction of the remaining stake, and thus the volatility of our fund's returns can get progressively higher.

However, betting the same amount every month makes it very easy to calculate the average expected return over several periods. If we were to bet $10,000 a month with a 20 percent payoff for 12 months, we know immediately that our expected return for the year is $24,000, and that a graph of our possible returns would form a normal distribution with this figure as the center, and the width of that graph would depend upon the standard deviation of the investment.

Of course, this assumes that the repeated investments are not positively correlated with each other. If there is even a weak correlation between one month's returns and the next month's, then we would get an increased chance of having higher gains or higher losses in the year. On the other hand, if every month was negatively correlated to the next, then the annual volatility would decline.

Also, as the investment increases, the wagers become smaller as a proportion, which decreases the overall risk. For example if after one year the fund had $124,000, then the next $10,000 investment would only be 8 percent of the portfolio. Risk decreases as the fund gains value, but so does the potential rate of return as well. Still, this may be what we want over time in order to provide some increased predictability.

INDEX REGIME CHANGE

It is very common to see options strategies that are predicated on specific assumptions about the index, work well for a period and then stop working as a result of an index regime change, that is, a long-term change in the volatility or, to a more limited extent, the average return of the index.

In these situations, strategies that have high-expected profitability before the index regime change can now have neutral or negative profitability. Unfortunately, that analysis and conclusion may not be readily apparent because of the random factor in the index.

Imagine that an investor has developed a profitable repeated strategy using the index, using for instance calendar call spreads. For three years, the strategy has been generating profits, and then for six months in a row it either makes very little money or loses money, and the investment fund takes heavy losses.

With enough data, the investor would be able to review the implied volatility and compare it to the actual volatility of the index and identify the mismatch. Perhaps the spread between implied volatility and historical volatility has broken down, or maybe implied volatilities and/or the bid-ask spreads have increased significantly on the long options used in the position. Any of those changes could reduce the profitability of the strategy.

For example, in 2002 the underlying volatility of the index appears to have changed significantly at the beginning of the year, but the average level of the VIX did not change until the middle of the year. Traders writing calls or selling puts during the first five months were mispricing the risk and selling their options too cheaply, in retrospect.

Then, when the actual volatility of the index fell in 2003, for several months implied volatilities still remained high. This made option-selling strategies abnormally profitable, but this level of profitable strategy could not be sustained, and by 2004 the implied volatilities eventually fell to a level more commensurate with risk in which profits were adequate, but not a windfall.

When developing forecasts for portfolios that depend on specific volatility assumptions, it is critical to change these assumptions and determine the results. The best approach is to select strategies that have assumptions that seem to cover a wide range of market conditions, to combine multiple strategies on multiple securities, and always to keep as many assets liquid as possible. After all, liquid assets provide the only assurance that we have the ability to continue to invest.

SUMMARY

This chapter presented three similar options positions that can be used for capturing index appreciation: the bull call spread, the diagonal call spread, and the calendar call spread. All three are debit spread positions in which the long option is more costly than the short option, and the objective of all three positions is that the long call option increases in value while the short option loses value.

Debit call spread positions sometimes have early exercise risk, due to the underlying option gaining in value and creating a situation where it can be advantageous for the holder of the option to exercise it. This is only an issue for American-style options, and is most likely when a dividend is involved and the option is deep-in-the-money, but could potentially occur at any time.

The most effective way to construct a bull call spread is to combine a long in-the-money call option with a short at-the-money or out-of-the-money option. This ensures that the long option has primarily intrinsic value, while the short option merely has time value. Then, if the index appreciates, both options gain intrinsic value, but the short option loses time value, resulting in additional appreciation for the position.

The payoff structure of in-the-money bull call spreads is such that the position generates profits most of the time, but then every so often will take very high losses. This can make these investments difficult to include in a portfolio as the risk/return ratio is very high and makes forecasting and reinvestment problematic.

Bull call spreads also need to be held to expiry in order to realize maximum profitability. Selling them even a week early can result in the investor forgoing a third or more of the profits from the position due to the remaining value of the short option and the bid-ask spread.

Another issue with bull call spreads is that the fixed maximum payoff can create situations in which expenses that seem relatively minor reduce profitability significantly. One of these expenses is the volatility skew, which makes the hedging property of the long options in a bull call spread more costly than the short option. Another is the bid-ask spread, and commission costs can also contribute to the problem.

Diagonal call spreads, or spreads in which the long option and the short option have different strike prices and expiration dates, can eliminate these difficulties, but sometimes also create new ones. Diagonal call spreads have an unlimited maximum payoff, but also create an unpredictable short-term liability that must be addressed. The worst-case scenario is that losses are taken on both the long and the short option.

However, when properly constructed and when conditions are favorable, diagonal call spreads can be very profitable. A long option with a high intrinsic value, a high delta, and a long period of time to expiry is combined with a short option with only time value, and as the index appreciates the short option loses or barely maintains its value, while the long option builds more equity.

If a diagonal position is created every month, the result is a portfolio of long and short call options. Portfolios like this are ideal for capturing appreciation over time due to their high delta and low theta. The effect is that the monthly return of the index is multiplied several times.

A diagonal position is most effective when the short call is at- or near-the-money. If the underlying index rises or falls significantly, the short option can lose time value and situations can be created where the position has a negative expected return. When this happens, it is better to take the loss immediately and enter a new position rather than hold the existing position to expiry. Typically when the short option has a high intrinsic value and very little time value, the position is unlikely to build further value.

The third options strategy discussed in this chapter, the calendar call spread, is one of the most capital efficient positions for capturing index appreciation. Calendar call spreads are formed by purchasing a call option at a specific strike price and expiry and then selling an identical option, but with less time to expiry.

Calendar call spreads have extremely high leverage, and as a result can be extremely profitable, especially in high volatility environments, but have some unusual properties. The position can lose value in the event of a sharp decline in the index price or volatility. Also, like bull call spreads, relatively minor costs such as a difference in the volatility skew or high bid-ask spreads can severely impact the profitability.

In this chapter, using short-term strategies with high potential returns but high standard deviations, and then reinvesting the cash in the same strategy again and again, is referred to as cycling rather than compounding. Cycling is a way to rapidly increase the value of a portfolio, but is also extremely risky, as any position has the potential to lose 100 percent of its value.

When cycling, the ideal would be to use uncorrelated positions for all of the investments, but because correlations can change suddenly and dramatically, this can provide a false sense of security. Another approach is to only invest a constant amount of a portfolio's assets in any strategy or across all of the strategies, and one way to determine the ideal fraction to use is by applying the Kelly criterion, which takes into account both the payoff and the likelihood of loss.

In any event, it is important to understand that all short-term strategies are based upon assumptions about the market environment, and the random nature of index returns can make it very difficult to determine when these assumptions have fundamentally changed. When this situation, often known as regime change, occurs, any strategy predicated on older market conditions will often fail dramatically in the new environment.

CHAPTER 9

Cycling Earnings Using Spread Positions

In this chapter, we build long-term investment strategies around call spreads on the S&P 500. These strategies benefit from call option characteristics introduced in earlier chapters, including the long-term appreciation of the index, the leverage of call options, the lower marginal cost of longer-term call options, and the differences between implied and historical volatility.

Even when call spread positions are constructed with positive returns, it can still be a challenge to manage the risk and reinvestment of portfolio capital. The standard deviation of investment returns tends to be high, making rapid gains and losses possible and the end result unpredictable. And in diagonal spreads specifically, the use of long and short options with different expiration dates and corresponding cash flows will complicate risk management.

Three strategies are presented in this chapter: a six-month/three-month diagonal call spread held to expiry, the same spread sold after the expiry of the three-month option, and a shorter-term strategy that cycles a portfolio through twenty-four investments a year (making rapid reinvestment possible). We also discuss long-term approaches to modeling volatility and present a relatively simple approach to constructing simulations of weekly or monthly changes in returns and volatility. For more complex strategies, we will need methods like these in order to go beyond historical analysis and model potential market scenarios and associated future returns.

SHORT OPTION SELECTION

What can happen in three months? According to the historical data, quite a lot. While the average three-month return for the S&P 500 index is 2.81 percent, the standard deviation is 6.69 percent. This results in frequent sharp moves: 37 percent of all rolling 3-month periods have a gain or loss of 5 percent or more, and almost 15 percent of the periods have a gain or loss of 10 percent or more.

It is not that three-month holding periods or options are unusually volatile—it is just how the math works. The roughly 4 percent standard deviation in monthly returns allows enough randomness and combinations of probabilities to generate many possible return scenarios during this time frame and make 10 percent gains and losses relatively common occurrences.

As a result, a three-month at-the-money call option is extremely expensive, at least in relation to the underlying. Depending upon the volatility, the cost can be from 4 percent to 5.5 percent of the value of the S&P index, and more for other, more volatile indexes. Historically, the average payoff for this call option on the S&P 500 is 4.23 percent. Sellers typically hedge their positions with futures contracts, which then makes them more concerned with the cost of capital and the risk of loss.

In our analysis, the average loss taken by writing a three-month call option is −1.48 percent historically, and 70 percent of the time there was no loss on the option for the seller. This leaves 2.50 percent to 4.00 percent of profit available to the seller of the option, or about 0.83 percent to 1.33 percent a month, before hedging and interest expenses, and this profit can be increased through leverage.

Ten percent of the options analyzed had a loss greater than the premium, and in the worst case, one three-month period resulted in a 17 percent drop in the underlying. Thus the premium is not free money by any means—it is compensation for a willingness to repeatedly write a call in volatile circumstances and risk an occasional double-digit loss.

LONG OPTION

The challenge in finding a long option for a spread strategy is that as we move deeper into the money and select longer time frames in order to reduce hedging costs, implied volatilities also rise and this cuts into profits. All too often we arrive at combinations with an 8 percent expected return but a 60 percent standard deviation in returns, or something similar. This is essentially a random return and the results would only be predictable over hundreds or thousands of investments.

One solution is to sell the long call option before expiry. If we have a holding period of six months, it may be more valuable to hold a nine-month option for six months and then sell it. This allows us to recover some of the time value, and creates a situation in which the option's loss of intrinsic value will be offset by some time value if the underlying security drops. Also, a 5 percent in-the-money nine-month option will have a lower implied volatility than a 5 percent six-month option.

Six months is a reasonable holding period for the index and the average return during that period is 5.57 percent, with a 9.63 percent standard deviation. The highest six-month return is 26.84 percent and the lowest is −31.48 percent. Almost a third of all returns are over 10 percent.

A nine-month, 5 percent in-the-money option with average implied volatility (that is, 19 percent) when held for six months has an average return of 16.6 percent with a 64.5 percent standard deviation. This assumes that the option can be sold at the same implied volatility, but that of course will depend upon the current level of short-term volatility, and the skew associated with the current market price as related to the strike price, so there is some additional risk.

CREATING THE DIAGONAL SPREAD

A spread on the index is created by buying a nine-month, 5 percent in-the-money call option, and selling a three-month at-the-money call option. The short call option is allowed to expire, which may create a liability and a cash outflow if the index appreciates. Still, in that event the long option would have gained in value also, and could be sold for a profit.

Under average conditions, as the index appreciates, the long option builds appreciation faster than the time decay, but the short option does not, resulting in profits on both positions. When volatility rises and falls, it affects the profitability of both options and should still maintain the spread, although of course any difference in implied volatilities between the two options should always be monitored, as that will contribute to profitability.

Of course, the index can also be unpredictable, and two other scenarios are possible. Windfalls happen when the index is flat for three months and then rises suddenly, and liabilities are created when the reverse happens. The latter is sometimes known as a "deadly" diagonal, as cash would be consumed at the midpoint of the investment, but no profits are ultimately realized. The occurrence is statistically rare and doesn't happen very often in the historical data set for the S&P 500, but the scenario still needs to be considered.

The percentage gain on the diagonal, assuming average appreciation and a sale of the long option at the same volatility, is 24.79 percent in the six-month period. This is the total return, and doesn't take into account the difference in the timing of cash flows, that is, the fact that a cash outflow occurs at the three-month mark that isn't recovered until the end of the six-month period. In this circumstance, the long option holds its value while the short option decays.

Using S&P 500 return data from 1990 to 2007, we can calculate the cost and payoff of the two call options assuming average volatility. We find that the position costs 7.05 to enter (if the index is scaled to a value of 100), the average payout at the three-month mark is −4.23, and the total payout at the six-month mark is 13.32, for a 14.5 percent return over the six-month period (see Table 9.1).

Although the possibility of a loss of both options due to a sharp rise followed by a decline tends to attract attention and does lead to a few losses in the historical data set in excess of 100 percent (4 out of 167), most of the negative returns are simply the result of poor performance in the underlying security. There is an 80 percent correlation between the six-month index return and the return of the call spread.

TABLE 9.1 Cost and Expected Returns of the Diagonal Spread

Now	Days	Market	Strike	Years	Rate	Vol.	Price
			Initial Purchase				
Long	270	100.00	95.00	0.74	0.05	0.20	11.63
Short	90	100.00	100.00	0.25	0.05	0.19	4.38
Cost							7.25
		Average Appreciation, 2.5% in 3 Months, 5% in 6 Months					
Long	90.00	105.00	95.00	0.25	0.05	0.20	11.80
Short	0.00	102.50	100.00	0.00	0.05	0.19	2.50
Cost							9.30
% Gain							28.28%

	% Return	Cost	3-Month	6-Month
Avg.	14.5%	−7.05	−4.23	13.32
Std.	62.5%	0.00	4.51	7.27
Min.	−100.0%	−7.05	−20.17	0.00
Max.	183.8%	−7.05	0.00	33.01

OPTION PORTFOLIO

The holding period of the two options would lead to a long-short portfolio and a quarterly timeline, as follows:

Long call @ 95 expires in 9 months

Short call @ 100 expires in 3 months

Long call @ 92.5 expires in 6 months

The third option is the "holdover" from last quarter—the nine month @ 95 call option after three months of average appreciation. The combination of the three options creates a leveraged position on the index with relatively high delta, and our six-month deep-in-the-money is designed to capture index appreciation cost-effectively.

We can calculate the cost potential return for this options portfolio given potential returns on the underlying and an average volatility and not including the volatility skew, which has a minor effect on the profitability of the long options (see Table 9.2).

From this perspective it becomes clear that a sharp positive index return that makes the short call option a liability isn't a real concern. If the index were to increase 10 percent suddenly, the appreciation would be captured by both of the long options, and when the short option payment is due, the second long call option would also be sold, ensuring no significant cash outflow.

Again, the real danger is simply that the underlying performs poorly, wiping out the value of the long options. If the drop is small, some of the loss will be offset by an increase in time value, but if it is large, then significant losses are unavoidable. Our only consolation is that such losses would be statistically rare, and over the life of our investment we would expect more sharp gains than losses. This portfolio would be characterized as neutral-bullish.

It should be noted that this options, portfolio provides uneven leverage—the leverage ratio is greater on the downside than the upside. For example, a 5 percent gain in the value of the underlying index is a +17.4 percent increase in the portfolio, but a 5 percent decline in the underlying leads to a −33.8 percent drop.

This asymmetry is a consequence of the expiration dates and strike prices selected and is somewhat offset by the portfolio's ability to provide positive returns even when the underlying is flat—a characteristic that a typical leveraged investment would not have. However, it needs to be well understood; otherwise, an investor may be left wondering how an 8 percent decline in the underlying index over three months could lead to a

TABLE 9.2　Option Portfolio Returns Based upon Index Returns

	Long #1	Short #1	Long #2	Cost		
Initial Value	11.3	−4.38	11.77	19.01		

% Return	Long #1	Short #1	Long #2	Value	% Return	Leverage Multiplier
−10%	3.88	0.00	3.13	7.01	−63.1%	6.31
−9%	4.34	0.00	3.61	7.95	−58.2%	6.46
−8%	4.83	0.00	4.14	8.97	−52.8%	6.60
−7%	5.36	0.00	4.71	10.06	−47.1%	6.73
−6%	5.91	0.00	5.31	11.22	−41.0%	6.83
−5%	6.49	0.00	5.96	12.45	−34.5%	6.90
−4%	7.10	0.00	6.64	13.74	−27.7%	6.93
−3%	7.74	0.00	7.36	15.10	−20.6%	6.86
−2%	8.41	0.00	8.11	16.52	−13.1%	6.56
−1%	9.10	0.00	8.89	17.99	−5.4%	5.38
0%	9.82	0.00	9.70	19.51	2.6%	
1%	10.56	−1.00	10.53	20.09	5.7%	5.66
2%	11.32	−2.00	11.39	20.71	8.9%	4.46
3%	12.11	−3.00	12.26	21.37	12.4%	4.13
4%	12.91	−4.00	13.16	22.07	16.1%	4.01
5%	13.73	−5.00	14.07	22.80	19.9%	3.98
6%	14.57	−6.00	14.99	23.56	23.9%	3.99
7%	15.43	−7.00	15.93	24.35	28.1%	4.01
8%	16.30	−8.00	16.87	25.17	32.4%	4.05
9%	17.18	−9.00	17.83	26.01	36.8%	4.09
10%	18.08	−10.00	18.79	26.87	41.3%	4.13

−53 percent loss, while a 10 percent gain in the underlying delivers only a +32 percent profit.

CYCLING FRACTIONAL AND FIXED

The difficulty in using this diagonal call spread in a cycling strategy is that each investment is not unique. If a single six-month call is purchased in January, February, March, and so on through June, then we would expect for the returns of those calls to be similar, as many of the months that make up the corresponding six-month returns would overlap.

This means that any monthly investment strategy we choose would have a high chance of several positive or several negative returns in a row. If the cycling strategy required the investor to invest 10 percent of the available cash on hand every month, then over a six-month period, they would find that almost half of the portfolio was invested in positions with a high degree of correlation, and if the index faltered, all of this money would be lost.

Distributions of returns in which positive and negative returns are clustered rather than independent and leverage is applied can lead to peak-and-valley effects in which the fund can lose 80 percent in a downturn and then grow 500 percent when the market recovers. This creates a lot of risk, and of course success becomes very dependent upon market timing, that is, exactly when the investor enters and exits the portfolio.

The risk is also increased because there are circumstances in which the diagonal could have a loss in excess of 100 percent of its investment—that is, when the short call is bought back at a loss, and then the index declines and the long call has a loss as well. This makes trying to determine a "safe" amount to invest difficult.

Instead of cycling a fraction of our portfolio through the options position, we could standardize on a fixed amount, and increase it gradually. This would help prevent overinvesting during an upturn or downturn and would reduce the volatility. Also, the risk and payoff of a fixed investment is conceptually easier to understand and predict.

For example, $10,000 worth of diagonal calls is purchased on the index every month and the average return is about 20 percent, providing roughly $2,000 of income per month. However, the income is uneven, and in some twelve-month periods $15,000 is gained, and in others $10,000 is lost. Figure 9.1 shows the net cumulative gain.

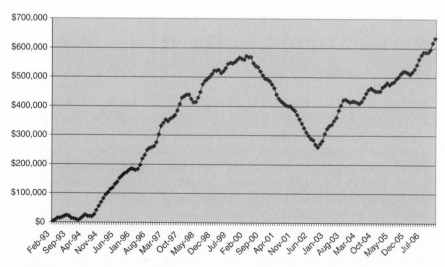

FIGURE 9.1 $10K + 5% Annual Repeated Investments

This portfolio starts at zero and has the potential to go negative when losses outpace gains for a period, but over the long term would be expected to return $24,000 a year. In this example, it never goes negative, but does have some close calls—once early in the life of the investment, and once during the 2003 downturn.

When the portfolio has $500,000+ in gains, continuing to invest $10,000 or $15,000 a month may seem needlessly conservative, but there is still always the possibility that an investor could invest for 24 months at that level and receive little or no return, or perhaps even negative returns, and that has to be taken into account.

FASTER REINVESTMENT

Could we make our options portfolio more amenable to a cycling strategy? First, instead of using a six-month holding period for our long call options and a three-month period for our short call options, we could use the same holding period—that is, three months. This eliminates the cash flow timing issues and the possibility of losses in excess of 100 percent.

Then we have to ensure that our investments are independent. Investments will only be made once every three months rather than monthly, and this helps us ensure that losses on one set of options won't spill over into another. Of course, extended downturns are still possible, but one quarter's losses would only result in a single loss, rather than three.

Selling our nine-month option after just three months rather than continuing to hold it for the six-month period reduces our returns, but also significantly affects the standard deviation of those returns. Our average three-month return becomes 10.76 percent, but with a 22.41 percent standard deviation.

Note that this return is calculated based upon our ability to sell our option at the same implied volatility that we bought it. As a rule, appreciation would result in an increase in implied volatility, and a decline would lead to a reduction, but it can be difficult to make categorical assumptions.

However, when we randomize the implied volatility used in pricing the long option's value at sale, neither the return nor the standard deviation change significantly, because in some quarters it results in a gain, and in others it's a loss, and that effect isn't as pronounced as the impact of market movements. It only adds about 3 percent or 4 percent to our standard deviation (see Table 9.3).

Next, we have to select a fraction to invest. Even though our standard deviation of returns is low, we shouldn't delude ourselves into thinking that multiple double-digit losses aren't possible. We can calculate

TABLE 9.3 Effect of Random Volatility on a Diagonal Spread

Long	270	100.00	95.00	0.74	0.05	0.21	11.92	0.58	0.40
Short	90	100.00	100.00	0.25	0.05	0.19	4.38	0.18	0.08
						Cost	7.54		

	Payoff	% Return
Avg.	8.35	10.57%
Std.	1.69	27.40%
Min.	1.53	−87.73%
Max.	10.02	72.90%

that at 40 percent invested per cycle, three back-to-back cycles with 50 percent losses would wipe out about 49 percent of our portfolio in a nine-month period (50% × 40%) ∧ 3 = 51.2%). We decide that this risk is acceptable due to our portfolio's long-term nature and its ability to recover from losses, and settle on that fraction. At this level of reinvestment, we grow our portfolio 10.4× over a period of about 13 years, as shown in Figure 9.2. This portfolio still has peaks and valleys, of course, and in the downturn gives up about 40 percent of its value due to circumstances similar to the above—multiple double-digit declines in a two-year period. But it

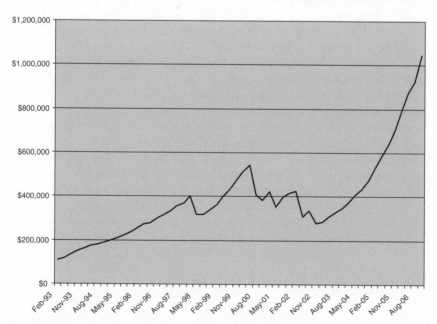

FIGURE 9.2 Weekly Calendar Call Strategy Cumulative Returns

recovers rapidly and climbs to new heights. Note that these calculations do include an estimated 5 percent annual interest earned on the withheld capital, which makes a significant contribution.

If this level of risk is too high, we can try a smaller fraction, for example 20 percent. If we multiply the average three-month return, 12 percent, by 20 percent we get a 2.4 percent average three-month return, which doesn't sound very exciting, but if we add in the 80 percent of the portfolio invested in risk-free securities, that adds another percentage point. But the real benefit would be the reduction in risk, and at some points portfolio volatility would be even lower than the S&P 500 itself.

TRANSACTION AND SPREAD COSTS

This analysis doesn't include transaction costs, which would be expected to be minimal on a quarterly strategy; after all, only four spreads are purchased a year. But there are some hidden costs that investors need to be aware of.

The first is that the bid-ask spread will have a significant impact on profitability. On SPX options, this spread is generally only about $1 or so on a $1,300+ index, and therefore, as a proportion to the underlying, it is very low. However, if the investor is buying and selling $40 spreads, losing $4 in the transaction represents a very large hurdle. This is one reason that it may be more cost-effective to hold a three-month or six-month position than three or six one-month positions.

The second is that differences in the implied volatilities between the long and short option will have an impact and could cut profitability significantly. Buying a call option with 22.8 percent implied volatility and selling one with 21.2 percent may seem like a minor difference, but there is enough of a shortfall in those two positions to cut the profitability significantly, especially if both options are at or near the money.

A combination that is used here and often works well is a long slightly in-the-money option (5 percent for example) and a short at-the-money option. Both volatilities are generally close in value, and in high volatility periods, the short option may even have a higher implied volatility than the long option. Then, if volatility remains high beyond the expiry of the short option, the long option can be sold at a premium.

FAST CYCLING WITH CALENDARS

We've seen how adjustments in the long and short options can create a position that is independent enough for cycling, but still profitable. What if we selected options with even shorter time frames and higher average profitability? Could we get dozens of cycles every year and have the opportunity to grow our portfolio exponentially?

We can modify our strategy by using calendar call spreads on front month and second month options. In a calendar call spread, we profit when the volatility of the underlying security is low, but take losses when the index rises or falls sharply.

Using front-month options would limit our number of cycles to twelve per year, one per month of options, but actually we can purchase multiple calendar call spreads a month and sell them before expiry. If we make our first purchase four weeks from expiry, and then sell that spread two weeks from expiry, and then purchase a new spread that is held to expiry, we would be able to cycle our investment twice per month, or twenty-four times a year. (See Table 9.4)

The issue that we would run into is transaction costs, so this strategy is only feasible for investors who work with brokers with low transaction costs and bid-ask spreads. The bid-ask spread is also dependent upon the index used, and this constraint would certainly restrict us to only the most liquid of indexes, such as the S&P 500.

Also, a hidden cost is the implied volatility spread between the front-month and second-month option. Because long-term options tend to have higher implied volatilities than short-term options, there will be a tendency for an option's implied volatility to drop a little over time, and this effect would be independent of the volatility skew. For many options positions

TABLE 9.4 Calendar Call Spread Purchase Schedule for March, April, and May

Week	Buy	Sell	
0	April Call @ 100	March Call @ 100	
3	March Call @ 100	April Call @ 100	
3	April Call @ 100	March Call @ 100	
5	March Call @ 100	April Call @ 100	March Expires
5	May Call @ 100	April Call @ 100	
7	April Call @ 100	May Call @ 100	
7	May Call @ 100	April Call @ 100	
9	April Call @ 100	May Call @ 100	April Expires
9	June Call @ 100	May Call @ 100	
11	May Call @ 100	June Call @ 100	
11	June Call @ 100	May Call @ 100	
13	May Call @ 100	June Call @ 100	May Expires

this may not be significant, but given the razor-thin margins on repeated front-month calendar calls, every penny matters.

Sample Run

In the following example, we use actual weekly S&P 500 index ETF returns for a thirteen-week period in the start of 2007. The call options are priced according to the level of the VIX on those dates. A 5 percent interest rate is used, and prices are dividend-adjusted. The results are shown in Table 9.5.

The returns for the six calendar spreads range from −27.6 percent to +51.4 percent. If we start with an initial portfolio of $100,000, and allocate 25 percent of it to each two or three week cycle, our portfolio grows in some cycles and shrinks in others, but ends the period with $128,393, not including any accumulated interest.

Of course, large drawdowns are also possible with this strategy due to subsequent negative returns, and there is the implicit assumption that the weekly returns are uncorrelated and independent.

This model assumes no transaction costs, and that an investor can sell their option for the implied volatility of the current level of the VIX. The simplest way to add in extra costs is to reduce the amount of the return for each calendar spread by 10 percent, a catchall expense that reflects the bid-ask spread, transaction costs, and slight increase in implied volatility for the longer-term options.

TABLE 9.5 Calendar Call Strategy Returns, First 13 Weeks of 2007

Weekly	Index Return	Cost	Payoff	No Transaction Costs		With Transaction Costs	
				Return	Equity	Return	Equity
1	1.49%				$100,000		$100,000
2	−0.02%						
3	−0.58%	1.22	1.49	+21.7%	$105,419	+11.68%	$102,919
4	1.84%						
5	−0.71%	1.49	2.02	+35.6%	$114,800	+25.59%	$109,505
6	1.22%						
7	−0.30%	1.29	1.49	+15.8%	$119,334	+5.80%	$111,092
8	−4.41%						
9	1.13%	1.49	1.08	−27.6%	$111,092	−37.63%	$100,642
10	−1.13%						
11	3.54%	1.29	1.41	+9.6%	$113,772	−0.35%	$100,554
12	−1.06%						
13	1.61%	1.49	2.26	+51.4%	$128,393	+41.40%	$110,962

When this expense is added in, the returns drop significantly and $17,000 is lost. For repeated strategies, management of expenses is crucial, and this means doing whatever it takes in order to uncover the security and brokerage with the lowest transaction costs.

VOLATILITY MODELING

Before going much further in our cycling strategy, it's important to highlight a critical aspect of the model: volatility. Modeling volatility is one of the most difficult aspects of financial modeling and forecasting. Over time, both the historic and implied volatility of the index changes; and this affects the return distribution.

The standard approach to this problem is to vary the volatility over time and generate a series of returns using this volatility. In order to better approximate the conditions of financial markets, this volatility is "clustered," and the series will have periods of low volatility interspersed with periods of high volatility; this makes volatility mean-reverting over time.

These approaches are referred to as a stochastic process, and this specific method would be a GARCH process. GARCH or similar models can be used for modeling both discrete and continuous prices, that is, either daily or weekly prices, or prices that change every minute or second, which is a requirement for traders. Of course, continuous prices will also have jumps, or points in time in which the prices move suddenly, such as after an earnings release.

When using investment performance models with complex volatility calculations, the returns are often a function of the inputs, and the internal behaviors can be difficult to follow. A hidden assumption may show a strategy as more profitable than it actually is.

A problem is that modeling one single volatility is not enough—the implied volatility relationships between options must also be calculated, and at some points the long-dated options have lower volatility than shorter-term options, or the spread may change between in-the-money and out-of-the-money options, or between puts and calls. Or perhaps the market just breaks down and bid-ask spreads widen so much that no option is profitable.

In our opinion, the best models are those that are simple and have assumptions that are easy to vary, and that even under standard conditions generate many different types of profitable and unprofitable scenarios that can be analyzed. This makes it easy to determine the boundary conditions for a strategy and to be able to identify potential market conditions that could make it more or less successful.

WEEKLY VOLATILITY SIMULATION

In order to simulate the long-term return of the rapid cycling strategy, we start with an average weekly compounded return of 0.18 percent, which, when annualized, equals the 10 percent historical average. Then every week, we allow the volatility to drift upward and downward at random and use that figure to generate a return based upon the long-term appreciation assumption and the current volatility.

For example, if our model starts at a volatility of 15 percent, the long-term average for the S&P 500, that translates into a weekly volatility of 15%/sqrt(52), or 2.08 percent, and the index return for that week is calculated using that random factor. But if next week the volatility increases to 18 percent, then the return is calculated using the same weekly appreciation, but the new, higher volatility.

The weekly increase or decrease in volatility is calculated as a random percentage based upon observed volatility fluctuations over the 1990 to 2007 time period. On average, volatility increased 0.6 percent a week but with an 11.47 percent standard deviation. We can use that variation as the basis of an assumption that allows us to vary our volatility by a random amount that in turn increases or decreases the standard deviation of our index returns.

As an aside, this 11.5 percent would vary over time—if we analyze 52-week sets of VIX returns, we find that the standard deviation of the weekly percentage changes in the VIX varies from about 8 percent to 15 percent. What's important is that we ensure that the VIX is capable of either doubling or halving within a three-month period and then remaining at that level for a significant period of time.

Of course, the VIX is not the actual volatility—it is a market estimate of future volatility that generally trades at a premium. We can simulate that premium by simply multiplying our internal volatility by 25 percent, the long-term difference between implied and historical volatility. This premium changes over time and is higher some years and lower in others, but has averaged 25 percent from 1990, and this assumption is discussed further in a later chapter.

In Table 9.6, the VIX rises from 18 percent to 30 percent while the actual volatility increases from 15 percent to 25 percent. The index remains flat during most of the period, but then suffers an 8 percent decline in the last two weeks due to the volatility spike and bad luck—the returns could have just as easily been 8 percent higher.

The weekly returns provided by this relatively simple model look reasonable and like a scenario we would expect to see in the actual index. While this type of series would not be sufficient for a complex

TABLE 9.6 Random Volatility Influencing Returns

Week	Index Start	Vol.	VIX	Weekly Vol.	Index Return		Index Volatility	
					Rand()	Change	Rand()	Change
0	100.00	15.00%	18.00%	2.08%	0.41	-0.30%	0.40	-3.02%
1	99.70	14.55%	17.46%	2.02%	0.48	0.10%	0.66	4.73%
2	99.80	15.24%	18.28%	2.11%	0.86	2.44%	0.75	7.90%
3	102.24	16.44%	19.73%	2.28%	0.63	0.96%	0.79	9.19%
4	103.22	17.95%	21.54%	2.49%	0.37	-0.63%	0.31	-5.68%
5	102.56	16.93%	20.32%	2.35%	0.42	-0.31%	0.91	15.30%
6	102.24	19.52%	23.42%	2.71%	0.62	0.99%	0.34	-4.77%
7	103.26	18.59%	22.31%	2.58%	0.20	-1.97%	0.34	-4.61%
8	101.22	17.73%	21.28%	2.46%	0.19	-1.96%	0.61	3.13%
9	99.24	18.29%	21.94%	2.54%	0.76	2.00%	0.89	14.24%
10	101.22	20.89%	25.07%	2.90%	0.41	-0.49%	0.93	16.81%
11	100.72	24.40%	29.28%	3.38%	0.04	-5.62%	0.59	2.69%
12	95.07	25.06%	30.07%	3.48%	0.22	-2.49%	0.38	-3.43%
13	92.70							

program-trading simulation that used required accurate daily pricing, as a simple technique for providing realistic sample weekly index returns and implied volatilities it is sufficient.

WEEKLY STRATEGY RETURNS

In a Monte Carlo analysis, we assumed that both the long or short at-the-money call could be purchased at the current level of the VIX. Given these assumptions, our average return for a two- or three-week calendar-call spread is about 10 or 11 percent with a 45 percent standard deviation. Interestingly, there is not a significant difference between the average returns of two-week or three-week calendar-call spreads, or between calendar-call spreads exited at expiration or sold two weeks before.

A 10 percent return in two weeks is excellent, but clearly the risk is high. However, suppose we use this call spread position as the basis of a cycling strategy in which 25 percent of the portfolio is invested (see Table 9.7). Over the thirteen-week period, the portfolio gains approximately 16 percent on average with a 32 percent standard deviation of returns, and in four thirteen-week periods (that is, one year) the average return is +60 percent with an 88 percent standard deviation.

However, most of the standard deviation is a result of upside risk rather than downside, and annual returns ranged from −50 percent to +190 percent. The avoidance of sub-50 percent returns, which is partly a result of the 25 percent cycling strategy, prevents the portfolio from ever falling into a pit that can't be climbed out of.

TABLE 9.7   Weekly Strategy Returns for Three Months and One Year

Three-Month Portfolio Return, Cycling 25% Every Two Weeks	
Average	17.5%
Median	12.7%
Stdev	31.5%
Min.	−40.7%
Max.	137.4%
One-Year Portfolio Return, Cycling 25% Every Two Weeks	
Average	96.2%
Median	55.6%
Stdev	196.2%
Min.	−48.6%
Max.	192.3%

Like most leveraged, risky portfolios, over time the level of risk decreases and the returns become somewhat predictable. Also, the averages are pulled up as a result of the highest performing portfolios resulting in a mean higher than the median.

Over a five-year period, 74 percent of portfolios are profitable, one-third of portfolios have doubled in value, and 14 percent have tripled or better. The median portfolio return is only +50 percent, but the mean portfolio return is +90 percent, and the top 10 percent of portfolios have gained +300 percent to +400 percent.

Note that this portfolio has no built-in transaction costs. With options held for only one or two weeks, managing these costs would be critical, as it would be very easy for a wide bid-ask spread to eliminate all of the profit from a two-week option.

Therefore, while cycling daily or even hourly calendar-call spreads would be possible with no transaction costs, their existence requires the investor to make some trade-offs as to the holding period of the position and the cycling frequency. Generally, the higher the transaction costs, the longer the holding period required, and the longer the associated cycle would have to be.

With reasonable transaction costs, four- or six-week positions would likely provide higher returns on highly liquid securities such as the S&P 500 index or Russell 2000. For other securities with higher costs, the investor may be limited to only three-month positions.

SUMMARY

In this chapter, we developed profitable call spread strategies using both diagonal call spreads and calendar call spreads on the S&P 500 index. Like all spreads, these two option positions allow us to purchase a more profitable call option and fund that purchase through the sale of a less profitable call option.

In previous chapters we determined that longer-term options and in-the-money options are more cost-effective and have higher returns, on average, than shorter-term at-the-money options. A diagonal spread is constructed using an in-the-money nine-month call option and an at-the-money three-month option and we estimate its profitability under average appreciation and volatility conditions at approximately 25 percent for a six-month period.

When the long option position is held for six months, but the short option is held for only three, a long-short options portfolio is created, and we can use standard assumptions to value that portfolio given various appreciation conditions. We find that the payoff is asymmetric and our position can lose value quickly as the index declines, but will not gain in value quite as quickly if the index appreciates, and this lowers the expected six-month return somewhat and makes risk management a little more complex.

Diagonal calls also typically have issues with cash flow timings, as the investor may not have enough cash to pay for the liability created by the short call option. However, the holding period of the nine-month option exactly coincides with the selling schedule of the short option, eliminating this potential danger.

Still, the position can be made more predictable by holding the long option for only three months, rather than six months. While the average return of the position is lower, the increased predictability improves risk management and allows investment returns to be immediately reinvested, facilitating compounding.

Generally, cycling is done by repeatedly reinvesting a fixed fraction of the portfolio. However, when the standard deviation is high, even small fractions can result in investment returns that are, for all practical purposes, random. In these cases it can be better to instead invest a fixed amount each cycle, and slowly grow that amount over time by, for example, 5 percent per year.

Converting the diagonal spread into a position with a standard three-month holding period allowed us to reduce the standard deviation of the return and invest more of our capital. In an S&P 500 backtest analysis in which 40 percent of our portfolio capital was invested every three months in the position, over a thirteen-year period the portfolio grew from $100,000 to $1,044,400, an annual return of 17.4 percent per year, or at about twice the rate of the S&P 500.

This is a somewhat conservative cycling strategy, and we introduced one that is much more rapid and aggressive by using at-the-money calendar call spreads with a holding period of two weeks and investing 25 percent of the portfolio in this strategy. Over an average three-month period, this strategy bought and sold six call spreads, and in a sample three-month period in early 1997 would have gained almost 30 percent.

In order to develop a long-term forecast, it was necessary to develop a model for simulating volatility. We introduced a simple method where the real and implied volatility varied every month and returns were generated using this volatility. Using this model, the average three-month appreciation was calculated at approximately 16 percent for a three-month period and the average annual return is 90 percent due to the higher upside potential.

Still, call spreads are very sensitive to transaction costs, and a bi-weekly strategy would not generally be feasible unless the index used is extremely liquid and the bid-ask spreads are very low. When cycling is rapid, even small transaction costs can wipe out a large amount of profit and depress the ratio of reward to risk.

We should point out that neither of these strategies is specifically promoted as superior, and that these are primarily presented as a framework for creating profitable spread strategies. Call spreads that are long the index and hold intrinsic value and sell time will generally be profitable but with wide standard deviations. But, as always, a well-planned cycling strategy is needed to control the exposure of the portfolio to this reward and risk.

CHAPTER 10

Practical Hedging with Put Spreads

T he last few chapters presented a number of different investment strategies using long and short call options to capture long-term profits from the index. Typically the long call options provided the profits, while the short call options helped lower the initial investment and manage the risk.

This chapter presents investment strategies using long and short put options; as a result, the roles of the long and short options change. Long put options primarily control portfolio risk, while short put options help fund the purchase of long options and also provide investment profits.

Much of the emphasis of the chapter is on portfolio protection, and assumes that the investor is holding a leveraged long index portfolio using call options, index futures, or some similar security. However, because put options are very expensive, the addition of short put options is often needed to make a hedging strategy more affordable and cost-effective.

Two bullish strategies are also discussed: the bull put spread and the calendar put spread. Bull put spreads have some flaws that make consistent profitability difficult, and as a result more time is spent discussing calendar put spreads. These positions can be extremely profitable and can also provide enormous flexibility when used in conjunction with a leveraged portfolio.

ABOUT PUT OPTIONS

A put option is a hedging tool that allows an investor to eliminate some or all of the downside risk of a security in exchange for an upfront payment. Like call options, put options have a strike price, an expiration date, and a rate of interest built into the security, and are priced using a specific implied volatility.

This implied volatility is, on average, higher than the historic and actual volatility, which creates either an extra expense or profit opportunity, depending upon whether the position is long or short. Selling puts is profitable on average, but with occasional extreme losses that are many times the value of the premium.

Conversely, to own a put option is to own a security that has a negative expected return, but that still has enough volatility to deliver extremely high positive returns occasionally. A particular 50-cent put option might be expected to expire worthless 95 percent of the time but also to provide +500 percent returns in the rare event of a market crash.

Put options are referred to as out-of-the-money (OTM) when the strike price is lower than market and the owner has no incentive to exercise it, given current prices. OTM put options are less expensive than ATM or ITM put options in absolute terms, but are priced with a higher implied volatility. At the lowest strike prices, put options are either incredibly cheap or incredibly expensive, depending upon one's perspective.

An American-style put option provides the owner with the ability to exercise it at any time before expiry, and this gives it more value than a European-style option. Early exercise becomes advantageous when a put option is significantly in-the-money and its hedging value is low, because the owner can take the profits immediately rather than waiting for the option to expire, and as a result the options are priced higher than their counterparts.

SELLING PUTS VERSUS COVERED CALLS

Many beginning investors are eager to sell covered calls but shy away from short puts, not understanding that the two strategies are equivalent. In both strategies, an investor commits capital either by holding cash margin or purchasing a security, and then agrees to take an undetermined potential loss that could be several times the amount of premium.

Put options often have higher implied volatility than calls, which raises the premium, and short positions tend to require less capital. This makes put selling strategies more profitable, as a rule, but also increases risk. The liabilities associated with puts can sometimes arise suddenly and unexpectedly.

When American-style put options are used, an unexpected market drop may lead to the short option being exercised. When this happens, the investor's market position is essentially unchanged, as the purchased long stock will have the same delta as the deep-in-the-money short put option that it was exchanged for.

However, because stock is exchanged for the put option, the investor will likely be over the margin limit and will need to liquidate the shares. This would also effectively close out any spread strategy at a loss if the initial position is bullish.

While most options on ETFs are American-style options, generally options on indexes are European-style options and can only be exercised on the last day—or, more specifically, they are auto-exercised on the last day if they are in-the-money. This eliminates the early assignment risk, but theoretically adds one more risk for the mismatched positions.

If an investor is short a put option that expires in February, for example, and is long a put option that expires in March, there is no guarantee that when February arrives and that put option is in-the-money, requiring a cash payment, that the March option can be sold to offset this potential loss.

Of course, if the market is functioning properly, any other investor should be willing to buy the in-the-money March option for at least its intrinsic value and then those proceeds can be applied to the February liability. But the investor that holds this type of position should be aware that the risk is that there could be turmoil in the market, and that they would not be able to sell their March option and close out the February option except by taking a loss.

SELLER RISK IN PRICING

Put options are extremely expensive. It can cost as much as 2 percent to 3 percent to insure against a potential drop in the S&P 500 for a single month, and prices rise even further when the market has fallen, investors are fearful, and demand for put options is high.

The prices in Table 10.1 may seem especially high given the average historical appreciation of the S&P 500, which is only about 10 percent a year or 0.78 percent a month. But put option prices have nothing to do with expected appreciation, but instead are priced based upon the potential loss on the security within the given time frame. In the short-term, the index is very unpredictable, and that drives the security pricing.

TABLE 10.1   Put Option Pricing vs. Expected Index Appreciation

Days	Market	Strike	Years	Rate	Vol.	Price	Expected Appreciation
30	100.00	100.00	0.08	0.05	0.19	1.97	0.80
60	100.00	100.00	0.16	0.05	0.19	2.67	1.60
90	100.00	100.00	0.25	0.05	0.19	3.16	2.41
180	100.00	100.00	0.49	0.05	0.19	4.13	4.88
360	100.00	100.00	0.99	0.05	0.19	5.18	10.00
720	100.00	100.00	1.97	0.05	0.19	6.10	21.00

If we consider the situation from the perspective of the seller of the put option, it becomes clear from the historical data that it is not easy to implement a profitable and predictable strategy around put selling.

From January 1990 to November 2007, a 214-month period, the S&P 500 lost value in 78 months, lost more than 2 percent in 48 months, and lost more than 5 percent in 16 months. The average loss on a put option, calculated by dividing the 78 months, worth of losses by the 214 total months, is −1.2 percent, and if the average put option costs about 2.5 percent of the value of the index, then the profit on each option is approximately 1.3 percent.

The two worst losses occurred in August 1998 and September 2002, in which the index lost −14.6 percent and −11.0 percent respectively. This suggests that in order to write an option for a month, a seller would need to be absolutely certain that he or she could withstand at least a 15 percent loss in the index and remain solvent.

This requires having reserve capital in place, and then additional capital beyond that in order to continue to write more options—after all, no trader wants to get wiped out by a single transaction.

But even that amount of margin may not provide safety. In 2002, the S&P 500 suffered five monthly declines in excess of 5 percent, and fell more than 25 percent for the year. If losses follow each other in quick succession, then it is difficult to say what starting level of capital would be sufficient for a put writing strategy to withstand an extended downturn.

Put option prices are also impacted by the role of the exchange, which has the goal of minimizing or eliminating counterparty risk. The exchange is certainly aware of the historical data, and wants to ensure that in the event of significant market movements, the funds are available to pay the holder of an option, and thus has an incentive to set the cash margin requirements for an uncovered put option as high as possible.

When the cash margin requirements are high, then the costs of selling OTM put options rises, and put option sellers then raise their own prices in order to compensate. And many also believe that supply and demand plays a role in OTM put option pricing, as there are generally more market participants that are willing to purchase portfolio protection rather than provide it.

PROTECTING PORTFOLIOS

Faced with the historical data, perhaps puts seem cheap, as they create a situation in which an investor can take a smaller, guaranteed loss immediately rather than maintain an expensive cash reserve in anticipation of a potential large loss. Reducing risk in one part of the portfolio can provide the opportunity to invest more aggressively elsewhere.

Still, it is also critical to understand how the addition of a put option to a portfolio changes its return distribution. Any investment portfolio has not only an expected return, but also a range of potential returns, from extreme losses to flat performance to extreme gains.

Adding a put option to a portfolio eliminates or reduces potential losses, and the result would always be a higher expected return for the portfolio. However, this is before one takes into account the cost of the put option.

If the cost of a put option were less than or exactly equal to the portfolio losses it prevented, then buying a put option would be an easy decision. Investors would always purchase the hedge, and thereby reduce their portfolio risk.

Of course, there would be many situations in which the hedge would be unnecessary, but those would be balanced out by the scenarios in which it was helpful. The average portfolio return would remain the same or improve, and the volatility would decline.

Unfortunately, in the financial markets, the price of a put option is significantly higher than the average financial benefit provided. The result is that hedging is expensive and reduces the breakeven point and the expected returns for a portfolio.

As an example, suppose that an index investor has the opportunity to purchase a put option that protects against a drop of 10 percent or more in the value of the index in the next year, but it carries a cost of 3 percent of the value of the index. We will assume a $100,000 portfolio, and the cost of the hedge is $3,000.

The maximum loss for this portfolio is not $10,000 but $13,000, due to the cost of the hedge. We know that we will have at least $87,000 to invest at the end of next year, and that provides some certainty. Also, the potential gains are unlimited, and if the index appreciates 10 percent as expected, we will make $7,000 after hedging costs.

However, $7,000 is not the best estimate for our one-year return. If we assume that the put option is somewhat overpriced and only delivers $1,800 in real value, then $8,800 would be a better estimate. On average, $1,800 of protection is provided for a cost of $3,000.

Would the average investor be better off with this protection in place? In order to simulate the effect on this kind of hedge on long-term performance, 300+ index portfolios were simulated over a twenty-year period to find the answer, using historical average returns and volatilities.

Only one hedged portfolio out of the sample set had a significantly higher result at the end of the twenty-year period than its unhedged counterpart. Several others had comparable results, but on average the hedged portfolios had 40 percent less capital at the end of the twenty-year period. In more than 99 percent of portfolios with these characteristics, hedging either impaired performance or had no significant effect.

This is not to say that hedging is never needed or that a portfolio can never benefit, but given a sufficiently long period of time, the ability to compound at a higher rate is much more important than the ability to withstand losses. Single years of double-digit losses may seem catastrophic but actually have little effect on the portfolio; in contrast, the cumulative reduction of investment returns can do a lot of damage.

PUTS, FUTURES, AND LEVERAGE

When an investment portfolio uses leverage, gains and losses in the underlying security are magnified, and a market drop can be catastrophic. In this case, even if a put option is expensive, having one in place at the right time could be the difference between being able to recover from a loss and losing everything.

Leveraged portfolios can be created using futures contracts, and then protection can be purchased with put options. A futures contract on an index can be held with only 5 percent margin, resulting in a position that is leveraged 20:1, and then a put option limits the potential loss and protects the cash reserve.

The characteristics of the put option dictate the maximum loss of the position and as a result, the maximum leverage and cash reserve needed to keep investing. This could be done in either shorter or longer time frames.

For example, after the September 11, 2001, attacks the S&P 500 lost 11 percent of its value in a single week, and this type of event would wipe out any investor with 9× leverage or more. An investor could buy cheap weekly put options that prevent a 5 percent loss and thereby push the portfolio to 10× leverage, and would still have the confidence that if a drop of that magnitude occurs, about half of the portfolio would remain intact.

Or, an investor could prevent large drops over longer periods by purchasing LEAPS. During the post–dot-com downturn, the S&P 500 index fell more than 50 percent in a two-year period, and even a 2:1 leveraged investor could have been bankrupted. A LEAPS put option that limited this loss to 25 percent would allow the investor to hold on to their portfolio and continue investing for many more years.

Of course, for every hedging strategy that could be imagined, there is a corresponding series of returns that could devastate the portfolio. If the investor hedges against 3 percent monthly drops in the value of the index, then clearly twelve monthly drops of 2.9 percent in a row would lead to almost half of the portfolio being wiped out in a year's time. Still, the odds of that particular combination of returns occurring would be extremely unlikely.

DIVERSIFICATION AND CORRELATION

The high cost of hedging a portfolio through put options is a strong encouragement to find other, more cost-effective forms of portfolio protection. The first and often the best choice is generally intelligent diversification through security selection. With smart asset allocation, the downside risk of a portfolio can be reduced substantially.

If portfolio assets had no correlation, then in theory it would be possible to create portfolios with little or no risk and highly predictable returns by purchasing hundreds or thousands of securities. Unfortunately for investors, just about all equities are correlated to some degree, and this limits diversification opportunities.

However, the level of correlation is often misunderstood and overstated. Indexes that have an 80 percent or 90 percent correlation can still have very different returns on a weekly or monthly basis, and by the end of the year, the cumulative differences could be very large. If the difference every month is one to two points, then by the end of the year one index may be ten points higher than the other.

Also, correlations will change over time. One challenge of investing during a cyclical downturn is trying to determine exactly what kinds of stocks will be perceived as "defensive" at any point, as the classification isn't always consistent.

Still, if two securities are correlated and provide similar returns, then a put option on one security may help protect against a decline in the other.

This technique can sometimes be used to cost-effectively hedge a position by purchasing a put option on the less volatile and therefore less expensive security.

For example, if an investor has a position in finance industry stocks and finds them expensive to hedge, he or she could instead purchase a put option on the S&P 500 index, with the reasoning being that the overall performance of securities in the finance industry would be expected to be closely correlated with those of the broader economy.

Of course, many securities or indexes have a beta coefficient that's higher than the S&P 500, and as a result would be expected to fall faster than the index in any broad downturn. In this case, to provide adequate protection an investor would have to buy a correspondingly higher ratio of index puts.

COLLARED PORTFOLIOS

Another method of portfolio protection is the collar. A collar is a transaction in which an investor owns an asset and then buys put options and sells call options on the underlying security, creating a price floor and a ceiling for a specified amount of time. The expense can be low or even zero if the proceeds from the sold call options are applied to the purchase of the put option.

Collars can help prevent large losses and can be very useful for leveraged investments in which such a loss would be magnified to the point where a portfolio is wiped out. A collar could be put in place for months or years and may have a very wide range.

In Table 10.2, puts are purchased and calls sold on the Russell 2000 for two years. Note that a collar should provide an identical payoff to a bull call spread, as it provides essentially the same service. An investor could buy a bull call spread at the specific low and high strike prices, and then put the remainder of funds in risk-free securities and achieve the same financial result.

As with a bull call spread, a collar will also suffer from the volatility skew. The OTM put option will usually have a higher volatility than the out-of-the-money call option. This effect can be reduced by purchasing longer-term options in which the implied volatilities are higher, as the skew wouldn't be as pronounced.

According to historical data, collaring returns on the S&P 500 or Russell 2000 would generally lead to lower returns, as there are many more extremely high returns than extremely low returns in the historical data, and this mismatch of extremes pulls the average upward. Still, a collar

TABLE 10.2 One-Year Collar Transaction on the Index

			Call Option			
Days	**Market**	**Strike**	**Years**	**Rate**	**Vol.**	**Price**
365	100.00	125.00	1.00	0.05	0.15	1.01

			Put Option			
Days	**Market**	**Strike**	**Years**	**Rate**	**Vol.**	**Price**
365	100.00	80.00	1.00	0.05	0.27	1.91
Cost of Collar						0.90

would result in a considerable reduction in the volatility of the fund, which could then be used to increase leverage.

BEAR PUT SPREADS AND SPEED BUMPS

A bear put spread is created by purchasing an out-of-the-money put option and then selling a put option at a lower strike price. The position profits when the underlying security closes at or below the lower strike price and as a result is a bearish position. Table 10.3 shows an example of a bear put spread in which both strike prices are below the market price of the security.

The result of this transaction is that losses in a falling security within a specific range are transferred to the counterparty. A 10-point loss would still be taken, but a 25-point loss becomes a 10-point loss. The investor can get up to 15 points worth of index appreciation for only $2.13.

This position is sometimes referred to as a speed bump, as it does not prevent losses on a falling security, but instead merely slows them down. If the underlying security were to fall 40 or 50 points, then significant losses would still be taken and the short option would build a large amount of intrinsic value, and would probably be exercised if it were an American-style option.

TABLE 10.3 Speed Bump Created with a Long and Short Put Option

	Days	Market	Strike	Years	Rate	Vol.	Price	One Year Cost	Per Day
Long	365	100.00	90.00	1.00	0.05	0.21	2.51	2.13	0.006
Short	365	100.00	75.00	1.00	0.05	0.21	0.39		

There are two other benefits to this position. One is that if the index falls 10 points and there is still some time left before expiry, then the long option would build time value and, if volatility is relatively high, could be sold for a significant profit. The key is to close the position before the second option builds significant value.

The second is that the implied volatility of the short option is almost always higher than the long option, and this reduces the cost of the bear put spread. This allows a position with negative delta to be created relatively cheaply.

Speed bumps can be put in place for long periods of time, as expiration dates for put options on the broad index are often available for two to three years. The initial delta of a bear put spread is low, but increases rapidly as the underlying security rises.

Thus for the life of the position, any decline in the value of the index will result in an increase in the value of the bear put spread and vice versa. Still, as is true for any spread, the maximum value is realized only by holding a profitable position to expiry.

Selecting the appropriate strike price and time to expiry is difficult for these positions and depends upon the volatility of the underlying. The challenge is not to overpay for the time value of the long option, at least as compared to the remaining life of the option. In general, a longer-term position will be more cost-effective than a shorter-term position for strike prices that are within 10 percent of the money.

BULL AND CALENDAR PUT SPREADS

There are two bullish positions using put option spreads: the bull put spread, and the calendar put spread. Both positions write put options with the intent of having them expire worthless, and both can also be used as the foundation for other types of spread positions that provide both hedging and profits.

A bull put spread is created by selling a put option on a security at a higher strike price with a specific expiration date, and then buying a similar option but with a lower strike price. Because of the strike price mismatch, a potential liability is created, and this must be met by holding cash margin.

Current Market Price: SPY = $132.06

Buy @ 125 exp 6/2008, 151d for $5.70 (IV = 26.73)

Sell @ 135 exp 6/2008, 151d for $9.25 (IV = 23.61)

Max profit = $3.55

Cash margin required = $10 (includes premium)

This position will generate its max profit of $3.55 if the index ETF closes higher than $135 in June and will be breakeven at $131.45 ($135 − $3.55). If it moves lower, the max loss will be $6.45 ($10 minus the $3.45 as premium).

Note that this position has some early exercise risk. If in three months SPY fell from $132 to $125, the short put option could be assigned, which would likely force the sale of the long option as well. Calculating the likelihood of early exercise risk can be difficult, but it is much more likely to occur when a dividend payment is involved, or if the put option is deep-in-the-money.

Another problem with this position is that the IV of the long put option is quite high, and that means there is little profit to be generated by selling a spread between the two options. The max profit, $3.55 per share, is relatively low considering that $10.00 in cash per share is at risk.

The combined initial delta of the position is only 0.27 at purchase. By expiry, it will be almost 1 if the current market price is maintained, but the increase will be gradual until just about the final month. Like bull call spreads, a bull put spread must be held to expiry in order to be profitable in most cases, as the position has low delta initially, and an early exit will incur transaction costs and would require buying back the short put option.

Selling it just a week before expiry would likely reduce the profit potential by a third or more, and as a result, many traders don't even consider purchasing a bull call spread or bull put spread unless the position has only a few weeks to expiry and will be held until that date.

CALENDAR PUT SPREAD

In a calendar put spread, a put option is sold at a specific strike price, usually at the money or close to it, and a second option purchased at the same strike price but with a later expiry. The position is a debit spread and has a very similar payoff to the calendar call spread but benefits to some extent from the higher volatilities on put options as compared to call options.

The short put option is held to expiry so that it expires or can be bought back relatively cheaply, and then the long put option with the later expiration date is sold. When the market price is close to the strike price at that time, the long put option will have a high time value and will be profitable.

Like calendar call spreads, calendar put spreads are like throwing a dart and trying to hit a mark. If the market price is much higher or much lower than the strike price of the two options at the expiry of the short option, then the position will take losses. But both calendar calls and puts have a broad target, and within a fairly wide range of market conditions, the calendar put spread position will be profitable or at least breakeven.

The position has vega risk and benefits from higher volatility, and in market conditions with high or even moderate volatility but no significant losses, calendar put spreads can be extremely profitable. This is often the case after a market drop—investors are fearful and volatility rises, but share prices are low enough that another large drop is less likely.

The problems occur when the market price drops significantly, for example by 5 percent or more. Not only does the time value of the long put option become worthless, but the position is also exposed to early exercise risk, in the case of an American option. If the short option is exercised, the investor will likely have no choice but to sell the long option and take the loss.

Calendar put spreads are very highly leveraged positions in which $1,000 may hold an interest in $50,000 or $100,000 worth of the underlying security. When the short put option expires or is bought back early, the long option needs to be sold immediately or the investor will be left holding a short position. This situation reduces the flexibility of the investor and creates a defined trading schedule.

Backtests of calendar put spread strategies are very similar to the results of the calendar call strategy discussed in Chapter 8. A repeated strategy on the S&P 500 has a slightly higher average profitability but also a higher standard deviation of monthly returns.

Also, like calendar call spreads and other spreads, the profitability of a calendar put spread is very dependent upon both commission prices and the bid-ask spread between the two options, and a large bid-ask spread can wipe out most or all of the potential profits.

DEEP-IN-THE-MONEY CALENDARS AND DIAGONALS

In a bullish or neutral put calendar spread, the strike prices of both the long and short options are at-the-money or just above. This position provides the maximum payoff in the event that the market price remains relatively flat or provides a modest return.

Calendar put spreads can also be structured to provide profits when the price of the underlying falls significantly, thereby creating a portfolio hedge, and this is done by selecting a strike price well below market. The maximum payoff occurs when the market price falls to the level of the strike price.

Market price = 100

Buy @ 90 exp 180 days for $1.40

Sell @ 90 exp 90 days for $0.63

Debit: $0.78 per share

As market declines are statistically rare, this position will likely have a negative expected payoff and would only be valuable as a source of crash protection. Like other calendars, profitability is dependent upon the bid-ask spread and this strategy is generally only suitable for highly liquid index options like the S&P 500.

As a rule, this position will provide protection for the point in time between the expiry of the first option and the expiry of the second, but not before or after. If a market drop occurs immediately, the short put option would gain value and the spread would lose value, potentially wiping out the position.

Ideally, the market would remain relatively flat until the short put option expires worthless, and then the long put option would still have value. At that point, the long option could either be sold for capital gains, or kept in place as a hedge.

If the market advances in the short term, there may be an opportunity to buy back the short option but still retain the long option for hedging purposes. That hedge would allow the investor to invest more aggressively, knowing that their losses on the position are limited. Of course, if the market rises sharply, the hedge may be of little value.

Thus a deep-in-the-money calendar put spread can be a tool for putting a hedge in place at a future point in time, but not immediately, and not with certainty, but perhaps extremely cost-effectively if market conditions permit.

ROLLING LEAPS PUTS

Like LEAPS call options, LEAPS put options can be rolled forward indefinitely for periods of years or even decades. The roll-forward cost for the LEAPS option will be dependent upon the volatility of the underlying security and the distance between the strike price and the market price.

This technique can be used to create a long-term hedge on the portfolio, but it is an imperfect hedge because the price to maintain it will rise in unfavorable market conditions. When the index price falls and volatility rises, the roll-forward cost of the option will increase somewhat. However, the current option would also become much more valuable.

Typically, the delta of a LEAPS put option will be rather low, such that a $1 drop in the index may result in only a $0.30 to $0.50 increase in the value of the hedge. The delta would only climb to negative one when the option is deep-in-the-money and/or close to expiry.

Because the expected trend of the index is upward, a rolled LEAPS put option would become less and less valuable over time as its strike price would move further and further away from the market price and its delta would fall to close to zero. In this case, the LEAPS put option could be rolled up to a higher strike price, and this should be feasible if the investor has been able to benefit from the accumulated appreciation in the underlying index.

A rolled LEAPS put option could be very useful in conjunction with index futures or a similar leveraged position that has unlimited downside, as the LEAPS put would protect against extreme downward price movements. Also, a LEAPS put on the S&P could be used to hedge a wide range of equity index futures, including indexes based upon various sectors, countries, and styles, as the majority of these investments would be expected to correlate with the S&P 500.

ROLLING LEAPS CALENDAR SPREAD

A rolling LEAPS calendar call spread is a very useful position for an investor with a long portfolio of calls and/or futures as it has a relatively low cost and can create many opportunities for either portfolio protection or immediate profits. It combines many of the elements from the earlier strategies.

In the transaction shown in Table 10.4, a spread is created with a long one-year put option and a short three-month put option, both just a little out-of-the-money. The position is relatively inexpensive due to the high cost of the three-month option and the low marginal value of time.

TABLE 10.4 Rolling LEAPS Calendar Spread Position, Long/Short Put Option

	Days	Market	Strike	Years	Rate	Vol.	Price
Long	360	100.00	98.00	0.99	0.05	0.21	4.99
Short	90	100.00	98.00	0.25	0.05	0.21	2.66
						Cost	2.33

If the short option expires worthless, the long option can be held as a hedge for nine months, providing plenty of protection. Or, that option can be sold, and the proceeds applied to a longer-term hedge, such as a two-year put option.

Also, if the underlying security fails to appreciate at all, and the market price at expiry is very close to the strike price, the long option can be sold immediately for a significant profit, especially if volatility has increased.

The primary benefit of this position is flexibility. At the expiry of the short option, the investor can decide based upon the security price and implied volatility and the composition of their portfolio whether to choose immediate profits, a nine-month hedge, or a rolled longer-term hedge.

The position would lose value if the market price falls significantly in the next three months and the short put option becomes a liability. Security prices are extremely unpredictable on a quarterly basis, but on average, we would expect the losses on the short option to be well below its purchase price. However, early exercise is always a possibility for American-style options, and should be taken into consideration.

SUMMARY

Put option strategies can be used to provide either portfolio protection or profits. The options themselves are expensive because the downside risks for even a well-diversified index are extremely high. Historically, weekly and monthly losses have been as large as 11 percent and 14 percent respectively, and this can make it difficult to manage a put writing strategy that can withstand a moderate downturn.

However, because of the higher implied volatilities and the effect of index drift, the average weekly or monthly loss for an at-the-money put option is relatively low, and as a result writing puts is profitable, on average, with a profit margin of approximately one third. Very few investors would consider writing puts using cash margin, as it would be difficult to ascertain a reserve level that provides both security and leverage. Consequently, two bullish strategies are presented that use long put options as security in order to hold a short put position.

The first position, the bull put spread, uses a long option at a lower strike price and cash margin as security for the short put. As the index appreciates or holds its value, the short put expires worthless generating a profit. The difficulty with this position is that the implied volatility of the long option tends to be very high, the percentage profits are relatively low, and even small transaction costs can reduce profitability significantly.

The second position, the calendar put spread, provides more profit opportunities. A long put option is combined with a short put option at the same strike but with an earlier expiration date. When the short put option expires, the long put option is sold. The profits can be extremely high when the market price is close to the strike price and volatility is up.

When put options are used in conjunction with a leveraged long position, such as index futures, long call options, or neutral-bullish call strategies, they can help provide a hedge against a market decline. Hedges are, as a rule, losing positions and a hedging strategy would generally provide a drain on a portfolio and lower the expected return. However, hedging can be a necessity when leveraged portfolios are used due to the potential for steep declines that would be very difficult for an investor to recover from.

The least expensive form of downside protection is security selection. If asset correlations are well understood, portfolios can be created that have less downside risk. Also, purchasing put options on correlated but lower volatility securities can also result in less expensive hedging strategies.

Generally, simply buying and holding puts is not cost effective due to the high volatilities, the effect of index drift, and the accumulation of time decay. The economies are better for longer-term positions, such as those provided by two- or three-year LEAPS options, but these positions can also have low delta and may not be as useful in the short term.

Selling short options can reduce the cost of protection at the expense of some potential protection. One such approach is to use a bear put spread, a position composed of a long put option and then a short put option at a lower strike price. This position provides limited downside protection, but benefits from the higher implied volatilities of far out-of-the-money options. Collars can also be used if the investor is willing to lose out on potential upside in exchange for protection.

Innovative hedging strategies can be constructed through calendar and diagonal put spread positions in which the short put option is closer to expiry and also close to the money. At the expiry of this short option, the long option can be kept in place as a hedge and, if needed, rolled over for many more years. However, if the underlying security declines before the short put option expires, then the potential liability may lead to the position being exited at a loss.

CHAPTER 11

LEAPS Puts and Three Ways to Profit

I n the last chapter, we demonstrated that put option spread positions can be used to cost-effectively limit downside risk or as components of an investment portfolio that generate profits based upon index behavior. Spread positions are more cost-effective than using puts alone and provide a variety of both long and short alternatives.

In this chapter, we introduce three different strategies that use long LEAPS put options to either protect a portfolio or generate additional return. The first strategy is an out-of-the-money bear put spread, also known as a speed bump. This position provides cost-effective portfolio protection, and thereby allows an investor to take on additional leverage with a sharply reduced risk of catastrophic failure in the event of a poor return. Additional protection can be achieved through diversification, and two techniques for modeling diversified but correlated investment portfolios are shown here.

The second strategy presented in this chapter uses LEAPS calendar put spreads to generate high returns. These put spreads are extremely profitable but have both long holding periods and relatively high standard deviations. LEAPS calendar put spreads can be used in a repeated strategy, and a historical performance analysis is presented using a diversified fund made up of three S&P 500 sectors with low correlations.

The final strategy is a monthly put writing strategy in which LEAPS put options are used to secure the investment. This is a well-known and highly profitable strategy, but has some often unforeseen pitfalls that can make it difficult to manage and implement safely.

PORTFOLIO SAFETY NETS

The primary fear of any leveraged investor is that a moderate decline in the value of the underlying security will be magnified by the leverage ratio into a devastating loss. However, by using hedging positions, the impact of this scenario can be minimized, if not entirely eliminated, and this can allow a portfolio to reach higher levels of leverage.

The options position that makes this possible is an out-of-the-money bear put spread using LEAPS. A two-year LEAPS put option is purchased at a relatively low strike price, and then a second two-year LEAPS put option is sold at an even lower strike price. The sale of the second put option helps fund the position, but also limits the amount of downside protection created.

Example: Assume 100 is the current market price of the index.

Buy 2-year put @ 90 for 3.71 (IV = 21%)

Sell 2-year put @ 75 for 1.04 (IV = 21%)

Spread cost: 2.67

As a rule, the IV (implied volatility) of the deeper in-the-money option would be somewhat higher, reducing the cost of the spread, but for two-year options, this effect may not be that significant and will be ignored in this analysis.

This put spread creates a speed bump that limits the downside risk of the index for a period of two years. It creates 15 points of protection, but only after the initial 10-point loss. A 25-point loss is reduced to 10 points, and a 30-point loss would be reduced to 15 points.

This is a tremendous amount of protection for a two-year period and is made possible by the cost-effectiveness of LEAPS options. With LEAPS, the marginal cost of each additional month of protection is relatively small. In Table 11.1, we show the cost and protection provided by this spread if other expiration dates were used.

For an unleveraged fund, the initial cost of the put spread reduces the amount that can be invested in the security. For example, if the initial portfolio funds are $100,000 and the put spread costs $2,670, that would leave only $97,330 to invest. This suggests that the real cost of the portfolio protection is not only the initial cost, but also the forgone capital gains for the next two years.

But because we are using leverage, this is not an issue, and the investor can purchase both $100,000 of index exposure, and a put option on 1000 shares. With 20:1 futures leverage, this could be achieved with a

TABLE 11.1 Comparison of Protection Cost for Short-Term and Long-Term Positions

Days	Market	Strike	Rate	Vol.	Price	Spread Cost	Cost per Day
30	100.00	90.00	0.05	0.21	0.08	0.08	0.003
30	100.00	75.00	0.05	0.21	0.00		
90	100.00	90.00	0.05	0.21	0.63	0.62	0.007
90	100.00	75.00	0.05	0.21	0.01		
180	100.00	90.00	0.05	0.21	1.40	1.33	0.007
180	100.00	75.00	0.05	0.21	0.08		
365	100.00	90.00	0.05	0.21	2.51	2.13	0.006
365	100.00	75.00	0.05	0.21	0.39		
730	100.00	90.00	0.05	0.21	3.71	2.67	0.004
730	100.00	75.00	0.05	0.21	1.04		

$5,000 portfolio of index futures and $2,670 of put options. Or alternately, deep-in-the-money LEAPS call options could be used in place of index futures.

Example—Portfolio

$2,670 Put option

$5,000 Maintenance margin for the futures contract

$32,330 Cash in interest-earning account

EXPECTED RETURNS AND HEDGING ANALYSIS

On average, an investor would estimate the return on the index at 10 percent a year including dividends, or 21 percent for the two-year period, and the put option would be expected to expire worthless. A 21 percent return on the $100,000 portfolio is $21,000, but the cost of the put reduces the profits to $18,330 before interest expenses.

Interest costs would be $3,133, assuming 5 percent interest on the $62,670 borrowed. The final profit would be $15,196, or just about 38 percent on the initial $40,000 portfolio, which is an 18 percent annual return. Transaction costs would not be a significant factor as the LEAPS put spread is purchased only once every two years.

Expected Profits: $40,000 equity and $60,000 debt

Gains	$21,000
Hedge	$2,670
Interest	$3,133
Profits	$15,196

The next step in the analysis was to model 1,000 two-year investments using S&P 500-like returns, that is, 10 percent average appreciation with a 15 percent standard deviation. In Table 11.2, the two-year portfolio returns of the unhedged and hedged position are compared, assuming no leverage. The starting value of the portfolio is 1.0.

For the hedged position, the two-year returns are about two points lower, reflecting the cost of the hedge. The volatility is slightly lower, but the difference doesn't look significant. However, the minimum is a lot lower: 0.75 versus 0.63. In this case, the hedge reduced the downside risk by more than 12 points, before leverage. (The maximum protection is twelve points, not fifteen, because of the cost of the hedge.)

Table 11.3 shows the frequency distribution of portfolios with losses after two years. The total portfolio count for each category is 1,000. Note that the risk of a 15 percent or greater loss is cut by 75 percent, the risk of

TABLE 11.2 Average Value of Unhedged vs. Hedged Portfolio in Two Years

	No Hedge	Hedge	Diff.
Avg.	1.21	1.19	0.0198
Std.	0.23	0.22	0.0251
Min.	0.63	0.75	−0.1240
Max.	1.97	1.94	0.0260
Median	1.19	1.17	0.0260

TABLE 11.3 Count of Portfolios with Losses, Hedged vs. Unhedged, Cumulative

Loss	No Hedge	Hedge	Diff.
<5%	128	148	+16%
<10%	83	102	+23%
<15%	48	12	−75%
<20%	25	4	−84%
<25%	15	0	−100%
<30%	9	0	−100%
<35%	2	0	−100%

a 20 percent or greater loss is cut by 84 percent, and there are no unhedged portfolios that lost 25 percent or more. This is a much safer portfolio.

When 2.5× leverage is applied to the investment, the hedged portfolio returns +40 percent on average over the two-year period, while the unhedged portfolio returns +45 percent. Again, the standard deviations look similar, but compare the minimums. In at least one case an unhedged leveraged portfolio was wiped out during the two-year period, while the minimum hedged portfolio is 31 percent of the original amount. Of course, losing 69 percent of the portfolio isn't ideal, but it is certainly better than losing one hundred percent (as shown in Table 11.4).

Because the put spread limits the losses of the underlying security within the −10 percent to −25 percent range, when the 2.5× leverage is applied, the portfolio distribution still has losses in the −25 percent to −35 percent range, but has eliminated almost all of the losses in the −50 percent or greater range. Out of the 1,000 leveraged portfolios, only 9 out of 1,000 hedged portfolios lost more than 50 percent in the two-year period, as compared to 43 for the unhedged portfolios.

This is not to say that it wouldn't be possible for a portfolio with this type of hedge to lose everything. Because only 15 percentage points of downside protection has been purchased, a two-year loss of 40 percent or 50 percent in the underlying would definitely do a lot of damage. Based upon historical averages, this kind of loss would be a possibility but still extremely rare, and it does show up in the simulations occasionally.

TABLE 11.4 Two-Year Leveraged SPY Portfolio Performance, Hedged vs. Unhedged

	No Hedge 2.5×	Hedge 2.5×
Avg.	1.45	1.40
Std.	0.58	0.55
Min.	0.00	0.31
Max.	3.34	3.28
Median	1.41	1.34

Loss	No Hedge 2.5×	Hedge 2.5×	Diff.
<5%	128	148	+15.6%
<10%	83	102	+22.9%
<15%	48	12	−75.0%
<20%	25	4	−84.0%
<25%	15	0	−100.0%
<30%	9	0	−100.0%
<35%	2	0	−100.0%

Over a ten-year period, if this strategy is repeated and the level of leverage is maintained, about 4 percent of the unhedged portfolios have lost more than 75 percent of their value, and some have lost everything, as compared to only 0.7 percent of our hedged portfolios (see results in Table 11.5).

Generally the results are more favorable, with the hedged portfolio profitable 90 percent of the time, and growing in value 5.1× on average. The mean is higher than the median, and the best portfolios have returned 10× to 15× their value in the period.

CORRELATED INDEXES USING SIMTOOLS

The investment above is profitable on average, but still has a very high volatility and distribution of two-year and ten-year returns. We can improve the predictability and reduce the risk of the investment by building a diversified portfolio of equity indexes and then applying leverage. As stated again and again, diversification is the cheapest form of portfolio protection.

The issue with modeling this portfolio is that just about all equity returns are correlated due to the wealth effect and the global interconnections of the economy. For example, during 2007, the weekly returns of the S&P 500 and the MSCI EAFE were correlated at a 90 percent level.

There are two ways to address this. The first is to model a single "blended" index with the risk-and-reward characteristics that one would expect from an investment portfolio given historical averages. Then, just one set of portfolio returns is generated that is expected to be consistent with the expectations from that blended investment.

For example, in Chapter 3, we found that a rebalanced equal-weighted sector portfolio had higher returns and lower volatility than the S&P 500 during the last decade. We could study that portfolio over many years and use that analysis to estimate an expected level of future volatility at 13.5 percent. Then we could use this volatility and an expected 10 percent

TABLE 11.5 Ten-Year Portfolio Returns, Unhedged vs. Hedged

	10-Year No Hedge	10-Year Hedged
Avg.	6.08	5.11
Std.	6.27	5.15
Min.	−0.02	0.23
Max.	70.56	61.22
Median	4.24	3.57

annual return in order to generate the monthly or annual returns for the diversified set of indexes.

Another approach is to generate random returns for the base index, for example, the U.S. S&P 500, and then use a tool to generate correlated random numbers for the returns of other indexes. Correlated random numbers are random numbers that are selected in such a way as to share a correlation with another random variable. By using correlated random returns, the behavior of multiple indices that have an observed market relationship can be simulated.

Professor Roger Myerson of the University of Chicago has developed a plug-in for Excel named SIMTOOLS that is designed to help calculate the results of economic decisions under uncertainty. By using the CORAND() function included in this package, a correlated number can be generated based upon another random number, and this number can be fed into a normal distribution to generate an index return.

Example: (Excel calculations)

A1: = RAND()
> Generates a random number between zero and one.

A2: =CORAND(0.9, A1)
> Generates a second random number with a 0.90 correlation to the first one. (Note: Do not reverse the function arguments!)

A3: = NORMINV(A1, 0.01, 0.04)
> Uses the random number in cell A1 to generate a random monthly index return with an average of 1 percent and a standard deviation of 4 percent.

A4: =NORMINV(A2, 0.01, 0.04)
> Uses the correlated random number in cell A2 to generate a correlated monthly index return with the same average and standard deviation.

The plug-in is freely available on the Internet and is easy to install, and the function is simple to use. We are grateful to the creators for making what could be a very complex mathematical task very easy. Find it at this location: http://home.uchicago.edu/~rmyerson/addins.htm.

CORRELATED PROTECTED PORTFOLIOS

At this point, we can improve the earlier investment by diversifying the portfolio into S&P 500 MidCaps, but also maintaining the protection of the bear put spread. From September 1995 to June 2007, the correlation between the monthly returns of the S&P 500 and the MidCap index is 0.855.

The combination of the two created a portfolio with 2 percent higher returns than the S&P 500, but with only 0.5 percent higher volatility, as Table 11.6 shows.

In order to simulate the monthly returns of the MidCap index, we could use either the historical return of 15 percent, or, if we want to be more conservative, a lower return such as 12 percent that corresponds more to the expected 80-year long-term averages. Then we could use the historical volatility of 16.6 percent or 17 percent to generate the monthly or annual returns.

When a 90 percent correlation between the two indexes is assumed along with relatively conservative performance characteristics, a simulated portfolio created by combining the two indices has higher performance than the S&P 500 but without significantly higher volatility. A difference between 10 percent and 11 percent annual return is very significant, especially if the portfolio is borrowing investment capital at 5 percent.

We should also point out that although 90 percent sounds as if it's close to perfect, in fact there is usually considerable variation between the two market indexes over longer periods of time in the historical data. The standard deviation of the difference between the two returns is 2.48 percent per month, and in many months one index has a return five points higher or lower than the other.

If the two indices are combined into a portfolio, 2.5× leverage is applied, and two-year protection is purchased, the return is increased significantly, as can be seen in Table 11.7. (Compare the results to Table 11.4.) The average ten-year return also rises from 5.11 to 6.42, as shown in Table 11.8.

But what's even more interesting is that the likelihood of a 15 percent or 20 percent loss is cut in half. In a two-year period, only 6 of the unleveraged portfolios had a loss greater than 15 percent, and only one had a loss

TABLE 11.6 Historical Performance Comparison of SPY and MDY vs. a Blend (September 1995–June 2007)

	SPY	MDY	Blend
Monthly			
Avg.	0.88%	1.17%	1.03%
Std.	4.18%	4.78%	4.32%
Min.	−14.12%	−20.04%	−17.08%
Max.	9.69%	12.54%	9.55%
Annual			
Avg.	11.11%	15.02%	13.05%
Std.	14.49%	16.57%	14.96%

TABLE 11.7 Two-Year Performance of 2.5× Blended SPY and MDY Portfolio

	No Hedge	Hedge	
Avg.	1.50	1.45	
Std.	0.58	0.56	
Min.	0.00	0.31	
Max.	3.42	3.36	
Median	1.48	1.42	

Loss	No Hedge	Hedge	Diff.
<5%	109	132	+21.1%
<10%	75	84	+12.0%
<15%	44	6	−86.4%
<20%	29	1	−96.6%
<25%	11	0	−100.0%
<30%	2	0	−100.0%
<35%	1	0	−100.0%

of greater than 20 percent, as compared to 12 and 4 for an undiversified portfolio based on the S&P 500. These are reductions of 50 percent and 75 percent respectively.

These reductions in the unleveraged portfolio also lead to reductions when leverage is applied, and only 9 out of 1,000 portfolios had losses in excess of 50 percent in any two-year period.

The combination of diversification and portfolio protection allows an investor to leverage the fund to a relatively high degree, and still withstand moderate losses that would cause other portfolios to implode. While bad years may occur, the portfolio would still have the capacity to benefit from the next upturn.

TABLE 11.8 Ten-Year Blended SPY/MDY Portfolio Returns, Hedged vs. Unhedged

	10-Year Portfolio (No Hedge)	10-Year Portfolio (Hedge)
Avg.	7.66	6.42
Std.	7.38	6.10
Min.	0.00	0.16
Max.	52.15	44.67
Median	5.40	4.48

LEAPS CALENDAR PUT SPREADS

In this section, a high-profit options position is presented that takes advantage of index drift, the marginal value of time, and the implied volatility premium. The position is the LEAPS calendar bull put spread, and it can be used in a repeated strategy to accumulate profits over long periods of time.

To create this position, the investor purchases a two-year LEAPS put option slightly out of the money, and then sells a one-year put option at the same strike price. When the index appreciates, the short put option expires worthless, but the long put option still has some value and can generate very high one-year returns. As shown in Table 11.9, the spread is purchased at 105 percent of the market price.

When using a spread like this, it is important to ensure that unexpected liabilities aren't created by the timing mismatch of the options. As noted in the previous chapter, if a European-style short put option expires and requires a cash payment, the associated long put option in the calendar spread may still not have sufficient value to cover the liability, creating a shortfall.

The payoff structure for this position is very high, assuming the index holds its value. When the index gains 5 percent to 15 percent, the profit on the position is +350 percent to +800 percent before transaction costs.

TABLE 11.9 Calendar Put Spread Cost and Payoff as a Result of Index Return

	Days	Market	Strike	Years	Rate	Vol.	Price
Long	730	100	105	2	0.05	0.19	8.11
Short	365	100	105	1	0.05	0.19	7.50
						Cost	0.61

Days	Market	Strike	Years	Rate	Vol.	Price	Payoff	% Return
365	75	105	1	0.05	0.21	25.60	−4.40	−724%
365	80	105	1	0.05	0.21	21.28	−3.72	−612%
365	85	105	1	0.05	0.21	17.33	−2.67	−439%
365	90	105	1	0.05	0.21	13.83	−1.17	−192%
365	95	105	1	0.05	0.21	10.82	0.82	134%
365	100	105	1	0.05	0.21	8.30	3.30	542%
365	105	105	1	0.05	0.21	6.25	6.25	1027%
365	110	105	1	0.05	0.21	4.62	4.62	760%
365	115	105	1	0.05	0.21	3.36	3.36	553%
365	120	105	1	0.05	0.21	2.41	2.41	397%
365	125	105	1	0.05	0.21	1.71	1.71	281%
365	130	105	1	0.05	0.21	1.19	1.19	196%
365	135	105	1	0.05	0.21	0.82	0.82	135%

The position takes a loss when the index declines more than 5 percent in a year, and statistically this should happen only about 16 percent of the time, given a normal distribution.

Losses are also possible on the high end, that is, when the index gains more than 30 percent, but are statistically unlikely. These calculations are based upon an implied volatility of 19 percent and a final volatility similar to that at the start. Of course any calendar spread will have vega risk, and that can either improve or diminish the profitability and is simply another random element.

LEAPS CALENDAR PUT PORTFOLIOS

Building a strategy around LEAPS calendar put options can be a challenge, and there is also a psychological dimension that can be difficult. Because the value of the position can change so rapidly, especially when it is close to expiry, it can be very frustrating to watch six months of profits evaporate in a week because the underlying index declines or volatility falls.

Also, if a monthly strategy is used, the investor will over time accumulate a large number of put spread positions on the same security or on correlated securities, and in the event of a market decline, the entire portfolio could be devastated.

One suggested approach would be to rotate relatively small monthly investments among three different securities with low correlations. For example, an investor with a $50,000 portfolio could purchase $2,000 worth of put calendar spreads on the finance sector index in January, $2,000 worth on the energy sector index in February, and $2,000 worth on the health care index in March.

However, one issue is that bid-ask spreads have a significant impact on put calendar spread profitability, and these spreads can be high for LEAPS and especially for securities that aren't widely traded. This can make it difficult to build a position on an index with a low S&P 500 correlation.

Also, because LEAPS put options generally expire in December or January, the investor may need to close out the positions early rather than holding them all to expiry, otherwise the entire short option portfolio might expire on the same day, creating a very large amount of delta and vega risk in the few weeks before expiry.

HISTORICAL PERFORMANCE

For the historical analysis, we assume that we can create one-year and two-year spreads at an average volatility and continue to invest $2,000 a month indefinitely. Also, rather than take turns among the three funds, we simply invest one-third of the $2,000 in each sector in each month, and this provides less of a dependence on the ordering of the investments. Also, the losses on any individual put spread are capped at 100 percent.

The analysis starts in January 1999 and continues until June 2007, and monthly investments are made for six and a half years and held for one-year intervals. There is a 0.55 correlation between the monthly returns of the three sectors, and this helps to provide some diversification (see Table 11.10).

Over the six-and-a-half-year time period, the $2,000 monthly investment accumulated $450,000 worth of gains. Although the energy sector had the best performance, most of the gains came from the less volatile sectors that nevertheless managed to deliver reasonable returns.

During the 2001 downturn, the positions did take losses, but there were also sporadic gains that helped the portfolio and prevented any significant losses. Then in 2003, the portfolio gains value quickly and generates very high returns.

Note that this analysis is based upon fairly rudimentary assumptions about the implied volatility of each option and doesn't include the transaction costs. However, it gives some indication of what a repeated, well-diversified strategy can do over a several-year period.

The other issue is that while this strategy is expected to be profitable due to the index drift and the volatility premium, it is difficult to build a cycling strategy around this investment because the payoff doesn't occur for a full year, and if multiple investments are made within that year period, they will be correlated with each other because their holding periods will overlap.

When the index rises for a period and provides portfolio appreciation, it would be very tempting to invest more each month; however, a subsequent loss of even just 6 percent or 7 percent could be enough to wipe out half of the portfolio. And in fact, if American-style options are used, then there is always the risk of an early exercise on the short put that forces the

TABLE 11.10 Monthly Payoff on $2,000 Invested for Calendar Put Spreads

	XLE	XLF	XLV	Blend
Avg.	2,353	4,866	7,795	5,005
Std.	5,018	5,536	5,616	3,881
Min.	−2,000	−2,000	−2,000	−2,000
Max.	15,678	15,865	15,787	12,611
Sum	211,746	437,937	701,532	450,405

investor to sell the shares and then sell the long put, exiting the position and likely taking a large loss.

The calendar put spread is a high-profit indexing strategy, but is best used with a small portion of a portfolio, and on a diversified set of underlying indexes that have low transaction costs.

PUT WRITING WITH LEAPS

The third investment strategy presented is a classic strategy in which an investor writes one-month at-the-money put options on the index, and then holds an out-of-the-money LEAPS put option as collateral in order to satisfy the broker requirements for writing put options.

The profits are generated from the put option premiums that, on average, are expected to be higher than the actual loss taken from writing the put option. The LEAPS option will also decay, losing value, but it can be sold early while it still has some time value in order to help mitigate the loss.

The position will look like this (assume the share price is 100):

Buy Put @ 90 exp in 2 years for 3.86

Sell Put @ 100 exp in 1 month for 1.97

Continue selling put options for twelve months, then sell the LEAPS put option.

Expected Returns

On average, we would expect the index to increase and for the short put options to expire worthless. Still, we should be prepared for some losses. As a "back of the envelope" calculation, one could assume that on average the investor will keep a third of the short put premiums received and use the other two-thirds for payouts associated with losses. This is an estimate, but the precision of this calculation will be checked shortly.

Over the year, assuming average volatility, the investor will receive premiums of $26.86. Note that this is more than 12× the initial short put option cost, as the value of the index increases over the year, providing slightly larger premiums. If one third of this premium is retained, then this generates almost $9 in profits for the year. (See Table 11.11)

However, the LEAPS put option is also expected to decline in value over the year. We can estimate the starting and ending volatilities, and as a result assume that this option will lose approximately $2.75 of value over

TABLE 11.11 Writing Monthly Put Options Using LEAPS, Estimation Using Average Appreciation

Month	Index	Long Put	Short Put						
			Cost	Payout	Accum. Profits	Cash Margin	Profits Short	LEAPS Profits	Total Profits
0	100.00	-3.86	1.97			10.00			
1	100.80		1.99	-1.30	0.67	10.80			
2	101.60		2.00	-1.31	1.34	11.60			
3	102.41		2.02	-1.32	2.02	12.41			
4	103.23		2.03	-1.33	2.71	13.23			
5	104.05		2.05	-1.34	3.40	14.05			
6	104.88		2.07	-1.35	4.10	14.88			
7	105.72		2.08	-1.36	4.80	15.72			
8	106.56		2.10	-1.37	5.51	16.56			
9	107.41		2.12	-1.39	6.22	17.41			
10	108.27		2.13	-1.40	6.94	18.27			
11	109.13		2.15	-1.41	7.67	19.13			
12	110.00	1.15		-1.42	8.40		8.40	-2.71	5.69

the year. Nine dollars in profits from the short option minus $2.75 in losses from the short option equals $6.25 worth of profits per share.

But what is the capital base? The cost for the LEAPS put option is $3.86, but the investor immediately receives $1.97 in premiums, reducing this cash outflow to $1.89. However, cash margin is also needed to hold the position, and this amount is the difference between the strike prices, which is $10. Thus the total initial outlay is about $12 and the $6.25 profit reflects an expected one-year return of barely under 50 percent.

Still, as the index appreciates, this cash margin requirement will also increase, and by the twelfth month, the cash margin required would be $20, which is the current market price of $110 minus the strike price of $90. In fact, during the twelve-month period, cash margin requirements are expected to grow a little faster than profits. The cash would be accumulated until the LEAPS put option is finally sold.

This analysis shows that not only the returns, but the cash flows and margin requirements are going to be dependent upon the monthly returns of the index, and this creates quite a bit of uncertainty. It's critical to review the potential scenarios to determine exactly what conditions will lead to cash-flow issues.

Scenarios

We created 596 one-year scenarios based upon the assumptions listed above. In the simulation, the average payout for a put option was 32 percent, just about identical to our initial estimate of one-third. This is based on the average historical returns and volatility of the S&P 500 from 1991 to 2007, and is a reasonable long-term estimate. The one-year profit of $6.26 on the initial investment of $11.89 provides an annual average return of 52.6 percent.

The investment return has a fairly wide standard deviation of $6.71, and the max loss is quite high, at −$9.18 per share, which would represent a −77.2 percent loss on the initial investment. Theoretically losses in excess of 100 percent are possible, but nothing of that magnitude occurs in the generated scenarios.

The scenario presented in the first half of Table 11.12 depicts one of the scenarios with the largest loss for the period. During the year, the index appreciated, declined sharply, and then rebounded again. In months three and four, the index declines $11 and the losses from the short put options accumulate sharply. Over the rest of the year, the index recovers, but the strategy never does, as the subsequent put options don't provide any significant profit.

If the index had declined over the year, than perhaps the LEAPS put option would have provided some offsetting compensation. However, the

TABLE 11.12 Selected Scenarios, LEAPS Monthly Put Option Writing Strategy

Lowest

Month	Index	Long Put	Cost	Payout	Accum. Profits	LEAPS Profits	Total Profits	Margin	Days	Market	Strike	Years	Rate	Vol.	Price
0	100.00	-3.86	1.97					10.00	730	100.00	90.00	2.00	0.05	0.21	3.86
1	105.85		2.08	0.00	1.97			15.85							
2	101.30		2.00	-4.55	-0.50			11.30							
3	95.90		1.89	-5.40	-3.91			5.90							
4	89.61		1.76	-6.28	-8.31			-0.39							
5	98.68		1.94	0.00	-6.54			8.68							
6	93.57		1.84	-5.11	-9.71			3.57							
7	90.51		1.78	-3.05	-10.92			0.51							
8	96.54		1.90	0.00	-9.13			6.54							
9	94.42		1.86	-2.12	-9.35			4.42							
10	104.92		2.07	0.00	-7.49			14.92							
11	101.24		1.99	-3.68	-9.10			11.24							
12	103.53	1.96		0.00	-7.11	-1.90	-9.01		365	103.53	90.00	1.00	0.05	0.21	1.96

Higher

Month	Index	Long Put	Cost	Payout	Accum. Profits	LEAPS Profits	Total Profits	Margin	Days	Market	Strike	Years	Rate	Vol.	Price
0	100.00	−3.86	1.97					10.00	730	100.00	90.00	2.00	0.05	0.21	3.86
1	106.60		2.10	0.00	1.97			16.60							
2	104.82		2.06	−1.78	2.29			14.82							
3	107.13		2.11	0.00	4.35			17.13							
4	114.17		2.25	0.00	6.46			24.17							
5	116.19		2.29	0.00	8.71			26.19							
6	117.00		2.30	0.00	11.00			27.00							
7	124.71		2.46	0.00	13.30			34.71							
8	127.97		2.52	0.00	15.76			37.97							
9	126.27		2.49	−1.71	16.57			36.27							
10	128.03		2.52	0.00	19.06			38.03							
11	126.67		2.49	−1.36	20.22			36.67							
12	134.81	0.12		0.00	22.72	−3.74	18.98	36.67	365	134.81	90.00	1.00	0.05	0.21	0.12

243

index did end up +4 percent for the year, and the LEAPS put option contributes to the loss.

In the second scenario shown, the index surges, creating enormous profits for the index and generating profits for the strategy as well. Cumulative profits from the sold put options equal $22.72 as a result of the high payout ratio from the put options, 82 percent, and the increasing value of the options. The LEAPS put loses value, of course, but the loss is minimal.

This is an excellent return, +160 percent for the year, but note the increasing margin requirements. By the end of the year, the margin requirements from the put spread have increased from $10 to $36, and at one point they hit $38. This increase even outpaces the high profits, and likely means tapping additional reserves of capital. And as margin requirements grow, the risk of the position climbs higher and higher, and a sharp drop at the end of the year could wipe out $30 in profits.

One way to reduce the escalating margin requirements is to sell the LEAPS put option when the index rises sharply and then put a new LEAPS put option in place at a higher strike price. This prevents the escalating margin requirements, but creates two additional issues.

The first issue is higher cost. The LEAPS put option is still a relatively expensive component of the investment, and its negative delta works against the profitability of the strategy, reducing the overall returns. However, after a few months of appreciation, it is so far out of the money that it has very little value left to lose. If the depreciated LEAPS is then sold, and a new, higher strike price LEAPS is put in its place, this LEAPS will also decay, and profitability will suffer.

The second issue is simply predictability. This strategy is already a difficult one to manage in terms of selecting the overall level of investment, and if more cash is consumed through the purchase of higher strike price LEAPS at odd intervals, then if the index declines sharply right after that, all of the cash could be tied up in a LEAPS put that has increased in value, but is still out-of-the-money.

One question that is asked about this strategy is whether it is possible to increase profits by selecting a higher strike price. After all, if the index is expected to appreciate on a monthly basis, then it makes sense that one way to capture this positive drift would be to consistently write puts on out-of-the-money options.

However, when puts are written at a higher strike price, the implied volatility is lower due to the volatility skew, and this tends to cut into profits. If we lower the implied volatility in our model from 19 percent to 18 percent and raise the strike price by 1 percent, the value of the put options sold increases, but the payout ratio for the put options falls from 32 percent to 24 percent, and no additional profit is generated.

In fact, slightly higher annual profits can be generated by lowering the strike price by 1 percent, as shown in Table 11.13. We assume that the

TABLE 11.13 Historical Put Option Writing Profitability at Selected Strike Prices

	101% Strike Profit	100% Strike Profit	99% Strike Profit
Avg.	5.22	5.91	6.59
Std.	7.94	6.56	5.65
Min.	−15.68	−14.19	−14.55
Max.	26.26	24.79	21.01

implied volatility increases 1 percent, and this raises the payout ratio from 32 percent to 39 percent. The standard deviation of returns is also lowered from $6.71 to $5.83.

SUMMARY

In this chapter, we presented three strategies using LEAPS put options to provide long-term portfolio protection that can be used to either limit losses and make possible higher levels of leverage, or as security for a put-writing strategy. The put-writing strategy could be either a single one-year put option, or multiple short-term put options.

Because protecting an investment portfolio begins with diversification, we also show how to model a correlated equity index portfolio using either blended long-term averages or by simulating individual returns using SIM-TOOLs, a Microsoft Excel plug-in that can be used to create correlated random variables.

For leveraged investments in which a few percentage points of return can make a large difference, a position on a second security can provide sufficient diversification, even if the correlation is 90 percent or higher. Often those high percentages can be misleading, as monthly returns between two indexes with that high correlation can often be five points higher or lower.

The combination of portfolio diversification and a bear put spread for protection can allow an investor to leverage a portfolio 2.5× and hold the position for ten years with an average return of +540 percent for the period, or about 20 percent per year. While poor annual returns are still possible, the likelihood of a return on the underlying that wipes the leveraged portfolio out is reduced by 75 percent to 100 percent, depending upon the spread purchased and the underlying volatility.

Another strategy, the calendar put spread, can be used to generate very high returns of more than +100 percent a year on average, but with a very high standard deviation of about 250 percent. The short one-year option decays and expires worthless or close to it, and the long two-year put option retains its value.

However, the long time frame, the unpredictability of returns, and the inability to make repeated investments in a year without having overlapping periods and correlations can make it a difficult strategy to implement and incorporate into a cycling strategy. Also, there are risks present in the use of either European options, which can create timing liabilities, or American options that can be exercised early.

The safest way to utilize this strategy is to make regular, fairly small investments over time on multiple securities with low correlations. In the analysis, three sector investments with low correlation were used. Also, liquidity and transaction costs will always be a factor in any calendar spread strategy.

The last strategy presented in the chapter was a classic put-writing strategy using a LEAPS put option as the security. The average one-year return for this strategy was just over +50 percent with a 50 percent standard deviation, but losses well in excess of 100 percent are possible if the index is very volatile and rises and falls repeatedly.

While the strategy is well known, one often unforeseen issue is that the margin requirements needed to maintain the position can often grow faster than the accumulated profits for the position. When this happens, the investor may have to either tap their cash reserve, or sell the LEAPS put and purchase one at a higher strike price to reduce the margin requirements. This additional cost would lower the expected return and make the returns less predictable.

Further analysis also showed that selling put options with a strike price just below market provided the highest risk-adjusted return, on average, because of the higher implied volatility of these options. The profits were 10 percent higher than if at-the-money options were used, and the standard deviation was 10 percent lower.

Put-writing strategies can be psychologically challenging, as it can be difficult to take losses and continue to write put options in a falling market, especially when the financial press is constantly reminding investors how bad the investment environment is. However, at some point the market always turns around, and the strategy begins to generate high profits due to the high volatility.

Still, these types of strategies are generally recommended for supplemental income rather than as a primary technique for managing the portfolio, because it can be difficult to allocate capital and manage risk, and because the market can always change, rendering earlier assumptions invalid. Selling a put option with the intent of profiting from its expiry is a high-risk transaction, and the primary concern must always be how to limit the potential damage to the portfolio.

CHAPTER 12

Managing the Leveraged Multistrategy Portfolio

T he final chapter of the book addresses the challenge of creating and managing multistrategy leveraged index portfolios. It begins with an overview of the advantages and disadvantages of utilizing alternative assets in a portfolio. These assets have become increasingly mainstream, but we'll make the case that although they fit the definition of investments they are not suitable for most portfolios.

Next, the performance of the ProShares Ultra S&P 500 ETF is investigated. This ETF is one of the most popular and widespread leveraged investments available for retail investors, yet, during the period since inception, it has lagged its underlying index, the S&P 500. The causes for this underperformance are illuminating and a better understanding can help investors avoid similar underperformance.

This chapter ends with steps to build and manage your own leveraged multistrategy investment portfolio using principles of effective management. Management is the practice of setting shared objectives, creating a strategic plan, directing action, and measuring results, and the section covers how each of those steps apply specifically to leveraged asset management.

THE QUESTION OF ALTERNATIVE ASSETS

We start with an important portfolio management question: Should alternative asset classes be included in the investment portfolio? Alternative assets such as precious metals, commodities, real estate, and currency have become increasingly mainstream and options and futures contracts on these securities are now cheap and easy to purchase.

Many portfolio managers include alternative assets because their performance has a low, zero, or sometimes even negative correlation to the broader index. As the price of a barrel of oil or a bushel of wheat or an acre of land rises, the value of the S&P 500 index may fall due to the increased expenses and cost of inputs. These types of assets are thought to provide a hedge against poor equity index performance.

Of course, alternative assets tend to get much more attention when their performance is up and the broader market is weak. At those times, financial reporters look to areas of outperformance and frequently find them in "hard" assets such as commodities or currencies.

At those times it is critical to recognize the nature and influence of a thesis or "story" in the valuations of any asset, including alternative assets. Many investments in unique and fast-growing companies or industries are referred to as "story stocks" because there is a compelling story behind the company that draws in investors. A clear example is small Internet stocks during 2000, a time when investors believed that these stocks were destined to dominate their industries both online and offline.

Stories generally develop because of some favorable fundamentals. Potential investors watch market values climb and, not wanting to be left behind, also buy the investment based upon those compelling fundamentals and a favorable story, and that pushes prices up even further.

For example, in 2005 and 2006 Hong Kong was clearly benefiting from the rapidly growing Chinese market combined with its unique political and economic position, and stock market prices skyrocketed accordingly. But by October 2007, the Hang Seng was up +130 percent from its October 2004 level. Did the fundamentals support this gain? Evidently not, as the index lost 25 percent of its value in the following six months.

That change in perception could be an opportunity for an active investor to profit by rapidly moving their position from long to short. But for a passive investor who is trying to build investment income through a buy-and-hold strategy with rebalancing and leverage, there are only two choices, both bad: sell at a loss or endure a long decline.

At times like this, it helps to understand that stories tend to move ahead of markets. If analysts are predicting that the value of a barrel of oil will be $200 next year, but it's only $100 today, then clearly there are many in the marketplace who don't believe the story; otherwise, the price of oil would be much higher already.

A frequently repeated story about hard assets such as gold, real estate, and commodities is that they are hedges against inflation and stores of value that can help reduce the impact of a continually devalued currency.

Like most investment stories, there is some truth to this, but if inflation is 3.8 percent, yet the price of coal futures has risen 50 percent, then clearly there's some mismatch.

The consensus of economists is that real estate and commodity prices do respond to inflation, but are primarily cyclical. Over time, higher prices trigger increases in production and reductions in supply, and these factors eventually lower prices. The lower prices then promote use but discourage new production, and when a shortage emerges, producers respond by raising prices. In the meantime, investor sentiment continually adjusts as traders try to predict which part of the cycle they are in.

There's no question that a specific alternative asset can and will outperform the broader market for a period. The problem is that there's no way to select this asset or predict the period of outperformance. But because they do have diversification value, perhaps a portfolio should own them all and index them. But in fact, there's a better alternative.

The Solution: Own the Producer

The definition of an investment is very broad: any asset that is expected to climb in value. It could include anything from distressed debt to a rare stamp. In this section, we will make a case that for indexing to work and deliver equity-like rates of return, an investment must be made in a producer, and not the product.

The distinction is important. When oil prices are rising, it may seem that an investor could profit by either buying a stake in the oil company or by buying a barrel of oil on the open market. But there is a world of difference between these two investments.

While the barrel of oil may fit the very broad definition of an investment, as someone somewhere has the capability to purchase it with the expectation that it will go up in value, the oil company did not produce that barrel as an investment, but rather for immediate consumption by customers. And while the company's fortunes may be tied to the price of a barrel of oil, we have to assume it would not bother producing the barrel if it didn't have some way to profit from the activity.

A producer is a professionally managed firm with access to supply and distribution and inside knowledge of the market and of short-term and long-term pricing trends. It can make production, purchasing, and investment decisions using that knowledge in order to increase profits, and then can reinvest the operating cash flow in other investments in order to grow the asset base.

Because of these capabilities, the firm is viewed and valued as an investment and priced based upon its ability to deliver future returns as compared to other potential investments. The share price is not immune to speculation, but over the long term, market prices would be expected to reflect the fair values of the investments.

In contrast, the barrel of oil itself will only be valued according to its utility as an economic resource. The need for oil may increase in the future, making it more valuable, but supply and demand patterns could also make prices stay flat or fall as compared to the value of a unit of currency, a treasury bill, or any other risk-free asset.

Of course there are many in the market that disagree, and will try to make the case that gold, real estate, commodities, or currency are equivalent to an equity and can offer similar rates of return. The problem is that the historical data doesn't support this assertion. Over the very long term, gold, commodities, real estate, and other assets have underperformed equities, delivering only bondlike returns with much higher volatility.

There is simply no substitute for the professional financial management of equities. Effective management is able to use market conditions to grow and compound earnings, increasing the value of the asset, while ineffective management is replaced by disgruntled shareholders.

This is a powerful mechanism that, over time, has delivered impressive returns, and we would urge investors not to depart from that model merely to chase performance. If portfolio diversification is all that's needed, then simply purchase and index the producers.

PROSHARES ETF ANALYSIS

On June 21st, 2006, the Ultra S&P 500 ProShares ETF (ticker: SSO) began trading at a dividend-adjusted price of $64.90. This ETF was developed by ProShares as a security that delivered twice the daily return of the underlying investment, in this case the S&P 500. The security became extremely popular with both retail and institutional investors, and trading volume ramped up quickly.

On April 1, 2008, this security closed at a dividend-adjusted price of $70.55. This represents a total return of 8.7 percent for the just over twenty-one month period, and an annualized return of 4.8 percent. In contrast, the SPY ETF rose from $121.61 to $136.61 in the same period, a 12.3 percent total return for the 21 months and a 6.7 percent annualized return (see Figure 12.1).

Clearly the leveraged fund is designed to provide a higher, not a lower, return than the underlying index. What went wrong?

It would be easy to blame the poor performance on the S&P 500, and as a rule, a leveraged investment will underperform when the returns of the underlying are lower than the cost of capital. For example, if a fund

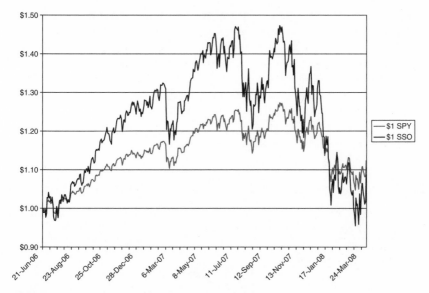

FIGURE 12.1   SSO vs. SPY, June 2006 to April 2008

borrows at 5 percent and invests at 4 percent, it is going to have a negative return for the leveraged portion of the portfolio.

However, the annualized return of the underlying index was 6.7 percent, and while somewhat disappointing, this certainly exceeds any imaginable cost of capital. Thus we should expect higher returns from any leveraged fund, and a 2× leveraged fund would be expected to provide an annual return in the 8 percent to 10 percent annual range. If we take the entire 21-month period into account, there's essentially a six- to nine-point return deficit that needs to be explained.

There are three issues affecting the performance. The first is that SSO has a relatively high management fee of 0.95 percent, and this lowers the performance. However, this would only contribute perhaps 1.8 percentage points to the shortfall over the period.

This fund uses futures contracts and equity swaps and rebalances daily in order to maintain a leverage ratio of 2×. In order to do so, this requires the fund to either increase or decrease their exposure to the index depending upon the previous day's return. For example, if the index falls 1 percent, then the fund must immediately thereafter sell index futures in order to reduce the leverage.

Daily rebalancing increases transaction costs somewhat, and this is the second issue. If we double the daily returns of the S&P 500 and then subtract a small amount that would be equal to an annual 6 percent expense, then the results are almost identical to the performance of the ETF on a daily basis and for the entire period.

The third issue is a little more complex and has to do with the leverage and volatility of the investment. During the 21 months studied, the volatility of the leveraged ETF is extremely high, reaching 31 percent on an annualized basis. This is expected, as the underlying index has a volatility of 15.5 percent for the period and the fund is leveraged 2×. But this high volatility creates the potential for sharp negative returns, which then occur in the latter part of the period.

Multiplier Leverage Effect

Then where exactly does most of the shortfall come from? The best explanation is that it is a consequence of daily rebalancing, and of taking on too much risk exposure as the index advances, and then too little exposure when the index decreases.

When gains and losses are multiplied, the results are asymmetrical and create situations which are difficult to recover from. Consider an underlying investment that loses 20 percent and a 2× leveraged fund based upon this investment that loses 40 percent of its value as a result of the leverage, as shown in Table 12.1. Then assume that the underlying investment recovers 10 percent of its value. What are the fund's results? For simplicity, assume no capital or transaction costs.

For the underlying investment, the 20 percent loss and 10 percent gain still leaves a significant shortfall. The fund has lost 12 percent total, and an additional +13.6 percent return would now be required for the fund to recover its initial value.

As the negative returns for the leveraged fund are magnified, the value has fallen much further, −28 percent, and a +38.9 percent return would now be required to recover the rest of the losses.

TABLE 12.1 Effect of Index Declines and Advances on a Leveraged Portfolio

	Underlying	Leveraged
Starting Price	$100	$100
After 20% Loss	$80	$60
After 10% Gain	$88	$72
% Shortfall	−12%	−28%
% Needed to Recover	+13.6%	+38.9%
After 15% Gain	$101.20	$93.60

Now let's assume that the index then rises 15 percent. This amount is just above the amount needed to bring it back to its original level, but is not enough to recover the losses in the leveraged fund. The difference in value between the two funds is now $7.60, a considerable disappointment for anyone expecting the leveraged fund to have higher performance.

And this is very similar to what happened to the leveraged ETF during the final months of the period. In the last several months of the period examined, the SPY falls from a peak of almost $155 to a low of $127, an 18 percent drop, but then recovers about 7 percent, leaving a shortfall of about 12 percent. The multiplier effect of leverage wipes out a third of the value of the leveraged ETF, but then recovers only a fraction of that loss.

By the end of the timeframe analyzed, the S&P 500 needs a +13.3 percent gain to recover its losses and hit its earlier peak, but the leveraged ETF would require a much larger +17.8 percent return from the underlying in order to do the same. It is easy to see how the shortfall in the leveraged fund could continue going forward.

Learning from Failure

This leveraged fund and return scenario holds valuable insights about leveraged portfolios. The first is that even with 2:1 leverage and an underlying investment with returns higher than the cost of capital it is very easy to lose money through a poor reinvestment strategy.

At the start of the period, one share of SSO is worth $64.90 and represents $129.80 of index exposure. As the index appreciates, this exposure climbs to $191.24, based on the SSO share price of $95.62. Then as the index falls, the fund exposure falls to $123.98. Aggressively increasing exposure during a bull market and then reducing it during a bear market may seem like smart trading at the time, but the result is a poorly positioned portfolio.

If improper selection of the level of leverage and index exposure can lead to a fund shortfall, then could a good reinvestment strategy increase returns as compared to the underlying index? Absolutely. Simply maintaining constant exposure to the index results in a 14.2 percent annualized return and a 20 percent increase over the period, a 7.4-point increase. The volatility of returns also decreases (see Figure 12.2).

We also show three reinvestment strategies in which the level of index exposure is constant. The annualized growth rates are +0 percent, +5 percent, and +10 percent. As Table 12.2 shows, all provide annualized returns much higher than the 6.7 percent annualized return of the underlying. In this example, the higher growth rates have lower returns, but this won't always be the case, as it depends upon the price trends of the underlying.

Reinvestment strategies were covered in earlier chapters, but there are a few important lessons to be found in this example. The first is that even a

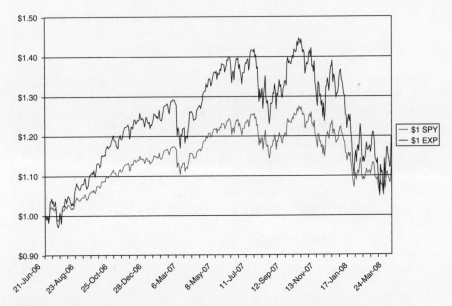

FIGURE 12.2   Effect of Maintaining Constant Leveraged Exposure

popular ETF can suffer from flaws in the reinvestment strategy that make it a failure as a long-term investment. In fairness to ProShares, the leveraged funds are marketed primarily to short-term traders, but undoubtedly there are some longer-term investors that purchase the security without understanding its limitations.

In a long-term leveraged investment, the level of index exposure needs to be constantly managed and maintained. This applies not only to a managed futures fund, which is technically what the leveraged ETF is, but to

TABLE 12.2   Return Statistics with Controlled Exposure Growth Rates

| | Annual Exposure Growth | | |
	+10%	+5%	0%
Daily	0.0530%	0.0530%	0.0531%
Std.	1.83%	1.71%	1.61%
Min.	−6.50%	−6.31%	−6.12%
Max.	9.64%	8.69%	7.82%
Ann. vol.	28.99%	27.19%	25.49%
Ann. Return	14.16%	14.16%	14.19%
Tot. return	17.63%	18.67%	19.67%

any investment that takes a leveraged long position on the index using any of the derivative strategies mentioned in the book.

And this becomes even more critical when high-leverage strategies are used. For example, what if the fund had been leveraged $3\times$ or $4\times$ and attempted to increase its exposure as the index appreciated? At $4\times$ leverage with a constant level of investment, the fund makes 16.36 percent annualized. But if the level of exposure is left to the market, the downturn at the end of the period wipes out all of the earlier gains, and the fund actually loses 10 percent in the period.

ASSET MANAGEMENT OVERVIEW

According to business academia, management is the practice of developing strategic plans, directing resources, and making required adjustments in order to meet a shared objective. This applies to managing any organization, including one that manages assets.

The objective of asset management may seem obvious—to make money. But of course there are many ways to make money within the discipline of finance, as both a neighborhood bank and a leveraged commodity hedge fund can attest to. The objective has to be defined more clearly; for example, to own leveraged positions on a portfolio of indexes in order to create higher returns than the underlying index while keeping risk relatively low in absolute terms.

Next, a strategic plan is developed that includes the selection of strategies and indexes and the proposed asset allocation. Included in this plan are assumptions about the long-term performance and volatility of the underlying indexes, and the corresponding effect on the leveraged portfolio.

Because the underlying assets are unpredictable, scenarios need to be created that address what actions will be taken if the market rises, falls, or holds steady in both the short and long term. In a traditional business environment, this would be called contingency planning, and is generally demanded by executive management to ensure that potential risks are being addressed.

After the planning is completed, all resources are directed and the results monitored. In the context of asset management, this is the launch of the fund, in which securities are purchased and held, and then repeated investments are made as required over time. For a leveraged portfolio, monitoring results would include not just daily security performance, but also volatility, correlations, and even changes in the investment environment, such as new investment products or brokerages, decreased liquidity, or new regulation.

During the life of the investment portfolio, management should expect to make adjustments to the strategic plan. This may be due to the afore-mentioned changes, but more often than not, it is simply because very few strategic plans are perfect and can be implemented without issue.

Management is one area in which it is widely recognized that additional expertise and experience is worth the extra cost. When organizations de-velop a reputation for poor management, they are deserted not only by their customers, but also by their employees, financiers, and other business partners. Any cost savings achieved through second-rate management are short term at best.

There are two traits that set the effective managers apart from the mediocre. The first is organization. While many people consider themselves organized if they clean their desk every day or have several e-mail folders, in management, organization is defined as the ability to arrange or group information in a manner that improves task efficiency. For the task of port-folio management, effective organization means having a clear plan, a de-tailed list of the actions that have been taken or will need to be taken to achieve the plan, and a precise accounting of the past results achieved and the future results expected.

The second trait is the ability to face reality. In management, the earlier in the process that mistakes are found, the less costly they are. When a mis-take appears in a strategic plan, it can be corrected with a few keystrokes. But, if the same mistake is never identified until after implementation, the cost to correct can be crippling.

Effective managers may be optimist or pessimist by nature, but they are also realists. When the facts on the ground don't fit the model, they in-vestigate the reasons and make changes accordingly. For a portfolio man-ager, this may mean eliminating specific strategies or indexes when it be-comes clear that some early assumptions were incorrect.

Security Selection

Most index investors start with the S&P 500 as the core of their portfolio. However, as we've seen earlier, a strategy that rebalances the eight sector funds, as represented by the sector SPDR funds, can have higher returns and lower volatility than the S&P 500. Thus, it may be more effective to own these eight funds rather than the single S&P 500.

The advantage to owning the single S&P 500 rather than the eight funds is that the S&P 500 itself is only one fund and widely traded, which low-ers transaction costs, and its volatility is lower, which reduces the hedging costs. Thus for options strategies that require higher levels of leverage and very low transaction costs, using the S&P 500 is likely the better approach.

However, a managed futures fund that blended the eight sector funds would have a very low cost if the fund is large enough, and would likely outperform the S&P 500 with less risk over the long term. Or alternately, the fund could sell calls on each of the sectors in order to earn income and reduce hedging expenses and thereby take advantage of the higher volatility.

Next, the investor would want to include additional indexes such as small-cap, value, and international in order to diversify further and potentially improve performance. For U.S. small-cap stocks, the Russell 2000 is the obvious choice due to its low transaction costs and high performance, although the SmallCap 600 is starting to emerge as a potential competitor.

Generally, it is difficult to find exposure to international indexes on U.S. exchanges except through ETFs and their derivatives. The MSCI EAFE index is a single ETF that contains foreign exposure and LEAPS on this index are available. Again, the investor would have to decide whether to select a single ETF with broad exposure, or to equally weight smaller indexes in order to reduce volatility. This may require purchasing derivatives on foreign exchanges.

An investor could also overweight specific industry indexes in order to further diversify. There are many index futures available that provide exposure to industries such as utilities, energy, health care, or consumer staples that historically have lower S&P 500 correlations, and these can be combined to create lower volatility portfolios.

For example, as mentioned earlier, gold itself would not be a recommended investment for a portfolio, but gold producers would be, as long as it's a small part of the portfolio and the industry isn't selected at an obvious peak and period of high volatility. A portfolio could achieve this exposure through the GOX index, an equal-dollar weighted index composed of 11 companies whose core business is gold mining and/or production with futures traded on the CBOE.

The total number of investments selected could be two or three, or could be thirty or forty, depending upon the size of the portfolio.(See Table 12.3 for an example of a ten security portfolio of both ETFs and indexes.) Working with more indexes would result in higher transaction costs, not only because of the sheer number, but also because it is likely that some of the more obscure indexes selected would have less liquidity and higher transaction costs and/or volatility than the more popular ones.

Long and Short Strategy Combination

One question that arises is whether it would be beneficial to adopt both a long-term and a short-term strategy on the same index, especially if both strategies are bullish or bullish-neutral. For example, suppose an investor

TABLE 12.3   Sample ETF and Index Option Portfolio

ETF Options

Ticker	Index ETF
MDY	MidCap
IWN	SmallCap Value
XLU	Utilities
EFA	Europe, Asia, Far East
EEM	Emerging Markets

Index Options

Ticker	Index ETF
RUT	Russell 2000
UKX	UK 100
OEX	S&P 100
TXX	Technology
GOX	Gold Producers

decided to enter the following positions on the Russell 2000 index. Assume the initial price is 100.

> Buy Call @ 70 Exp 2 years (LEAP)
> Buy Call @ 101 Exp 6 months
> Sell Call @ 101 Exp 3 months

This investor is using two strategies: the first, a deep-in-the-money LEAPS call on the index which could be held or rolled over, and the second, a calendar call spread at a strike price slightly above market lasting three months. One is a long-term buy-and-hold strategy, and the other is a shorter-term cash generation strategy that would be repeated every three months.

Over the three-month period, we would expect the profitability of the calendar call spread to vary widely, and the position could easily be up or down 50 percent. The LEAPS would be much more stable, and although highly leveraged, would be unlikely to gain or lose more than 10 or 20 percent unless the market makes a large move.

On the other hand, the LEAPS is a relatively large investment with an initial cost of at least $30 per share, based on its intrinsic value. The calendar spread would be extremely inexpensive, perhaps only $1 or $2. Therefore in absolute terms, the LEAPS' total returns would have a much bigger impact than that of a single calendar call spread. However, over the two year period, the eight quarterly positions may provide more profit or loss.

If the index declines significantly in the next three months, the LEAPS would lose value, but the investor could certainly hold the position and wait for it to recover. In contrast, the investment in the calendar spread would be lost, and the investor would have to tap into their financial reserve. This is why repeated shorter-term strategies are sometimes called "cash" strategies, as both gains and losses will be paid immediately.

If calendar call spreads were purchased every three months, and the LEAPS was rolled every year, then in theory income from the calendar call strategy could fund the roll-forward costs. However, this is risky of course, and the investor would also need to ensure that he or she still has the ability to roll the LEAPS forward next year even if they lose money on several calendar calls.

Both the long-term bullish and the short-term neutral-bullish strategies are vulnerable to negative returns. However, because the time frames of the strategies are different, it is possible for the LEAPS to do well but the calendar spreads to perform poorly, or vice versa, even with the same sequence of returns.

For example, let's say that the index rises 20 percent in two years, but the volatility is extremely high and most quarters have either large gains or severe losses. In this case, the LEAPS may perform very well during the period, while the calendar calls perform erratically and never turn a significant profit.

Thus, although these two investment strategies use the same underlying index, they should be seen as separate but correlated investments. The challenge is the unpredictability of the calendar call strategy, but if the repeated investments are small and roughly identical in amount, it should be possible to calculate the long-term averages and do the required forecasting.

Strategy Selection

The choice of strategies for a specific index is often limited by the availability of derivatives. While some indexes, such as the S&P 500 or Russell 2000 have a vast array of derivatives and very low bid-ask spreads and as a result are suitable for just about any strategy, other indices are not as liquid or don't have the same types of derivatives available, and as a result limit the strategies available.

As a rule, shorter-term strategies will work only for indexes that have very low bid-ask spreads and transaction costs. These strategies include calendar call and put spreads, diagonal call spreads, bear put spreads, or

TABLE 12.4	Sample Strategy Selection
Long-Term Strategies	Long LEAPS ITM Call Option rolled annually
	Long index future
Short-Term Cash Strategies	Long one-year ITM call option
Using Call Options	Short three-month ATM call option
Short-Term Cash Strategies	Long three-months ATM put option
Using Put Options	Short one-month ATM put option

other short option positions in which the short option is held for only three months or less. Table 12.4 includes a list of short and long-term strategies.

If the position is one that will be held longer, such as a LEAPS call that is rolled over or held to expiry, or a calendar or diagonal call spread using six-month and nine-month options, then liquidity is not as much of a factor, and the strategy would work on a variety of indexes.

Volatility is also an issue as it adds to the hedging cost for the index, and this cost is built into the pricing of any option position. Index volatility also leads to portfolio volatility, which results in unpredictable investments. Selling options on extremely volatile indexes can be a very frightening experience, as losses can emerge suddenly and accumulate quickly.

Futures are in a category by themselves, and there are many indexes that have futures contracts available but no options or vice versa. Usually if a futures contract can be found on an index, the transaction costs and the bid-ask spread are low and not a significant factor affecting profitability so long as the position is long term. Volatility is not specifically a factor in futures pricing, but as a rule higher volatility indexes would have higher margin requirements.

Minimum Investment Sizes

As in most investment strategies, a leveraged futures or options strategy will have a practical minimum level of investment. This minimum is a function of the share price, the options selected, the transaction costs, and the bid-ask spread.

For example, if a strategy involves purchasing deep-in-the-money LEAPS call options on SPY, the S&P 500 ETF, and the associated LEAPS options are trading at $35 per share and there are 100 shares in an option contract, then the minimum level of investment is $3,500. If a broker is charging $8 per options contract, then that represents 0.22 percent of the purchase price, a fairly small percentage.

However, that doesn't include the bid-ask spread. If the bid price of the option is $34.80 and the ask price is $35.40, then the sixty-cent difference would be multiplied by the contract size, and would result in a fee of $60. The total fee required to buy and sell the security then would be $76, or about 2 percent of the purchase price. The costs start to add up.

As the size of the investment increases, the impact of the bid-ask spread grows at the same rate unless the investor is able to get preferential pricing. Transaction costs may go up also, depending upon whether the broker charges significantly more as contract counts increase.

The minimum transaction size to own a LEAPS call on an index option can be very large for a retail investor because of the high absolute prices of these securities. A single in-the-money LEAPS call option contract on an index that trades at 1400 may cost $35,000. The benefit is that the investor can buy and sell $140,000 worth of index exposure with one single transaction.

Shorter-term strategies such as diagonal and calendar spreads will have much lower minimums, because the options held have much lower values. It's common for put-spread prices to be only $1 or $2 per share on a $100+ ETF, and in order to get $50,000 of exposure, an investor would need to trade 250 to 500 contracts.

Futures contracts are designed for institutional investors, and as a result the amounts moved in a single contract are also large, from a retail investor's point of view. Typically, the "mini" futures contracts are valued at $50 per point, and the "full-size" futures contracts are valued at $250 per point. For an index with an initial value of 1200, a mini would represent index exposure of $60,000 and a full-size contract would represent an exposure of $300,000.

Because only a 5 percent margin is required to hold a position on a broad index, a position on $60,000 or $300,000 of securities would not require a lot of performance margin in order to hold initially. For example, $50,000 can secure $1 million's worth of securities, and the transaction costs are extremely low.

This is why futures brokers sometimes advertise that an investor could start trading with as little as $3,000 for a mini contract. While this is technically true, it ignores the necessity of the cash reserve that is required to withstand any kind of downturn. When the reserve is gone, the broker closes the position and applies the reserve to the losses.

Index Exposure

The long-term performance of an investment portfolio is a direct result of its selected strategies and underlying securities and the amount of capital allocated to each. The higher-risk and higher-reward strategies raise the average returns, but also the probability that the portfolio could lose most or all of its value. This effect is mitigated by selecting securities with low correlations.

In fact, indexes such as the Russell 2000 and the NASDAQ-100 can be seen as a collection of high-risk investments that, when combined into a portfolio, have an acceptable risk-reward ratio. Many of the stocks on the NASDAQ can have implied volatilities of 50 percent or 60 percent, but the implied volatility of the NASDAQ itself averages in the 20s because of the power of diversification.

In an index fund 100 percent of assets are invested, but with higher-risk strategies, typically only a fraction of the portfolio is invested and the rest is withheld for future investment. This lowers the risk of the portfolio and makes the investment's long-term results more predictable, and also allows cycling strategies to be created in which the portfolio has the opportunity to grow rapidly.

Most index funds are also market-cap weighted, but as a rule equal-weighted asset allocation strategies will deliver the same or higher returns with lower risk due to their ability to evenly spread exposure across a variety of assets. This requires some rebalancing, which may be inexact when dealing with high-value options or futures contracts and would result in additional transaction costs.

As we've seen in the leveraged ETF example, strategy exposure needs to be carefully managed in order to prevent situations in which the portfolio posts rapid gains, but then crashes in a downturn and gets into a situation in which it cannot recover. Ideally, a portfolio should be able to commit a similar amount to the strategy every month or quarter. Steady levels of investment help to reduce the volatility of portfolio returns.

To take advantage of this requires some discipline and foresight. Simulations need to be run in which the index is flat or declines and correlations between assets increase in order to ensure that the portfolio still has enough cash to continue to invest at the same level. This may require slowly reducing the level of exposure over a period of months.

Not all problems will be found in simulation. If the portfolio is live and potential problems with dangerous levels of strategy exposure are later identified, they need to be corrected. The best time to do this is when the market is rising or flat—changing strategy in a falling market will become expensive, but there are times when large losses have to be taken in order to prevent a potential catastrophe.

The most important lesson that we hope to convey in this book is that errors in asset allocation are the leading cause of death in leveraged portfolios. Fortunes have been made and then lost again and again by disregarding this maxim.

SUMMARY

This chapter covers selected topics in asset management, security selection, and strategy exposure. The objective is to provide portfolio managers with the tools they need to implement the leveraged investment strategies discussed earlier within leveraged multistrategy index-based portfolios.

It begins by addressing and, we hope, discrediting the idea of using alternative assets such as commodities and real estate as diversifiers in a portfolio. A sharp distinction is drawn between equity in a professionally managed firm with the capability to build market knowledge and expertise and grow earnings, and the specific product that it sells.

While commodities and currencies may fit the loose definition of an investment, as someone, somewhere has purchased it with the expectation that it will increase in value rather than simply as an economic input, over the historical period equities have delivered higher returns, and, when appropriately indexed, have lower volatility. There will be periods in which alternative assets outperform the broad equity indexes, but this is caused more by isolated short-term factors rather than by any fundamental change in characteristic.

Then our attention is turned toward the ProShares Ultra ETF, a popular leveraged investment widely available to retail investors. Since its inception, this investment has delivered poor returns and has lagged the S&P 500, its underlying index, significantly. Based upon the level of leverage, the expected return for the period should be 10 points higher for the 21-month period examined.

While this ETF has additional expenses and transaction costs, the primary cause of the underperformance is that the fund increased index exposure too aggressively while the index was advancing, and then reduced it as the market declined. This activity increased the risks, and as a result the returns fell well below the underlying index. This is presented as a cautionary tale regarding index exposure.

FINAL WORDS

Our final piece of advice to investors is simple: Get started.

At any point in time there are plenty of reasons why the index should be 10 percent higher or lower next week, next month, or next year, and all of those reasons will be convincing. But the truth is that nobody knows what the future will hold. Historically, the best time to buy the index is sooner rather than later, and every day without index exposure is a lost opportunity.

Over several months, profits may come quickly, or the index may lose ground. In a leveraged investment, the results in that short a time will be relatively unpredictable. Rising markets may cause false optimism and encourage overinvesting, or falling markets may bring a loss of hope; but all this is completely normal, and long-term investors are best served by being skeptical in the short term but relatively optimistic over the long haul.

The performance differential of an enhanced index portfolio will probably become apparent only over a span of five or more years. Before then, the difference between a 10 percent and, for example, an 18 percent annual gain is certainly significant, but not astronomical. But after ten years, the portfolio that can compound at the higher rate will be worth twice as much, and after fifteen years it will be worth almost three times as much.

Investing for years or decades requires planning and discipline. It means not overinvesting when the markets are up, but continuing to invest when things look bleak. Because it can be difficult to exit a leveraged investment, it is often prudent to invest a smaller and more manageable amount in order to achieve the same objectives.

Begin accumulating indexes now and find a way to incorporate them into your strategy. There are always new indexes and ETFs appearing in the marketplace, and improved liquidity is making the existing ones more accessible. Each of these index investments offers diversification potential, which allows higher levels of leverage and higher returns.

Then begin collecting strategies. Start with a simple strategy, such as owning and rolling a LEAPS call option, and then move to the more complex repeated strategies, such as diagonal call spreads and calendar puts. Model each strategy and collect inputs from market prices to check the underlying assumptions that deliver the profits over time.

Forget about annual returns and think monthly or even weekly. Understand the small movements in market prices that combine to create the longer-term trends. Then, when the index gains 5 percent in a week, which it does every four or five years, make sure that you're positioned to get a year's worth of investing profits out of that one rally.

And because that move could happen at any time, even next week, you want to get started today.

List of Index ETFs and Futures

The tables provided in this appendix can be used as a starting point for selecting the underlying securities for a leveraged portfolio. The following listings identify the indexes and ETFs that have options available, and at the beginning of each list we highlight the most widely traded and well-known indexes.

Before selecting an index, be sure to track the pricing for a period of time and confirm that there is liquidity, both for the index or ETF overall, and for options at the specific strike prices and expiration dates that will be used in the strategy. Also, compare the implied volatility for at-the-money options on the security with the historical volatility and verify that the volatility premium is consistent.

More information can be found at the web sites for the exchanges, and at an excellent online resource provided by the Options Industry Council (www.888options.com), which also provides the original materials that were the starting points for this listing.

TABLE A.1 Index Options

Most Liquid Index Options

Ticker	Index
DJX	Dow Jones Industrial Average
NDX	NASDAQ-100 Index
OEX	S&P 100 Index (OEX)
RUT	Russell 2000 Index
SPX	S&P 500 Index (SPX)

Other Index Options

Ticker	Index
BKX	PHLX/KBW Bank Sector Index
BTK	Biotech Index
BYT	ISE Semiconductors
CMR	Morgan Stanley Consumer Index
CRX	Morgan Stanley Commodity Related Equity Index
CYC	Morgan Stanley Cyclical Index
DFI	Defense Index
DFX	PHLX Defense Sector
DOT	TheStreet.com Internet Sector
DRG	Pharmaceutical Index
DUX	Dow Jones Utility Average
DXL	Jumbo DJX Index
EPX	SIG Oil Exploration & Production Index
EUR	EUROTOP 100 Index
EXQ	CBOE Exchange Index
GOX	CBOE Gold Index
HAI	Hapoalim American Israeli Index
HGX	PHLX Housing Sector
HKO	Hong Kong Option Index
HSX	ISE-CCM Homeland Security
HUI	Gold BUGS Index
HVY	ISE Gold Index
IIX	Inter@ctive Week Internet Index
IXK	ISE 50
IXX	ISE 100
IXZ	ISE 250
JLO	ISE US Regional Banks
JPN	Japan Index

TABLE A.1 *(Continued)*

Other Index Options

Ticker	Index
KRX	KBW Regional Bank Index
MFX	KBW Mortgage Finance Index
MID	S&P MidCap 400 Index
MNX	Mini-NDX Index
MSH	Morgan Stanley High-Technology 35 Index
MVR	Morgan Stanley Retail
NBI	Nasdaq Biotechnology
OIX	CBOE Oil Index
OSX	PHLX Oil Service Index
PMP	ISE Integrated Oil and Gas
POW	ISE-CCM Alternative Energy Index
RMN	Mini-Russell 2000 Index
RMN	Mini-Russell 2000 Index Options
RND	ISE Pharmaceuticals
RUF	ISE Homebuilders
RUI	Russell 1000 Index
RVX	CBOE Russell 2000 Volatility Index
RXS	PHLX Drug Sector
SIN	ISE SINdex
SML	S&P SmallCap 600 Index
SOX	PHLX Semiconductor Sector Index
UTY	PHLX Utility Sector Index
VIX	CBOE Volatility Index
VXN	CBOE Nasdaq-100 Volatility Index
XAL	Airline Index
XAU	PHLX Gold and Silver Sector Index
XBD	Securities Broker/Dealer Index (The)
XCI	Computer Technology Index
XDB	British Pound Currency
XDE	Euro Currency
XEO	S&P 100 Index European
XMI	Major Market Index
XNG	Natural Gas Index (The)
XOI	Oil Index
XSP	Mini-SPX Index

TABLE A.2 ETF Options

Most Liquid ETF Options

Ticker	Index
DIA	Options on DIAMONDS®
EFA	iShares MSCI-EAFE
EEM	iShares MSCI-Emerging Markets Index Fund
IWM	iShares Russell 2000
IWN	iShares Russell 2000 Value
IWO	iShares Russell 2000 Growth
MDY	Standard & Poor's MidCap 400 SPDRS
OEF	iShares S&P 100 Index Fund
SPY	SPDRS SPY
QQQQ	Nasdaq-100 Index Tracking Stock
XLB	Select Sector SPDR-Materials
XLE	Select Sector SPDR-Energy
XLF	Select Sector SPDR-Financial
XLI	Select Sector SPDR-Industrial
XLK	Select Sector SPDR-Technology
XLP	Select Sector SPDR-Consumer Staples
XLU	Select Sector SPDR-Utilities
XLV	Select Sector SPDR-Health Care
XLY	Consumer Discretionary Select Sector SPDR

Other ETF Options

Ticker	Index
ADRE	BLDRS Emerging Markets 50 ADR Index Fund
AGG	iShares Lehman Aggregate Bond Fund
BIL	SPDR Lehman 1–3 Month T-Bill ETF
BIV	Vanguard® Intermediate-Term Bond ETF
BLV	Vanguard® Long-Term Bond ETF
BND	Vanguard® Total Bond Market ETF
BSV	Vanguard® Short-Term Bond ETF
CGW	Claymore S&P Global Water Index ETF
CSD	Claymore/Clear Spinoff ETF
DBA	PowerShares DB Agriculture Fund
DBB	PowerShares DB Base Metals Fund
DBC	Powershares DB Commodity Index Tracking Fund
DBE	PowerShares DB Energy Fund
DBO	PowerShares DB Oil Fund
DBP	PowerShares DB Precious Metals Fund
DBS	PowerShares DB Silver Fund
DBV	PowerShares DB G10 Currency Harvest Fund
DEF	Claymore/Sabrient Defense ETF
DES	WisdomTree SmallCap Dividend Fund
DGL	PowerShares DB Gold Fund

TABLE A.2 *(Continued)*

Other ETF Options

Ticker	Index
DGT	streetTRACKS®—DJ Global Titans Index Fund
DHS	WisdomTree High-Yielding Equity Fund
DLN	WisdomTree LargeCap Dividend Fund
DSI	iShares KLD 400 Social Index Fund
DTD	WisdomTree Total Dividend Fund
DTN	WisdomTree Dividend Top 100 Fund
DVY	iShares Dow Jones Select Dividend Index Fund
EEB	Claymore/BNY BRIC ETF
ELR	streetTRACKS DJ Wilshire Large Cap ETF
EMG	streetTRACKS DJ Wilshire Mid Cap Growth ETF
EMM	streetTRACKS DJ Wilshire Mid Cap ETF
EVX	Market Vectors Environmental Services ETF
EWA	iShares MSCI Australia Index Fund
EWC	iShares MSCI Canada Index Fund
EWD	iShares MSCI Sweden Index Fund
EWG	iShares MSCI Germany Index Fund
EWH	iShares MSCI Hong Kong Index Fund
EWJ	iShares MSCI Japan Index Fund
EWM	iShares MSCI Malaysia Index Fund
EWP	iShares MSCI Spain Index
EWT	iShares MSCI TAIWAN Index Fund
EWU	iShares MSCI United Kingdom Index Fund
EWY	iShares MSCI South Korea Index Fund—ETF
EWZ	iShares MSCI Brazil Index Fund
EXB	Claymore/Clear Global Exchanges, Brokers & Asset Managers Index ETF
FBT	First Trust Amex Biotechnology Index Fund
FCG	First Trust ISE-Revere Natural Gas Index Fund
FDL	First Trust Morningstar Dividend Leaders Index Fund
FDM	First Trust Dow Jones Select MicroCap Index Fund
FEZ	DJ Euro Stoxx 50 ETF
FIW	First Trust ISE Water Index Fund
FPX	First Trust IPOX-100 Index Fund
FXA	CurrencyShares Australian Dollar Trust
FXB	CurrencyShares British Pound Sterling Trust
FXC	CurrencyShares Canadian Dollar Trust
FXE	CurrencyShares Euro Trust
FXF	CurrencyShares Swiss Franc Trust
FXM	CurrencyShares Mexican Peso Trust
FXN	First Trust Energy AlphaDEX Fund
FXS	CurrencyShares Swedish Krona Trust
FXU	First Trust Utilities AlphaDEX Fund

(Continued)

TABLE A.2	*(Continued)*

Other ETF Options

Ticker	Index
FXY	CurrencyShares Japanese Yen Trust
GAF	SPDR® S&P Emerging Middle East & Africa ETF
GDX	The Market Vectors—Gold Miners ETF
GII	SPDR® FTSE/Macquarie Global Infrastructure 100 ETF
GKD	Ameristock/Ryan 10-Year Treasury ETF
GKE	Ameristock/Ryan 20-Year Treasury ETF
GMF	SPDR® S&P Emerging Asia Pacific ETF
GMM	SPDR® S&P Emerging Markets ETF
GSG	iShares GSCI Commodity-Indexed Trust
GXC	SPDR® S&P China ETF
HHJ	HealthShares Emerging Cancer ETF
HYG	iShares iBoxx $ High Yield Corporate Bond Fund
ICF	iShares Cohen & Steers Realty Majors
IDU	iShares DJ® US Utilities Sector
IEF	iShares Lehman 7–10 Year Treasury Bond Fund
IGM	iShares Goldman Sachs® Technology Index
IGN	iShares® Goldman Sachs Networking Index Fund
IGV	iShares Goldman Sachs Software Index Fund
IGW	iShares Goldman Sachs Semiconductor Index Fund
IJH	iShares S&P MidCap 400 Index Fund
IJJ	iShares S&P MidCap 400 Value Index Fund
IJK	iShares S&P MidCap 400 Growth Index Fund
IJR	iShares S&P SmallCap 600 Index Fund
IJS	iShares S&P SmallCap 600 Value Index Fund
IJT	iShares S&P SmallCap 600 Growth Index Fund
ILF	iShares S&P Latin America 40
IPE	SPDR Barclays Capital TIPS ETF
ITE	SPDR Lehman Intermediate Term Treasury ETF
IVE	iShares Trust S&P 500 Value Index Fund
IVV	iShares Trust S&P 500 Index Fund
IVW	iShares S&P 500 Growth Index Fund
IWB	iShares Russell 1000
IWC	iShares Russell Microcap Index Fund
IWD	iShares Russell 1000 Value
IWF	iShares Russell 1000 Growth
IWP	iShares Russell Midcap® Growth Index Fund
IWR	iShares Russell Midcap Index Fund
IWS	iShares Russell Midcap Value Index Fund
IWV	iShares Russell 3000
IYC	iShares Dow Jones US Consumer Services Sector
IYE	iShares Trust—DJ US Energy Sector Index Fund

TABLE A.2 *(Continued)*

Other ETF Options

Ticker	Index
IYF	iShares Dow Jones U.S. Financial Sector Index Fund
IYG	iShares Dow Jones US Financial Services Sector
IYH	iShares Trust—DJ US Healthcare Sector Index Fund
IYJ	iShares Dow Jones US Industrial Sector Index
IYK	iShares Dow Jones US Consumer Goods Sector
IYM	iShares Dow Jones U.S. Basic Materials Sector Index Fund
IYR	iShares Dow Jones U.S. Real Estate Index Fund
IYT	iShares Dow Jones Transportation Average Index Fund
IYW	iShares Dow Jones U.S. Technology Sector Index Fund
IYY	iShares DJ US Total Market
IYZ	iShares Dow Jones U.S. Telecommunications Sector Index Fund
JPP	streetTRACKS Russell/Nomura PRIME Japan ETF
JSC	streetTRACKS Russell/Nomura Small Cap Japan ETF
KBE	streetTRACKS ETF KBW Bank
KCE	streetTRACKS ETF KBW Capital Markets
KIE	streetTRACKS ETF KBW Insurance
KLD	iShares KLD Select Social Index Fund
KRE	streetTRACKS KBW Regional Banking^{SM} ETF
LQD	iShares GS $ InvesTop^{TM} Corporate Bond Fund
MOO	Market Vectors-Agribusiness ETF
NXT	NYSE Arca Tech 100 ETF
OIH	Oil Service HOLDRS Trust
ONEQ	Options on Fidelity® Nasdaq Composite Index® Tracking Stock
OTP	Claymore/Ocean Tomo Patent ETF
PBE	PowerShares Dynamic Biotechnology & Genome Portfolio
PBS	PowerShares Dynamic Media Portfolio
PBW	PowerShares WilderHill Clean Energy Portfolio
PDQ	PowerShares FTSE RAFI Asia Pacific ex-Japan Small-Mid Portfolio
PEZ	PowerShares Dynamic Consumer Discretionary Sector Portfolio
PFI	PowerShares Dynamic Financial Sector Portfolio
PFM	PowerShares Dividend Achievers Portfolio
PFP	PowerShares International Listed Private Equity Portfolio
PGJ	PowerShares Golden Dragon Halter USX China Portfolio
PGZ	PowerShares Dynamic Aggressive Growth Portfolio
PHJ	PowerShares High Growth Rate Dividend Achievers Portfolio
PHO	PowerShares Water Resource Portfolio
PID	PowerShares International Dividend Achievers Portfolio
PJB	PowerShares Dynamic Banking Portfolio
PJF	PowerShares Dynamic Large Cap Portfolio
PJM	PowerShares Dynamic Small Cap Portfolio

(Continued)

TABLE A.2 *(Continued)*

Other ETF Options

Ticker	Index
PMR	PowerShares Dynamic Retail Portfolio
PRF	PowerShares FTSE RAFI 1000 Portfolio
PRN	PowerShares Dynamic Industrials Sector Portfolio
PSP	PowerShares Listed Private Equity Portfolio
PTF	PowerShares Dynamic Technology Sector Portfolio
PTH	PowerShares Dynamic Healthcare Sector Portfolio
PTJ	PowerShares Dynamic Healthcare Services Portfolio
PUW	PowerShares WilderHill Progressive Energy Portfolio
PVM	PowerShares Dynamic Deep Value Portfolio
PWB	PowerShares Dynamic Large Cap Growth Portfolio
PWC	PowerShares Dynamic Market Portfolio
PWJ	PowerShares Dynamic Mid Cap Growth Portfolio
PWO	PowerShares Dynamic OTC Portfolio
PWT	PowerShares Dynamic Small Cap Growth Portfolio
PWV	PowerShares Dynamic Large Cap Value Portfolio
PWY	PowerShares Dynamic Small Cap Value Portfolio
PXE	PowerShares Dynamic Energy Exploration & Production Portfolio
PXH	PowerShares FTSE RAFI Emerging Markets Portfolio
PXJ	PowerShares Dynamic Oil Services Portfolio
PXN	PowerShares Lux Nanotech Portfolio
PYZ	PowerShares Dynamic Basic Materials Sector Portfolio
PZD	PowerShares Cleantech Portfolio
PZI	PowerShares Zacks Micro Cap Portfolio
RFV	Rydex S&P Mid Cap 400 Pure Value ETF
RPV	Rydex S&P 500 Pure Value ETF
RSP	RSP—Rydex S&P Equal Weight Index Fund
RSX	Market Vectors Russia ETF Trust
RWR	streetTRACKS® DJ Wilshire REIT ETF
RWX	streetTRACKS® DJ Wilshire International Real Estate ETF
SDY	SPDR Dividend ETF
SHY	iShares Lehman 1–3 Year Treasury Bond Fund
SLX	Market Vectors Steel ETF
TLO	SPDR Lehman Long Term Treasury ETF
TLT	iShares Lehman 20+ Year Treasury Bond Fund
TMW	streetTRACKS DJ Wilshire Total Market ETF
UNG	United States Natural Gas Fund, LP
USO	United States Oil Fund, LP
VAW	Vanguard Materials VIPERs
VB	Vanguard Small-Cap VIPERs
VBK	Vanguard Small-Cap Growth VIPERs
VBR	Vanguard Small-Cap Value VIPERs
VCR	Vanguard Consumer Discretionary VIPERs

TABLE A.2 *(Continued)*

Other ETF Options

Ticker	Index
VDC	Vanguard Consumer Staples VIPERs
VDE	Vanguard Energy VIPERs
VEU	Vanguard FTSE All-World ex US ETF
VFH	Vanguard Financials VIPERs
VGK	Vanguard European VIPERs
VGT	Vanguard Information Technology VIPERs
VHT	Vanguard Health Care VIPERs
VIG	Vanguard Dividend Appreciation VIPERs
VIS	Vanguard Industrials VIPERs
VNQ	Vanguard REIT VIPERs
VO	Vanguard Mid-Cap VIPERs
VOE	Vanguard Mid-Cap Value ETF
VOX	Vanguard Telecommunication Services VIPERs
VPL	Vanguard Pacific VIPERs
VPU	Vanguard Utilities VIPERs
VTI	Vanguard Total Stock Market VIPERs
VTV	Vanguard Value VIPERs
VUG	Vanguard Growth VIPERs
VV	Vanguard Large-Cap VIPERs
VWO	Vanguard Emerging Markets VIPERs
VXF	Vanguard Extended Market VIPERs
VYM	Vanguard High Dividend Yield ETF
XBI	SPDR® Biotech ETF
XES	SPDR® Oil & Gas Equipment & Services ETF
XHB	SPDR® Homebuilders ETF
XME	SPDR® Metals & Mining ETF
XOP	SPDR® Oil & Gas Exploration & Production ETF
XPH	SPDR® Pharmaceuticals ETF
XRT	SPDR® Retail ETF
XSD	SPDR® Semiconductor ETF

About the Author

T ristan Yates researches and writes about global index investing, leveraged portfolio management, and derivative strategies for many publi-
cations, including Futures & Options Trader, Seeking Alpha, and Investopedia, and his articles are distributed through Yahoo!Finance, Forbes,
Kiplinger, and MSN Money. As an industry expert on leveraged ETFs, his
research has been cited in the *Wall Street Journal*.

He has an MBA from INSEAD, a leading international business school,
and began his career with Coopers & Lybrand, providing risk-management
services for the $400B GNMA MBS portfolio. More recently, he helped lead
the $1T securities restatement at the Federal National Mortgage Associa-
tion (FNMA) and a $100m enterprise-wide knowledge management initia-
tive at a leading defense contractor.

Tristan Yates lives in Bethesda, Maryland, and welcomes your ques-
tions and comments. He can be reached at tristan@indexroll.com.

Index

Active investing:
   definition of, 3–4
   reconciling with indexing, 5–6
Allocation of assets:
   covered call strategy and, 117–118
   leveraged portfolios and, 46–50
Alternative asset classes:
   including in portfolio, 247–249
   owning producer, 249–250
American-style options:
   debit spread, 164, 165
   put, 212, 213
Annualized percentage return,
      calculating, 72, 73
Annual return backtests, covered call
      strategy, 113–114
Appreciation:
   average, of index, 7
   bull call spreads and, 166–168
   converting annual to weekly, 102
   as delta, 125
Appreciation, capturing:
   with calendar call spreads, 180
   with LEAPS call options, 134–135,
      136
   with options, 90–97
Asset management:
   allocation of assets, 46–50, 117–118
   alternative asset classes, 247–250
   index exposure and, 261–262
   long and short strategy combination,
      257–259
   minimum investment sizes, 260–261
   objective and processes of, 255–256
   security selection, 256–257, 258

strategy selection, 259–260
   See also Security selection
Asymmetric payoff, 102
At-the-money (ATM) call options:
   description of, 86
   Greeks of, 123–125
   hedging costs of, 142
   LEAPS, 122–123
   three-month, 192
Auto-exercising call options, 165
Average annual return, 113

Backtests:
   calendar put spread strategy,
      222
   covered call strategy, 113–114
Balvers, Ronald, 11
Bear put spreads:
   correlated indexes using
      SIMTOOLS, 232–233
   correlated protected portfolios,
      233–235
   description of, 219–220, 226, 245
   expected returns and hedging
      analysis, 229–232
   OTM, using LEAPS, 228–229
Bid-ask spread, 200, 201, 237
Black, Fischer, 42
Black-Scholes option pricing model,
      42, 54, 83–84
Blending sectors in portfolios, 47
Bogle, John, 2
Book-to-Market metric, 19, 21
Break-even points for options, 96
Bremer, M., 12

Volatility (*Continued*)
  description of, 14–17
  diagonal call spreads and, 178, 180
  forecasting returns and, 27
  hedging cost and, 260
  LEAPS call options and, 122–123,
      139, 140
  of leveraged index portfolio, 63
  modeling, 203
  options and, 86–87
  profit margin and, 85
  rebalancing portfolios and, 50
  roll-forward cost and, 128–130
  weekly simulation, rapid cycling
      strategy, 204–206

See also Implied volatility; VIX
    (volatility index)
Volatility skew:
  bull call spreads and, 169–170
  call options and, 94–96
  collars and, 218
  LEAPS call options and, 127

Weekly returns, generating, 102
Wilshire Value ETF, 38
Wu, Yangru, 11

XLB (materials index), 159–160

Zell, Sam, 36